GW00374526

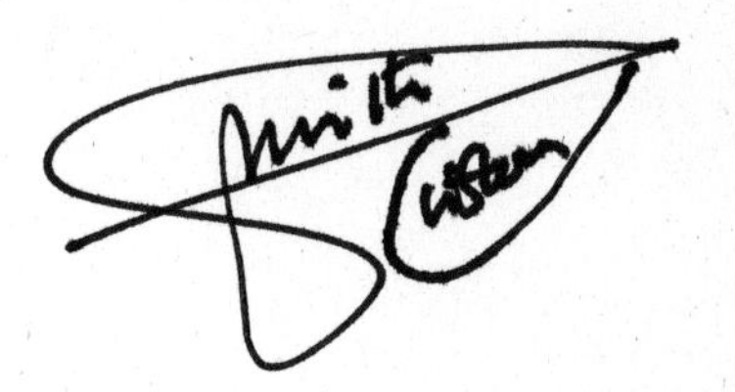

Workhouse To Westminster

Trevor Smith

Published by the Caper Press, London

www.caperpress.com

Cover Design and Illustration by Abigail Smith, ARLSdesign © 2018

First published 2018

Printed by Clays

ISBN: 978-0-9955384-3-6

By the same author:

Smith, Trevor, Anti-Politics: Consensus, Reform & Protest in Britain. London: Charles Knight & Co, 1972.

___________, British Politics in the Post-Keynesian Era. London: The Acton Society Trust, 1986.

___________, The Politics of the Corporate Economy. Hoboken NJ: Blackwell Publishers, 1979.

___________, Town & County Hall: Problems of Recruitment and Training. London: The Acton Society Trust, 1966.

Smith, Trevor, Michael Argyle, Training Managers. London: The Acton Society Trust, 1962.

Smith, Trevor, Robert Benewick (eds.), Direct Action and Democratic Politics. London: Allen & Unwin, 1973.

Smith, Trevor, Anthony M. Rees, Town Councillors: A Study of Barking. London: The Acton Society Trust, 1964.

Smith, Trevor with Alison Young, The Fixers: Crisis Management in British Politics. London: Dartmouth Publishing Company, 1996.

Trevor Smith, (ed.)Economic Dilemmas and Political Choices 1973

Contributor to:

Dench, G., T. Flower & K. Gavron (eds), Young at Eighty. Dench, Geoff, Kate Gavron, Young at Eighty: The Prolific Public Life of Michael Young. Manchester: Carcanet Press, Ltd, 1995.

Hayward, Jack & Michael Watson (eds.), Planning, Politics and Public Policy: The British, French and Italian Experience. Cambridge: Cambridge University Press, 2009.

Vernon, Richard (ed.), Big Business and the State: Changing Relations in Western Europe. Cambridge MA: Harvard University Press, 1974.

CONTENTS

This book is dedicated to my dear family and to the memory of my late parents and particularly my father who knew much more than a thing or two about life.

ACKNOWLEDGEMENTS

My greatest debt is to my dear wife, Julia, for enduring my writing of these memoirs intermittently over many years and reading through many revisions. She showed great forbearance.

I am most obliged to Joy Boaden for meticulously typing successive drafts, checking details and offering comments, all of which she did in an exemplary manner. And I have to thank my daughter-in-law Catherine Smith, for completing the task.

A number of friends, relatives and colleagues have read parts of the book, confirming details and making helpful suggestions. My daughter Naomi read the later chapters on Northern Ireland and my different political activities. My cousin, Alan Scales, read the early chapters and encouraged me to persevere. Another cousin, Leslie Fyffe shared his family records with me. Three close friends from childhood, David Ives, Michael Nutt and Michael Parsons helped to confirm the accuracy or otherwise of my memories. Lawrence de Arth helped confirm some details and pointed out I have plagiarised the title of G Haws' biography of Will Crooks MP. Initially, this was inadvertent; now it is intentional. My friends and former colleagues from Ulster University, Paul Arthur and John McCaffrey commented on Northern Ireland and Geoff Potter read through the entire manuscript and made very many useful comments and corrections.

Robert Dudley employed his professional skills also reading through it, offering some useful advice which I gladly accepted. My granddaughter, Abigail, helped design the cover for which I thank her. My niece, Sophie, prepared it for publication and puts me in her debt. Dr Paul Dimmock compiled the indexes and offered further editorial advice.

Finally, I am extremely grateful to my good friend, Stuart Weir, for employing his extensive journalistic talent in thoroughly editing the penultimate draft which greatly improved the final version.

In thanking them all, I remain wholly responsible for the end result and for any errors it may contain or omissions.

Trevor Smith

PART 1

CHAPTER 1

THE MAKING OF A MONGREL: ENGLISH, IRISH, SCOTTISH GENES AND A WELSH FORENAME

I was born to Vera and Arthur (later called René) Smith at 5 am on 14 June 1937 in Clapton at 21 London Road, (now Clapton Way) in the same bedroom where my mother had entered the world some twenty-two years earlier. She was the surprise child of a mother of forty-two and was fourteen years younger than her youngest sibling. Stillborn, she was rejected by a Dr Smith of Kenninghall Road who was in attendance. A midwife, however, who was also present, placed the baby in a very hot bath which revived her, gasping for air, and bringing her to life.

In his childhood autobiography, Bryan Magee, the former MP, debates whether or not the neighbourhood of Hoxton, where he grew up, was part of the East End of London because it was to the north-east of the City and certainly beyond the sound of Bow Bells. Similarly, the Metropolitan Borough of Hackney, in which Clapton was a district, may not be regarded by true Cockneys as being part of the East End. In my main career post I was to work in what was unquestionably the East End, namely Stepney, as a member of the academic staff of

Queen Mary College in the Mile End Road. Because of this and the similar culture, therefore, I agree with Magee's broader definition and consequently regard Hackney/Clapton as being part and parcel of the wider East End.

After their marriage in 1935, my father and mother lodged with her parents in the house they had rented for most of their own married life. My parents, however, were anxious to own their own home. My great aunt Lucy and her husband Ernest had recently moved from Clapton to Boston Manor in west London. He was a master-builder and we moved to the same newly- built suburb in 1938. It had the advantage of its own new Underground station serving both the Piccadilly and District Lines of London Transport.

Boston Manor also benefited from being a mile or so from the Great West Road which had been constructed in 1925 as the main western artery in and out of London. It naturally attracted many modern industries including Gillette's razors, Pyrene fire extinguishers, Firestone tyres, Beecham's pharmaceuticals, Sperry's gyroscopes, Trico's car windscreen washers and Maclean's toothpaste. The stretch of the road these firms occupied was known as the "Golden Mile". It represented most starkly the awakening from the Depression with the promise of a new prosperity, conjuring up a very real sense of economic and industrial renaissance. The area around Boston Manor hit the headlines in 2014 following a prolonged search for a murdered teenage girl. It had not previously attracted much publicity since the Civil War.

Neighbours

As Philip Roth asserted "the perceptiveness of a kid – neighbourhood", is a lasting reality and a sentiment which, I guess, resonates so strongly with most of us. The move to Boston Manor was to be my first experience of the relationship between geographical and upward social mobility. The house my parents bought – No 4 - was brand new, in a cul-de-sac called Boston Vale. It consisted of nineteen houses, eighteen of which were semi-detached in nine different designs with one fully detached mock Tudor house situated in the U-turn at the head of the road.

Although more modern, our house was not dissimilar in many respects to that in which Sir Roy Strong grew up. His was a terraced house built in the 1920s, with a crazy paved path leading up to the front door just as we had. Both were three-bedroomed. In both the two downstairs reception rooms were not called the lounge and dining room but referred to as the front and back rooms. Like the Strongs, we also sported a print of Millais's The Boyhood of Raleigh which must have been very popular at the time.

Almost all the purchasers of these houses were either established or aspiring members of the middle class. Our immediate neighbours on both sides were reasonably well-off. At No. 2 Harry Field was "a real gentleman" of good breeding. His wife had been injured in a car accident, when he was driving. She emerged totally paralysed. He had the house adapted to her needs and waited on her hand and foot. She was a very demanding patient as we could overhear from the instructions constantly shouted to her husband.

On the other side at No. 6 was Ernest Fenwick and his two maiden daughters who cared for him. They were clearly quite well-off. He was a retired ironmonger who once had a shop in Chiswick High Road. His daughters, Lois and Sadie, belonged to that legion of spinsters, victims of the First World War, in which so many eligible young men had been slaughtered with a resulting paucity of husband material.

Directly opposite us were the Corbetts; he was the owner/manager of a firm of local builders that his father had established. Next to them was a detective who worked in a back office of the Metropolitan Police headquarters at Scotland Yard. His wife, a piano teacher clearly thought she had married beneath herself to judge from the airs and graces she assumed.

There were three artisans in the road. One, Mr Poulsen, a Danish watchmaker, was married to a British woman, and worked in munitions during the war. Another was an engineer employed in a local factory and the third was a butcher from Deal in Kent. He was Philip Parsons, otherwise known as "Bib". He had risen from relatively humble origins to become a very superior Mayfair butcher during the war years and after as manager of Allen & Co., Mount Street, W 1, which supplied meat to many of the embassies, gentlemen's clubs and top restaurants in the West End. The shop flourishes to this day with its reputation intact.

There was one rather mysterious couple who kept themselves to themselves but about whom rumours abounded. She was always very highly made-up and would leave home on the dot at eleven o'clock in the morning to travel up to the West End, returning late at night. He was a rather dashing man with film star good looks who kept similar working hours. It was assumed she was a high-class call girl and that he was her pimp living off her earnings. This may have been entirely scurrilous but it was common currency amongst the tut-tutting residents of the Vale.

Prior to leaving Clapton, I had contracted scarlet fever and had been hospitalised in isolation for a couple of months, as was the medical practice then, before the introduction of antibiotics. This internment probably saved my life. My father possessed a rather flashy two-seater open-roofed Wolsey sports car. My parents were house-hunting and travelling at speed along the Great West Road, when they crashed and my mother received a broken nose. I would normally have been sitting on her lap and might well have had my skull crushed. So, in its way, the crash served as something of a good omen for the move from Clapton to Boston Manor as far as I was concerned.

Parents' Upbringings

As to my parents' backgrounds, most of what I know comes from family folklore – doubtless based on a good deal of myth, a short taped interview of my father's memories and a written record of my mother's experiences growing up between the two world wars.

My paternal grandfather, James, was born in Dunbar in 1879, the son of an English father and a Scottish mother. She came from the west of Scotland which is how James acquired a smattering of Gaelic. He became a groomsman and had a natural way with horses. At the turn of the century he spent a prolonged period in Germany training polo ponies that extended his language accomplishments to acquiring a working knowledge of German.

On returning to the UK, the coming of the motor car reduced the demand for grooms and he moved south seeking employment ending up in Maidstone. He secured a job as a groom-cum-chauffeur to a landowner where he met his future wife. She was Hilda, born in 1889 in Tovil, the daughter of Arthur Betts, head gardener and his wife Jemima (nee Coomber). Hilda's parents separated when she was young and she was effectively raised by a neighbouring pub-owning couple who were friends of her father's. They were able to send her at weekends from Maidstone to the Chiswick School of Music and Drama where she became proficient at both singing and playing the piano.

My paternal grandparents, then, met in Maidstone. James was ten years her senior and had seen very much more of the world. He seduced Hilda and as a consequence she became pregnant with my father. The disapproving mores of the time dictated they had to leave Kent and hastily marry. They sought work as a chauffeur and housekeeper in Central London and lived either in tied or rented accommodation in the areas of Marylebone and Fitzrovia.

A second son, Norman, arrived in quick succession the following year just as the First World War broke out. James avoided the army until he was forcibly conscripted into the King's Own Royal Lancaster Hussars in August 1916 as a Private (no.28388). As a cavalry regiment it was very appropriate for him having been a groom. Within three months he had deserted and in four days of freedom he committed a felony – most likely theft – and received a six weeks sentence in a civilian jail. He was returned to the army and court-martialled receiving a six months sentence in the Glasshouse for desertion.

Before the expiry he was sent to serve in France with the British Expeditionary Force. On the front line he received shrapnel wounds to his stomach, into which mustard gas penetrated. After a time in a field hospital he was sent back to England and transferred to Horton Military Hospital in Epsom. Horton was a London County Council mental asylum but was commandeered by the army for the duration of the war. Following treatment he was sent to Purfleet Camp, Essex, from where he was demobilised in February 1919. His medical records cite his physical wound and a mental condition - "debility". He received a disability pension and, perhaps surprisingly given his record, both the War and Victory Medals.

Time in the Workhouse

A consequence of serving prison sentences meant that his wife, two sons and infant daughter were despatched to a workhouse in Wiltshire. During WWI the workhouse system was nationalised to expedite the sending of indigent people from any part of the country to wherever there were vacancies. In peace time they would have been confined to facilities nearer their localities.

The management of each workhouse, however, was still locally based. My father remembered having to clean and polish the stone floors before going to school; being compelled to sing in the church choir; and being smacked across the face by the local vicar who, customarily, was also chairman of the board of guardians which ran the workhouse. In his adult years, my father had a twitch to his face which he said had been induced by him trying to avoid the slaps from the vicar. His experience made him a confirmed atheist – and a vehemently anti-religious and anti-church one - for the rest of his life. The records of the workhouse in Wiltshire have been destroyed (probably on purpose as was the practice in some other counties) but my father retained a very vivid memory for what he had endured.

When James was discharged from the army, he telegrammed his wife, saying she and the children should make their way to Markyate in northern Hertfordshire. There, he had secured a job as a caretaker-cum-hearse driver with a firm of undertakers that also provided living accommodation above the funeral parlour. My father recalled to me how his mother took her young family from pub to pub in Wiltshire singing and playing the piano in order to raise the railway fares to join her husband; her earlier musical training at Chiswick proved its worth. Having to beg in this way was a very humiliating experience and one which remained firmly etched on my father's memory.

I can testify that my paternal grandfather had a bad wound to his stomach which, because of the gas seepage, never healed and remained as an open, oozing ulcer that required him to wear a new daily bandage for the rest of his life. I saw this with my own eyes. What was also clear is that he suffered from what was then officially termed "debility", more popularly known as, "shell shock". At the time this carried the implication there was a lack of moral courage on the part of the injured individual; indeed, "cowardice in the face of the enemy" was a chargeable offence under martial law. These days, of course, it is recognised as a form as "post- traumatic stress syndrome" and carries none of the opprobrium that previously attached to shell shock.

The motivation behind his parallel career as a petty thief, which continued long after, may well have been exacerbated by his battle scars - both physical and mental. As it was, he was a very incompetent thief, according to my mother, being almost always instantly apprehended by the police. Horse skills apart, James Smith after WWI was certainly a very feckless, rather pathetic person and a mere shadow of his pre-war self.

London Again for My Father

The stay in Markyate must have been relatively brief for the Smith family moved back to London to a flat in Park Crescent Mews at the back of Harley Street. It was familiar territory. This mews accommodated many chauffeurs who lived above the stables turned garages.

The family moved again, this time to Hackney, where James resumed his funeral work. He became ill after collecting a body from Devon and lost his job but soon worked for another undertaker in Clapton.

It was at this point that my father left school at fourteen to become apprenticed to Whites Hairdressing, next to Russell Square Tube station. Like Leonard Bernstein's father, my father too was a hairdresser. The training was for three years and he received a sound grounding in men and women's hairdressing, cosmetics and wig-making. During this time he left home and acquired a rented room of his own.

On completing his apprenticeship, he was taken on by Manny Samuels in Dalston Lane – a return to Hackney once more. He worked a gruelling six and a half day week, with only Sunday afternoons free for rest and recreation. He became skilled in the new French-imported technique, invented by Marcel Grateau, of Marcel Permanent Waving and he later demonstrated this technique for Marcel in different parts of the UK.

He also sought to hone his expertise further by enrolling in, what was colloquially known as, "the French Academy" in Charlotte Street, Fitzrovia. This was in fact the London branch of L'Institut du Progrès Coiffeur where all the leading hairdressers, many of them French, assembled offering advanced training and organising competitions. My mother often acted as my father's model.

He won various medals and in 1937 the Members' Cup of the Academy of which he was later made an honorary *professeur*. It afforded him a very good network and my father's career began to blossom by leaps and bounds. At the Academy he met Raymond Bessone who worked for Vasco, a salon in Dover Street near Antoine's – the top Mayfair stylist at the time. Bessone later became famous in a series of TV programmes where he earned the sobriquet "Mr Teasy Weasy".

My father went to work for Harry Goldstein (trading as Honri of Knightsbridge) and was put under contract, although my father claimed Goldstein verbally promised not to enforce it. Twelve months later, Bessone opened up his own salon in Grafton Street and offered work to my father as a manager. Goldstein, contrary to his word, sued both Bessone for enticement and harbouring and my father for breach of contract. Bessone employed Gilbert Beyfus KC and won. My father represented himself and counter-sued for having to work too long hours contrary to his contract. He called for the appointments books to prove this but Goldstein's daughter, his receptionist, said she had burnt them. My father was found to have no case to answer and plaintiff Goldstein had to pay his own costs and those of Raymond that amounted to £1,000 - a considerable sum in those days. The legal battle took place in the King's Bench Division of the High Court of Justice in 1937, some months after my father had already begun working for Bessone.

To work with Bessone was to enter a new world. As was the fashion amongst Mayfair hairdressers in those days, my father took a French name – René - which was suggested to him by Bessone. My father certainly took Bessone as a role model and grew a moustache like him and the two were often taken for brothers.

René was certainly highly skilled and much in demand by clients. These included the J Arthur Rank actresses: Elsa Lanchester, Margaret Lockwood, Valerie Hobson, Evelyn Laye, Flora Robson and Martita Hunt.

Another client was a wealthy Mrs Schweid. Her brother had made a fortune developing the railways in Turkey. She lived in Belgrave Square in the week and Paris at the weekends. At one of her soirées at her London house, my father met the tenor Richard Tauber. My father and Bessone would be flown at her expense to France at weekends for her to have her hair done.

In Paris, Bessone introduced my father to many fine restaurants and high living in general (about which I can only speculate, though it certainly raised my mother's ire). My father worked for Bessone until he was called-up for military service in the Middlesex Regiment in 1940, although Bessone contrived to get him deferred on the grounds that he was assisting the war effort by sustaining the morale of actresses and other public figures who were important in sustaining, in their turn, the morale of the public. Not surprisingly, this ruse did not succeed.

The experience of my father working at the heart of Mayfair with top-class clients, travelling regularly to Paris, plus the influence of Bessone, propelled him into a wholly new life trajectory. The experience gave him a taste of cosmopolitanism - including foreign travel and added a sophisticated dimension to his natural flair for style and design. All of this induced in him a new self-confidence and further stoked his ambitions.

My Mother's Origins

My maternal forebears contributed a different set of elements in my genetic make-up that rounded off my mongrelism. The English component received a further element in the form of metropolitan London which would reinforce that coming from provincial Kent, while Northern Ireland was to complete the inheritance.

Much more is known about the maternal sides of my family. My grandfather, Henry - known as Harry - was born of an Ulster mother who, at a young age, was said to have walked from Ballywillan, near Portrush in Co. Londonderry, to London via the Stranraer to Larne ferry. She ended up in Shadwell, by the docks in East London and was married by the time she was nineteen. She had three children, two boys and a girl. After the death - or desertion - of her first husband, Tom Cross, she was penniless and forced to send her sons to the nearby poorhouse orphanage, maintaining contact with them at weekends, while keeping her daughter, Lucy, at home with her. Thus my maternal grandfather and his brother, like my father and his brother, all experienced the workhouse in their younger years.

Harry's mother was a redoubtable woman by all accounts. Jane or Janet McShannon or McShannock (names on the certificates of marriage and birth differ), having trekked from Northern Ireland to East London, had no immediate family, no-one to turn to and she was rendered destitute with no recourse to any State support in those days. Without help of any kind, her situation must have been desperate as she tried to scratch a living for herself and her baby daughter.

At first, she worked for a pittance all day and half the night as an outworker, machining shirts and blouses. My mother said that her grandmother always called to mind the poem by Thomas Hood entitled "The Song of the Shirt". She thought it captured her grandmother's lot. The first verse goes:

> "With fingers weary and worn,
> With eyelids heavy and red,
> A woman sat, in unwomanly rags,
> Plying her needle and thread –
> Stitch! Stitch! Stitch!
> In poverty, hunger, and dirt,
> And still with a voice of dolorous pitch
> She sang the 'Song of the Shirt.'"

George Haw quotes Will Crooks describing a very similar description of his mother as an out-working shirt-maker, working all hours for a pittance. It goes on, of course, in

Bangladesh and other third world countries to this day.

My mother admired her for never losing touch with her sons. Later her lifestyle improved in that she turned her undeniable beauty to good advantage.

By all accounts, she co-habited for some years, with a comparatively wealthy Mr Mitchell. Subsequently, she took a job as a housekeeper and became very "friendly" with a certain Jeremiah Rotherham who owned a large warehouse and a wholesale and retail factory business in Kingsland Road, London E1.

In addition to these liaisons she also contracted two subsequent marriages. After Tom Cross had been presumed dead, she married a Mr Stephen Holman, a farmer in Laindon, Essex. She was forty-seven and he was seventy-four. They were married in 1889 and when he died in 1908 she inherited the farm. Later that year she married George Orchard.

Although her material circumstances greatly improved she was profligate and in her old age dependant on a meagre "Lloyd George" pension and handouts from her sons and daughter. By this time she was reduced to two rented rooms in Whitby Lodge, a detached house, at No. 1 London Road.

My mother recalls that she visited her frequently and even in old age she remained a handsome woman. "Upright in statute, prepossessing, always dressed in black as widows were at the time – with a jet-encrusted shawl about her shoulders. She wore a white doilie-like cap on her still luxuriant hair. She had small even features, good complexion, pink cheeks and blue penetrating eyes". (Extracted from my mother's memoirs). She surrounded herself with a good deal of high quality furniture that she had accumulated during her various liaisons and husbands.

Her elder son, Harry became an apprentice French polisher, a trade which he continued until his death, working for Maples, Heals and other famous furniture stores. During WWI he worked in munitions at Woolwich Arsenal – a dangerous job because of the numerous explosions that occurred. He was very musical, playing the banjo and indeed making such instruments with inlaid mother-of-pearl surrounds. He was a staunch trade unionist and Labour party member.

He married Emma Harvey who was one of thirteen children all of whom, remarkably for the times, were reared to maturity. I, therefore, had numerous great-uncles and aunts who flitted in and out of my early childhood. Most of them remained living in parts of north-east London such as Dalston, Walthamstow and Stoke Newington as well as some remaining in Clapton. Whipps Cross was the local hospital but its reputation at the time was poor. Most of my relatives, it was said, "left feet first" from Whipps Cross. Conditions seem not to have improved as I noted it received a poor grading in 2015.

The oldest relative from my grandmother's extended family was Aunt Mary and it was always rumoured that she was the mother and sister of my youngest great uncle, Teddy. Apparently, my maternal great-grandmother, after twelve children concurred in sub-contracting her conjugal duties to her eldest daughter. This incest was one of the many skeletons in the ancestral cupboard; incest was not an uncommon feature of family life at the time being grotesquely termed "a game all the family can play".

My maternal grandmother worked in her father's shop selling gas mantles; these were the fine net meshes (the equivalent of light bulbs) through which coal gas was vented and would be ignited with a match to turn the lamps on which, I vividly recall, created a distinctive whoosh sound. Coming from a shop-keeping family, my grandmother would have been on the cusp of the lower middle class/upper working class by social background, although the thirteen children must have made considerable inroads into the family's fortunes.

She bore four children: Emma – the first name was continued in accordance with tradition – became an expert carpet mender and was called upon, well into old age, as a specialist to repair expensive Indian and Persian carpets. For many years she worked for Lamerton's, the high-class carpet shop in Ealing. Her boyfriend, John, was killed in the Great War and she married Joseph Blumson.

He was the son of a reasonably prosperous greengrocer. I remember him living with his son and daughter-in-law in his old age during WWII and being referred to as "old Blum". He had two sons, one of whom became a senior manager with the Associated Equipment Company (AEC), the bus builders in Southall, but Joe was made of much weaker stuff. He was probably what we would now call dyslexic, was illiterate and worked in a scrap metal dealers in Enfield where he rescued an intact bugle for me from amongst the cast-offs destined for the manufacture of weaponry during WWII.

The second daughter was Edie, and a very sweet aunt as I recall, became a typist and married unhappily as it turned out. Sadly, she successfully committed suicide at a second attempt by placing her head in a gas oven. She was thus an addition to one of the many ghosts in the family history cupboard.

A son was the third child to emerge, called Harry after his father. He secured a scholarship to the Grocers' School which later, as Hackney Downs Grammar School, produced many illustrious academics and also Harold Pinter. Subsequently, it declined very badly and was shut down after failing an Ofsted (Office for Standards in Education, Children's Services and Skills) inspection. It later re-opened as a successful Academy school.

The school was the foundation of the Grocers' Livery Company. Its expressed mission was to produce educated boys fit for clerical jobs in the City and hence did not provide any sixth form teaching for brighter pupils lest, diverted, they proceeded onwards to tertiary education. Accordingly, Harry passed the School Certificate examination and went to work for Sir Henry Lunn, founder of the travel agency Lunn Poly that specialised in up-market tours. Harry prospered as a backroom boy there, collating European routes and timetables for clients. Later, as a tour guide, he took the opportunity to draw pen and ink pictures to illustrate brochures of various destinations on the continent. I possess one of a scene in Paris.

Because of his intimate and detailed knowledge of the railway network in Europe, he was immediately called-up at the outbreak of hostilities in 1939 and commissioned into the Royal Engineers, then the Corps responsible for troop movement control. He received no basic military training and found himself at Dunkirk with a pistol in his hand and no idea of how to fire it. In 1945 he was sent to Washington DC for a year to supervise the rehabilitation of British troops who had been Japanese POWs but were too ill to be returned quickly to the UK. He was kept on after the war for some years and ended up as a Lieutenant-Colonel, collecting an OBE for his services. He later worked as the manager of Southend Airport before joining Sir Freddy Laker and his Airtours Company.

And, finally my mother, Vera, was born fourteen years later, being very much an afterthought. She was nevertheless lovingly spoilt by her elder siblings. During her school years she suffered from bouts of ill-health that included an attack of diphtheria which required many months in hospital. She left her only school, Bethnal Road Elementary, at fourteen.

Like Harry, she secured a grammar school place but, somewhat inexplicably given his political views, her father turned down the opportunity on grounds of cost; again, such sex discrimination was not unusual at the time and moreover continued well into the 1970s. She later trained as a Pitman shorthand-typist and book-keeper, working in the West End. At the age of seventeen, she met my father, who was living locally and they courted on Hackney Downs with another couple, Albert Sadler, always known to me as "Uncle Stan" and Elsie, my mother's longstanding chum from her school years. Stan was an insurance salesman going from door to door to collect weekly instalments for premiums. He was like the "man from the Pru" but actually worked for the Norwich Union. To my mother, together with her brother Harry, Stan was a role model of financial stability which she would want me to emulate in later years.

On marriage my parents lived with my maternal grandparents

who, as I have said, rented their house in London Road for £3 0s 0d per calendar month. The two top rooms were rented for eight shillings a week and the back kitchen and the top back bedroom for a similar amount. This totalled a satisfactory £3 4s 0d, a surplus of which Mr Micawber would have approved; it meant, in effect, my grandparents lived rent-free. My grandmother also ran a clothing club at each of the two local departmental stores – Z Dudley of Kingsland Road and Spokes of Lower Clapton Road. All twenty or so members of the club paid one shilling a week and after twenty weeks the accumulated money was shared out to purchase goods at one or other of the two stores. My grandmother received extra shares as a commission.

An assiduous Co-op member and collector of her dividends my grandmother's membership number of the London Co-operative Society was 165912, which I faithfully used when, avoiding school meals, I lunched in the restaurant at the Hounslow branch of the Co-op during my secondary schooldays.

The close, extended family pattern that had obtained amongst my maternal forebears was about to break up. My Uncle Harry moved into a modern semi-detached house at 70 Parkfield Avenue, Headstone Lane in the north-west part of the Borough of Harrow. Likewise, as I have told, after living for two years with my maternal grandparents, I moved with my mother and father to Boston Manor, an equally salubrious suburb at the time.

The Second World War

World War II was another cause hastening the family diaspora.

The East End was targeted heavily in the Blitz and the families of my two aunts moved to Boston Manor, together with my grandmother who had been widowed some three months after I was born. While this family network was not on the same large scale as at Clapton and its environs, the successive moves to Boston Manor transplanted, more modestly, something of an extended family in close proximity with one another. Thus, I experienced some of the closeness my mother had felt more intensely during her childhood. Many in the next generation would be denied such close extended family ties.

CHAPTER 2

A CHILD OF THE WAR: GOSPORT, SCOTLAND AND THE LONDON BLITZ

The 1940s were to prove the most volatile decade of my life both in terms of lifestyle and social mobility, on the one hand, and geographical mobility and travel on the other – though this pattern was to be repeated in my later years.

New Suburbs and the Neighbourhood

As I have recalled, the move from the East End to the west London suburbs in 1938 coincided with a considerable improvement in my father's income once he had become established as a Mayfair hairstylist. As a family, we fitted well into the new middle-class, or more accurately aspirant middle-class, of the area. And then, of course, in less than twelve months the Second World War was to break out. This changed everything, not least it hastened the creation of something of a community out of the newly-built series of somewhat anonymous semi-detached roads of the neighbourhood – we were all in it together and it quickly fostered a collective 'Blitz mentality'.

The wider locality in which the Boston Vale cul-de-sac was situated was much more mixed. Along Boston Road towards Hanwell Broadway, up to the parish church of St Thomas the Apostle, there were slightly older semi-detached houses. Beyond that, and until you reached Hanwell itself, the area was distinctly more proletarian with a mixture of Edwardian working -class homes and a council estate. Further west from Hanwell Broadway, was to be found Church Fields and a rather exclusive road called Golden Manor. West of Hanwell there was Southall which was aggressively proletarian with a lot of light industry that included the AEC, which built buses, and Quaker Oats, the cereal manufacturer. To the west of Hanwell, going on towards Ealing, there was first West Ealing, working-class for the most part, and then Ealing Broadway which was a main shopping centre that included Bentalls – an up-market departmental store whose main branch was in Kingston. The Broadway was more established boasting a magnificent parish church and the Town Hall. Close by were a number of well-built traditional Edwardian and even Victorian villas. As befitting its title of "Queen of the Suburbs" there were the lush green areas of Walpole Park to which the famous Ealing Film Studios abutted, and Ealing Common; and further away, various other parks and open spaces such as Horsenden Hill.

To the south of Boston Manor station, going towards Brentford, the main thoroughfare Boston Manor Road consisted of a ribbon development of fairly recently-constructed semis that led to Boston Manor Park which, too, was a rather grand open space with its own lake, old manor house, and woods that stretched down to the Grand Union Canal. Beyond that, was the Great West Road, which helped to relieve the congestion of Brentford High Street. Brentford itself was very seedy and run-down at that time. It contained a municipal swimming baths and library of late Victoria origin, a green-tiled public house called "The Beehive", which had the appearance and smell of a public urinal, and a fleapit cinema called "The Queens".

At the bottom end of the Half Acre was the High Street that led eastwards towards Chiswick which, like Ealing, was generally more salubrious. To the west came Isleworth with its magnificent Syon House and the popular "London Apprentice" pub by the Thames.

To the east of Boston Manor was Northfields, which also sported a Piccadilly Line station. Largely working-class, it was comprised of mainly artisan terraced cottages. Like so many other areas in outer London, the rising cost of housing has led, more recently, to a gentrified promotion. The western boundary of Boston Manor was defined by the Green Belt that encircled the metropolis. It consisted of playing fields, allotments, a golf course and Bluebell Woods. These were bisected by the Grand Union Canal which ran from the Thames at Brentford through to the London Docks before which it divided and had a more northerly branch that linked to the Midlands.

The north of Ealing was bisected by the Western Avenue. Like the Great West Road, this was another recently laid major thoroughfare and similarly attracted light manufacturing which included Hoover's, the vacuum cleaner manufacturer. This led on to Alperton and its Guinness brewery and then on to Northolt with its airport made notorious by Prime Minister, Neville Chamberlain, who returned there from his meeting with Adolf Hitler, waving a piece of paper and exclaiming "peace in our time". The A40 highway led on to Beaconsfield, High Wycombe, Oxford, the Cotswolds and further to the West and Wales.

As already noted, going west from Brentford one passed Syon House, where one could turn south to Isleworth or carry on down the Bath Road to Hounslow whose Heath was made famous in the Civil War. Keeping westwards on the Great West Road one would arrive in the district of Osterley. This was largely a ribbon development of recent semi-detached housing but its tube station was a splendid example of the Art Deco architecture of the period and has since had a preservation order placed on it. You could drive on to Slough, the western equivalent of Dagenham which lay to the east of London. It boasted a modern Trading Estate – one of the first of its kind – and the town was much reviled by John Betjeman in his wartime poem calling on bombs to fall on Slough. Such, then, were the hubs and parameters of my new home.

Declaration of War – September 1939

At first nothing much changed from the "phoney war" of the previous three months. My father continued to work in Mayfair as a hair stylist but was called up for military service in early 1940. I vividly remember him going off to the army. At the time we had a Ford saloon car which I loved playing in but, much to my chagrin, was sold off. My father also possessed a Red Panther motorcycle on which he rode off to basic training.

He was recruited into the Middlesex Regiment and later joined its machine gun battalion. The family's income plummeted. My mother went out to work at Maclean's Toothpaste factory as a secretary to one of the senior managers. She would take me to my Aunt Emmy who, with her family, had rented a house in Boston Manor Gardens, just across the Underground line. They had moved from Beecholme Road, Clapton which was soon to be destroyed by the Luftwaffe. She would look after me during office hours. Not only did she have to cater for her family, that included "Old Blum", her extremely tetchy father-in-law, but also to put up with my insistent demands. I remember her sawing some plywood to make me a toy in the shape of a rifle.

With the absence from home of my father, I was made very conscious of the war and, in addition to the improvised rifle, had a toy tin helmet which I wore for most of the day. Bombs fell on the London Playing Fields – thus falling short of their Great West Road intended target - which were at the bottom of my aunt's garden. A unit of Italian prisoners of war was brought in to fill up the holes. They camped in bell tents for three weeks while restoring the pitches and were watched over by one British squaddie. I regarded such meagre security with alarm, so I took out my cousin John's air rifle from its cupboard, loaded it with a slug pellet and served many hours of sentry duty looking over the garden fence lest any of the Italian POWs took the opportunity to escape. I assumed this voluntary conscription on my part as an obligatory patriotic duty.

Gosport

I think at that time there was an embryonic romance starting between my mother and her boss. My father got wind of this and, as he was about to be posted to Gosport in Hampshire, insisted that my mother and I went with him. At Gosport, he was commanded to help guard the submarine pens against possible German attack by sea. The army commandeered 'digs' for us which consisted of a front room in a semi-detached house owned by a young woman called Bunty. Her parents had died so there was plenty of room to accommodate lodgers. In the garden was a recently built Anderson shelter. These structures had been designed by William Patterson and Oscar Carl Kerrison, yet named after Sir John Anderson, the Lord Privy Seal. In this, not particularly well designed shelter, my mother and I spent most nights along with our immediate neighbours.

As a major naval base, Gosport was being heavily blitzed by the German Luftwaffe. My father was stationed on one of the off-shore forts that had been built at the time of the Napoleonic Wars to prevent any French invasion. Now, however, they were used to stop a German one. He had to spray his machine gun in a *180 degrees arc* once every thirty minutes to discourage any forays by German warships.

Home Again and Scotland

I can't quite remember how many months we were in Gosport but we returned when my father's regiment was preparing to be shipped out to the Far East. My maternal grandmother and my younger Aunt Edie and her husband Noel had moved into our house in Boston Vale. My uncle had dug up the lawn and planted potatoes as his contribution to the "Dig for Victory" Government campaign. My father was very annoyed. He and Uncle Noel, however, built a very solid semi-subterranean shelter at the end of our garage with concrete and spare iron furnished with half a dozen bunk beds. The family, joined by the three Fenwicks, slept there most nights during air raids.

My father went off for further training and returned on embarkation leave, prior to being sent to Burma. I have in my possession a photograph of the platoon he was in. On his last Sunday night we received a telegram instructing him to go to

Lanark in Scotland and present himself at the Officer Cadet Training Unit (OCTU). The rest of his platoon went to Burma and were all wiped out. He had had a very lucky escape. As before with Gosport, my mother and I were required to follow him to Lanark which was my second long excursion away from London and, once again, we were billeted by the army who had sequestered the front room of a very large family Council house. I remember there was a family of six other children in the house.

Lanark was to provide me with three stark experiences. First, it was the farthest I had ever travelled from home. Secondly, was the trauma of moving from a respectable London outer suburb to the barbaric architecture that characterised so much of twentieth century Scottish municipal building. Here was a large Council estate, built between the wars in beautiful countryside, with hardly any regard for design or minimal taste. It competed with the worst kind of Soviet building styles. It was, in effect, an updated version of the Glasgow Gorbals.

Thirdly, there was the impact in the change to our social status. My father was en route not, thankfully, to almost certain death in the Far East but to becoming "an officer and a gentleman". I was acutely aware of the significance of the transition from a private to being an officer cadet. He had white flashes around the regimental badge on his cap as well as on his shoulder straps. He did not always return home and often had to stay with his cadet cohort in camp. He would tell of the remarkable change in comfort as evidenced by the fact that officer cadets were furnished with sheets on their beds in separate rooms instead of sleeping in rough blankets in communal barracks, as was the case for other ranks. This had a quite considerable effect on him for he could not understand the rationale behind this form of discrimination. It was, of course, all part and parcel of the army's induction process from the ranks to the officer class.

I pause to ponder on my father's success in becoming an officer cadet. It was remarkable. He came from a very deprived and unsettled childhood that included the workhouse and endless moves which meant he went to a multitude of schools. He left central school at fourteen with no qualifications though, later, by dint of much application he had become a Mayfair hair stylist. How, one wonders, did he gain selection to OCTU?

In Richard Vinen's *National Service*; A Generation in Uniform (2014), the author tells of the great difficulties for non-public schoolboys to be considered for officer-training such was the sheer social snobbery and class bias inherent in the selection process. Even the exigencies of war could not explain my father's promotion, bearing in mind, too, that he was the son of a convicted WWI deserter. The odds could not have been more highly stacked against him.

My explanation, for what it is worth, says if you can manage to rise above extreme childhood deprivation, you will have developed into something of a "Jack the Lad" and, in the University of Hard Knocks, will have acquired a skill-set that fosters deep survival techniques. These will include a quick ability to read situations fairly accurately, perceive the strengths and weaknesses in those you meet and be ever-ready to seize the chance whenever circumstances occurred for a favourable opportunistic advantage to be gained. (It would be appropriate to say that life is not a bowl of cherries—it's a series of trade-offs, and one must always be on the lookout). My father clearly was of such a disposition.

In addition, working in Mayfair and attending to the needs of the rich and famous – often for hours on end – he could both cater to their desires and, more importantly, mimic their style and modes of behaviour. It meant he was thus enabled to pass muster in order to gain recognition as a POM (Potential Officer Material).

I was made fully aware of this elevation to superior status but I was soon to be shown its limits. On a visit to the Navy, Army and Air Force Institute (NAFFI), where my mother and I would go to collect our weekly food rations, I noticed my father being instructed in the finer arts of infantry tactics in a circle on the barrack square. I pointed him out to another snotty-nosed brat standing outside saying proudly "that's my Dad". He replied swiftly, "and you see the man instructing them, that's my Dad!" This immediate putdown was not just a personal blow for me but served as an object lesson in perceiving the hierarchical tiers implicit in the social strata. This may well have been influential in my choosing to take a social science degree and later becoming an academic in the discipline.

Another aspect of living *en famille* in a single room, both in Gosport and Lanark, was that I became aware of what young marrieds got up to nocturnally. Sex was very important to both my parents. And whether conditioned by this early nurture or by inherited nature, I strove later to maintain the family tradition.

Later, my father was sent on a forty-eight hours manoeuvres exercise which meant carrying full kit. He returned crippled with a very bad back injury. Local medical treatment was to no avail and he was despatched to the military hospital at Chester where he was to remain for a further six months. My mother and I returned to Boston Manor. At that time my aunt and uncle had moved to rented accommodation nearby and only my maternal grandmother remained. The one relief that Lanark had afforded was that it was not the target of German bombs whereas the return home meant that we were constantly awoken by the sound of air raid sirens. I felt I was back again on active service.

Another Return Home

Most nights were to be spent in the shelter my uncle and father had built. Torches, candles and endless mugs of cocoa were the enduring features of these nights. Unfortunately, with time, like many of the Anderson shelters that had been distributed throughout the country, the lack of drainage meant that it began to fill with water which later stagnated and made the shelter quite uninhabitable. We acquired a Morrison shelter, named after Herbert Morrison then Minister for Home Security. It was put in the living room and had the appearance of a large steel table with metallic mesh netting which could be put around the sides to protect occupants from bomb blast. A mattress and pillows were put at the bottom to enable us to sleep.

After six months at Chester no remedy was found for my father's back trouble and he was demobbed on medical grounds According to his discharge certificate he had served "in the Colours" from 17 October 1940 to 26 January 1942, in all a total of one year and 102 days. He received a small army pension. He wore a silver badge on his coat to indicate his status so that he would not be apprehended by the police or military authorities as a suspected "column dodger".

I remember his homecoming shortly before Christmas 1941. I recall it not only because the family had been reunited but also because funds had been plundered to buy me a large second-hand electric model railway set which was an unknown luxury in wartime austerity Britain. Ironically it had been made in pre-war Germany.

CHAPTER 3

RETURNING TO CIVVY STREET AND SCHOOL LIFE

Returning from Scotland and the demobilisation of my father evoked in me a feeling of returning to civilian life. While fully aware the war was still raging, it felt more normal and familiar after our billeted sojourns in Gosport and Lanark.

Reading the accounts of my slightly older, much more famous contemporaries, and their wartime childhoods, I realise how much mine departed significantly from theirs although inevitably sharing a great deal in common. Like Bryan Magee and John Gross, I had been born in the East End of London. Like Michael Frayn and Magee I had working-class forbears who became upwardly socially mobile, while John Carey hailed from a financially precarious but more middle class family. Roy Strong shared a suburban Middlesex childhood; he living in the north-west part of the county while I was in its west. Ken Morgan, a schoolteacher's son, was born and lived in London until 1939 and then after 1944.

Four of them were evacuated to safer homes. Gross was sent with his mother and sister to live in Egham, returning only occasionally to Whitechapel to observe the Jewish high holy days or attend family religious events. Magee was evacuated never to return to Hoxton, moving on to the Bluecoats School at Christ's Hospital, Horsham. Carey's family removed itself from Barnes to Radcliffe, near Nottingham, for the duration, while Frayn remained in Ewell, further out into Surrey, largely away from the Luftwaffe's main targets. Roy Strong spent most of the time in Winchmore Hill intertwined with brief periods of evacuation to the South Coast, Norfolk and, to avoid the deadly V2 rockets, to Wales in 1944. Morgan was born and lived in London until 1939 when he went with his mother to live in his family's ancestral seat in north Wales. They returned to join his father in Alexandra Park, a north London suburb, in 1944 just in time to experience the V1 doodlebug bombing attacks.

By contrast with these near contemporaries, in the early 1940s I had moved first towards the enemy and then to the other end of the UK to observe military manoeuvres in Scotland. When I returned to suburbia it was subjected to constant air raids during the Blitz and afterwards. Boston Manor did not receive the same merciless barrage as the City and inner London but there were regular aerial attacks on the factories along the Great West Road. Later, we suffered from the pilotless V1s or Flying Bombs and then the even more feared silent V2 rockets.

Coming back from Lanark, it was also time for me to begin my education. My parents were only too well aware of the appalling limitations of their own schooling. My father attended any number of schools as his father sought work wherever he could and was thus never able to settle in a school for any length of time. My mother was more fortunate having stayed at one elementary school until she left it at fourteen. Conscious of their formal academic limitations, but being ambitious and becoming better off, they were eager to give their children as good an education as they could manage.

Like the inter-war Surrey and Sussex of the distinguished historian Richard Cobb's childhood, Ealing and its immediate environs was littered with private schools. Cobb's were mainly boarding, or had boarding facilities. By contrast, those in Ealing were almost all day schools.

St Anne's Convent

I was enrolled at St Anne's Convent School in September 1941 and stayed until early 1944. It had been created in 1903 by the Sisters of Charity and was situated in Place House, a mid-eighteenth century mansion with extensive grounds, between Northfields and South Ealing – about a mile away from my home. In reasonably clement weather my mother and I would walk to school but, more usually with my friend Michael Nutt, I would take the Underground train one stop to Northfields and walk down the hill. It was a girls' school catering for pupils aged between three and a half to sixteen years. Provision was made, however, for boys to join the first two forms. Almost all the teachers were nuns wearing full habits, including pointed coifs and wimples with heavy rosaries dangling from their waists.

Although small boys were admitted, the lavatories had not been adapted specifically to meet male needs, so there were no urinals. One of the girls' toilet rooms was set aside specifically for the boys. These arrangements led to my first taste of authority. At the end of the first day I remember going home, proudly proclaiming that I had been made a monitor. My mother showed no surprise, saying she expected much of me, and was pleased at my swift elevation so early on in my schooling. She enquired what was involved. I replied that I was the lavatory monitor who had to take up duties in the mid-morning, lunch hour and afternoon breaks to ensure that the little boys aimed straight at the lavatory pan to avoid splashing urine on the floor. Her reaction was violent: "What, they've only made you the lavatory monitor because you're a Protestant!" The next day she scorched down to the school indignantly insisting that I should stop being monitor. I felt a grievous loss of status. For my part, I was quite prepared to carry on as toilet supervisor, but it was not to be. I am sure that this abrupt loss of my first public office, so keenly felt, influenced and fostered my all too over-weaning sense of ambition in later years.

The teachers were adept at instilling information in us by rote learning. There was a good deal of prayer, especially the Hail Mary, and a daily recitation of the alphabet in both upper and lower cases was de rigueur as was the repetition of the twelve times tables.

I was entranced by the rituals and trappings of a religious Order. Protestant boys were excused from attending chapel. I think I was the only one who voluntarily attended Benediction on Wednesday afternoons after school when a priest in full vestments officiated. I vividly remember the tinkling of the bells as the monstrance was circled before us. I sought to emulate this liturgical experience at home. In my bedroom I turned my dressing table into an altar on which I placed a crucifix and two candles. I borrowed my mother's dressing gown as a cope and her scarf as an orb; I set the bedroom alarm clock to ring to provide the sound of bells. My mother was amused but my father became extremely alarmed. Because of his experiences in the Wiltshire workhouse, where chapel had been compulsory and where the vicar had bullied and hit him, he was a convinced atheist. Indeed, he took this to extremes much to my embarrassment. When compelled by my mother to attend church for family weddings and baptisms he would sing obscenities to the words of the hymns.

Among other recollections I have of my convent school were the two contrasting infants' teachers. They were chalk and cheese. Sister Mary Thérèsa was beautiful, gentle and loving. (My daughter's second name is hers). The second was a Dutch nun, Sister Mary Jochandina. She was ugly, strict and possessed of an altogether nasty disposition. Once my family received a food parcel from a distant relative abroad. It contained a banana. I had never consciously seen one before as they were not imported during the war years. I proudly took it to school where Sister Mary Jochandina unzipped it and offered it to her favourite, a boy named Davis. Taking as large a bite as he could, he ate half of it before it was returned to me. It confirmed my impression of her as a complete bitch.

I also recall a striking girl pupil, Gaynor Letts, who was good looking and had an attractive personality. I always remember the names of girls with these attributes.

Shortly after I had left St Anne's, two pupils joined who later attracted widespread fame. One, in particular, was a young girl, named Mary Isobel Catherine Bernadette O'Brien, who became internationally renowned as the very successful pop singer Dusty Springfield. The other, Billy Treadwell, son of a local confectioner, became a well-known Rugby player, gaining three international caps as a hooker for England in the 1966 season.

Scotland Again – Edinburgh

My withdrawal from St Anne's Convent was precipitated in part by my father's fear that I was fast becoming a religious maniac but was also down to the activities of Adolph Hitler. My younger brother, Stephen, was born in January 1944 and three months later one of the first V2 rockets landed close to our home, bombing the Pyrene factory. It was decided that my mother, baby brother and I should evacuate once again to Scotland. This time we were to lodge with her brother, my Uncle Harry and his family in Edinburgh. This was the first occasion we had actively sought refuge from enemy action. Like the first period spent north of the Border, it also involved another insight into changes in social status as my uncle, then a captain, was the Railway Transit Officer (RTO) at Waverley Station, supervising troop movement control which was a very hectic time being just two months prior to D-Day.

We travelled up overnight on a crowded troop train from King's Cross. Much to my embarrassment, my mother was breast feeding her baby son under the lascivious eyes of our fellow passengers who were mainly soldiery. It was a nightmare journey of stopping and starting at almost every station where one was awakened by the sound of clattering milk churns being loaded on and off. Things looked up very much for the better when we arrived at Waverley to be met there by my uncle as we were accorded priority because of his rank. I was amazed how many soldiers saluted him – another impressionable example of differences in hierarchy and social status that was never lost on me.

The couple of months we spent in Edinburgh were not

otherwise a happy time for me. First, my Aunt Winnie was very strict but inconsistent, making it impossible to please her. Secondly, my cousin Michael, who was some years older than me, took a delight in bullying and teasing me. To get us out of the apartment, he was often told to take me on long journeys into the countryside or climb up Arthur's Seat, the steep hill that overlooks the city. He would frequently run away and leave me by myself. He was a pupil at the Royal High School, which later as a redundant building housed the first sessions of the devolved Scottish Parliament. I was much relieved, therefore, that after D-Day and the success of Royal Air Force (RAF) Bomber Command in obliterating the V2 launching sites, we could return safely home to London.

Rutland House School

I resumed my schooling in the summer term of 1944. Accordingly, I was sent to Rutland House Preparatory School in Hanwell. It was located in a large villa in the plush and aptly named Golden Manor Road. One of the lawns had been ashphalted over to make a playground.

The owner/head was a one John Freebairn-Smith, BA (Oxon). He himself had been educated at the All Saints' Choir School, in Margaret Street, close to the British Broadcasting Corporation (BBC), where Laurence Olivier had been his junior contemporary. All Saints' is one of the bastions of Anglo-Catholicism. Freebairn-Smith read Greats at New College, Oxford and had rowed for the College Eight. After graduating he returned to the Choir School and later became its headmaster. Towards the end of the 1930s he set up his own establishment in Hanwell opposite his mother's home.

He had a Swedish wife and two daughters (later four), Elizabeth and Tessa, who were the only girls to be allowed into an otherwise boys' school; I met up with them again in 2011. In the only school photograph I have there appeared eighty-four pupils and I can recall the surnames of about a third. I have the receipt for the first term's fees which amounted to £10 7s 6d.

In addition to an introductory class, the school consisted of four forms and accordingly had four members of staff plus a part-time art teacher. The first art teacher was an elderly spinster but her successor was a rather pretty young French woman. A Miss Carr ran the first form while the second form teacher was a Mr J Spencer, recently demobbed from the RAF. He was soon succeeded by the Rev G.T.M. Horne, AKC whom I got to know well as he caught the same bus as me. The third form was led by Mr John Thomas Pumphrey BD, King's College London, who also had recently been demobilised from the RAF. In 1945 he stood for the Ealing Borough Council being duly elected for the Labour Party. He was married to a rather exotic French artist and lived in a comfortable Edwardian villa in Castlebar Avenue, a stone's throw from Ealing Town Hall. I know this, because my parents paid for him to give me private tuition at his home. His young son Paul was a pupil at the school. Pumphrey later went on to found his own private prep school in Ealing called St Angelo's. At Rutland House the top fourth form was presided over by the headmaster.

I would catch the trolley bus to Hanwell Broadway and walk the next half mile to the school. This walk I undertook with a good deal of trepidation because halfway along there was a secondary modern school whose pupils, some of the more loutish of whom, would bully, rag and generally harass boys from Rutland House. We had a very distinctive uniform which consisted of a fawn blazer with brown edging, a pocket badge consisting of a quill pen and a Latin motto, Ex Usu Comodem ("Practice Makes Perfect"). Worse, we were compelled to wear a rather ginger coloured tweed hat which was more in the fashion of a golfer's cap or cor'blimey. The uniform was purchased from Abernathy & Sons, a Plymouth Brethren family of outfitters in West Ealing. It was not at all like a conventional schoolboy cap and made us stick out from the crowd. Later, I was allowed to cycle to school which I much preferred as it made it easier to speed by the louts.

At Rutland House quite a large contingent of the boys travelled from Iver in Buckinghamshire which was convenient for them travelling to Hanwell & Elthorne railway station. The pupils, for the most part, came from "respectable" lower middle class families whose parents, like mine, aspired to a good education for their sons. There were others who were socially a cut above that. Of those, I remember Paul Cox, who lived near the school and whose father had a successful umbrella shop close to the fashionable Selfridges store in Oxford Street in the West End. There was Wilberforce, a direct descendant of the great Parliamentarian who had helped to stop the slave trade and Roger Moate who later became the Conservative MP for Faversham and subsequently knighted.

The school worked a five and a half day week, including Saturday mornings. Tuesday and Thursday afternoons were allocated for games that took place on the Maclean's sports ground in Boston Manor, handy for my home. The morning breaks consisted of fifteen minutes of physical exercises and drill. The school operated on the 'muscular Christianity' principle of fostering a healthy body and a healthy mind. There were prayers each morning and classes started with a compulsory spelling test. We were issued with a spelling book and had to learn ten words every evening for homework. These were tested first thing next day and failure to get eight words right for three consecutive days resulted in a caning. We also had regular air raid drills ending up in the basement which was used as an air-raid shelter and we had to take our gas masks to school until VE day.

The school aimed to prepare its pupils for the Common Entrance examination, with a syllabus that included algebra, geometry, arithmetic, Latin, French, history, geography, religious knowledge and handwriting. Every day we had to complete a page of handwriting practice. In the books we were given there was an adage at the top of each page which had to be copied twelve times. I remember one of them: "Nottingham is the seat of the lace trade". I was a pretty average scholar but I always obtained top marks in RE and particularly handwriting. In one of my reports, Freebairn-Smith remarked I could reproduce perfect counterfeits of the printed sayings and accordingly awarded me 100 percent marks.

Rutland House reflected the personality of its head. He maintained strict discipline both in the classroom and on the sports ground. I was especially impressed by his ability to sketch an outline map of the British Isles on the blackboard. On the sports ground I also recall a cricket practice learning to catch.

The headmaster was in the middle of a circle of boys throwing the ball at random with much force. It hit one boy in the face who fell screaming to the ground. Attempting to illustrate how trivial the hurt was, the head threw the ball high in the air and successfully contrived to have it land on his nose. He rubbed it vigorously saying, "That's how to lessen the pain."

In class, as with spelling and tables, there was similar rote learning of tables of verbs and nouns from the ubiquitous Kennedy's *Revised Latin Primer,* first published in 1888 (In 1913, the copyright was challenged as Benjamin Kennedy's eldest daughter Marion who claimed that she, her younger sister Julie and two of Kennedy's former students, G.H. Hallam and Thomas Page, were responsible for this work). In the top set we stood on the desk seats to be tested. I recall a pupil named Bowden being unable to conjugate a verb when so ordered. He burst into tears exclaiming how he hated Latin. Freebairn-Smith strode up to him hitting him hard across the face and felling him to the floor. Bowden did not return to school.

While, as I say, there was the usual range of canings and detentions common at the time to maintain discipline, there were also many sports prizes, which provided me with the only sports medal I ever achieved. This was second junior long jump champion in 1947. The reason I got this was because the victor ludorum won six but was rationed to five medals and chose to deny himself the long jump prize so that the boy who came second was given the gold medal and I, who had come third, was promoted to second and received the silver medal.

Hove & Aldrington High School

I stayed at Rutland House until the end of the Easter term 1948. My mother was expecting her third child, who turned out to be my sister Janet. A Swiss au pair girl had been recruited to help her with the home and younger children – it was all getting a bit crowded in a three bedroom semi-detached house. The advice of Arthur Ratzer, the consultant chemical engineer at Ginsberg & Smith (and more importantly the possessor of a BSc) was sought and he suggested I joined his son, Martin, at Hove & Aldrington High School near Brighton. By this move my parents could achieve the twin objectives of reducing the overcrowding at home and sending me on to prepare for a boarding education at a public school. There was talk of my applying later to go to Brighton College after taking the Common Entrance exam.

My move to Sussex was one of the most traumatic of my life. My parents ought really to have checked out the school in advance and not blindly taken Ratzer's advice. It was housed in a Victorian/Edwardian villa and catered for both boarding pupils and day boys who constituted the vast majority.

The bedroom I was in consisted of six ex-WD camp beds. An enamel bucket served as a night urine receptacle that was monopolised by a nervous, maladjusted enuretic boy. There was also a rather engaging brash South American pupil, together with Martin Ratzer and one or two others. We were allowed a weekly bath in a conventional domestic enamelled tub which was supervised by the matron. She was a single parent mum who had a young daughter. The bath was filled with plenty of liquid carbolic and we all went in for a dip, towelling ourselves down afterwards. These very primitive facilities quite appalled me and I thought it must have been on a par with the deprivation suffered by my father when he was called up into the Army. Most of the boarders seemed to come from divorced homes and despite the imminent arrival of my sister, I wondered whether my parents' marriage, too, was on the rocks.

Our term's pocket money had been confiscated on arrival and was doled out to us on a weekly basis. We were allowed to write one letter home a week which was duly censored by a teacher. As at Rutland House the playground was simply the back garden asphalted over. The older boys seemed to dominate it, playing endless soccer matches. I remember them all being glued to the wireless set listening to the Wembley Cup Final.

The teachers seemed to me to be inferior to those I had experienced at Rutland House. This judgement was reinforced by the fact that the boys in the form above me would get me to do their maths homework on payment of 1s 6d. I was no great mathematician and, indeed, had to be coached in the subject by Mr Pumphrey; nevertheless, I was certainly better at the subject than those in the class above. I was dreadfully homesick. I had been with my parents through thick and thin, travelled the length and breadth of the country, slept with them in billeted accommodation and air raid shelters on a nightly basis, shared in all the decision-making that had gone on and now felt utterly rejected by them. I employed the tactics of my father when in the army; get out but in the meantime get on. I contrived to leave the place while at the same time adding to my pocket money and indeed to my status by doing the older boys' homework.

I wrote a clandestine letter to my mother telling her how unhappy I was and paid a day boy to post it. My mother must have realised something was amiss because she wrote to the school seeking permission for me to spend a weekend at home as my paternal grandmother was emigrating to Canada to live with her daughter and I needed the opportunity to say goodbye.

By good fortune, too, my elder cousin Ernie, I called him "uncle", was the resident engineer at the power station being built at Southwick, between Hove and Shoreham. He returned to Boston Manor at weekends to be with his family. It was arranged he would pick me up on the Friday evening to take me home. When I got home I informed my parents of the appalling standards at the school, both in terms of the poor teaching and primitive accommodation, and that under no circumstances would I consider returning. My father urged me to at least see the summer term out. I was aware that if I gave in to this I would have acquiesced in effect to staying on at the awful place. I was so unhappy and put up such resistance, crying my eyes out, that my parents relented and agreed to my not returning. The school never did return my outstanding pocket money which was all too symptomatic of the place.

State Schools

This meant that I had to spend the remainder of the summer term at the local primary school. Lammas School was the first time I had experienced state education. It was quite a good one. It was in Northfields and was situated between the Co-op laundry, that billowed smoke, steam and smells all over the playground and the adjoining Ealing Modern School (EMS).

This was located above the secondary moderns but below grammar schools in status, although it later became Walpole Grammar School. Miss Welham, Lammas's headmistress, had a formidable reputation and was a strict Christian Scientist. I recall vividly at one morning assembly when we were singing the hymn *Abide with Me*, Fast Falls the Eventide I remarked, giggling to those around me, that this was a very cheerful hymn. We all started laughing and she slapped me across the face on both cheeks.

The dawning of adolescence made me more aware of the attractions of the female sex. I was particularly drawn to the attractiveness of a one Ann Lewington, who to my chagrin soon moved away from the locality. Another girl was Margaret Angel, whom I never really got to know, but whom I always glanced fondly at when we passed by each other. Mary Cullen, however, had taken a shine to me and offered me her month's sweets ration as a token of her esteem.

The 11+ examination of that year had already been sat in the February and, in any case, I would have been ill-prepared for it having been concentrating on Common Entrance. I had not been rehearsed in the IQ tests which asked questions along the lines of: "As hand is to glove so condom is to......?" and you had to supply the right word. Actually, if that had been the question I would have been able to provide the correct answer.

My future education was looking rather bleak. In the autumn term I transferred to my second experience of state education by going to Borderston School situated between St Thomas the Apostle Anglican Church and Elthorne Park, halfway towards my old school Rutland House. I was to remain there for three weeks while my mother looked around for yet another private school.

At Borderston the school was built in a quadrangle; the classrooms had windows that faced inwards to the four corridors which were patrolled by a master with a cane who, if he detected a miscreant, went in and thrashed him without reference to the teacher holding the class. Again, like Hove & Aldrington, the quality of teaching was abysmal.

There was one exception in the person of the art teacher. In the first lesson he asked the new arrivals to draw any picture that came into their minds. I drew one of a country scene with a road moving away in perspective with a hillside of trees and verge side of grasses all presented as a black silhouette. I had copied it directly from one of my father's art books. Coming round to see how the boys were getting on he was brought up very short by my plagiarised design. He questioned me where I had got it from, had I copied it? I lied "No, it came from my imagination". With its sense of perspective and silhouette and general composition, it would have stood out from the run-of-the-mill attempts by the other boys. He must have thought he had a child artist prodigy on his hands. He said, "I'm sure we will be working closely together in the future". I thought to myself: "Yes, but only if I can't get out of this place".

Hounslow College

I knew this might be an eventuality as my mother had discovered Hounslow College for which I had to sit an entrance exam. It called itself an "independent grammar school". The architecture was familiar. Very similar to Hove & Aldrington

High School, it was housed in a Victorian/Edwardian villa or rather two adjoining villas. One was for the preparatory department and the other for the secondary grammar element.

Thus, in the space of six months, from April to September 1944, I attended five schools - two state and three private. Romani children have more stability than that. The normality of Rutland House returned with my entry to Hounslow College where I was to stay for the next five years.

It was situated in Lampton Road and had been founded in 1851 (it closed in 1999 in voluntary liquidation after a devastatingly bad Ofsted report). It was owned by a family trust which in 1926 appointed a Dr Norman Hindle, MA. DSc (Lond), a mathematician who came from the north of England. He appeared to be immensely over-qualified for the job if his degrees were authentic. It was very rare in those days to find someone with a higher doctorate, particularly at such a young age, a topic on which I will speculate further.

Hounslow College consisted of seven forms including an upper and lower sixth. According to the two school photographs I have, it comprised a hundred and six pupils in 1951, reducing to ninety-two by 1953. The fees were between £13 0s 0d and £15 0s 0d per term during my time there. In addition there were fifty-five pupils in the preparatory school in 1951, which had increased to eighty-two by 1953. The preparatory school had a headmistress, who also taught divinity to the secondary school, and four women teachers. The secondary school had eight staff in 1951 and two short of that in 1953. The small shortfall of staff was made up by Old Boys who either had done their *National Service* or, in some cases avoided it as conscientious objectors and served a term in prison, who were waiting some months before going up to university.

The staff were a sprinkling of itinerant graduates, with others completely unqualified. One such was Robert Hamblin, an Old Boy, who taught maths, geography and games, and was registered at Birkbeck College where he purported to be taking an undergraduate degree. In fact he never graduated and for that reason could only wear a student academic gown. This did not stop him later becoming deputy headmaster and indeed ultimately headmaster. C R Pearce, who taught history, was studying more assiduously at Birkbeck and graduated, after which he left for teaching in the state sector. His wife, who taught maths, had the appropriate initials L.C.M. (lowest common multiple) before her surname; she certainly had a B.Sc. from London University. My first form teacher was a Michael Hanley, a graduate from the National University of Ireland, whom I met up with much later as a colleague when I taught for a year in an East End secondary modern school after I myself had graduated.

The headmaster, Norman Hindle, never quite revealed his political preferences and was something of an enigma. He maintained very harsh discipline in the school with a highly contrived system of punishments. Apart from prefects' detentions, which could be handed out by those pupils holding such senior positions, there were form masters' detentions and more severely, housemasters' detentions. According to the misdemeanour a boy could be given one sort or go directly to a more serious one. At the apex were headmaster's detentions that were held on Saturday mornings. Two of those in a term would mean automatic expulsion from the school. In addition to this there was corporal punishment. Prefects could slipper boys on their backside as could the teachers (although, to my knowledge, Hamblin was the only one to have availed himself and I suspect that was to satisfy his personal gratification). Caning was the prerogative of the headmaster. There could be two kinds of thrashings. A public caning with reasons given for it, as a warning to the mob, or a private caning in his study which was usually on the bare bottom. For someone who had harboured and even cultivated pacifists on his staff and amongst his pupils, this use of sometimes excessive corporal punishment is almost inexplicable. I suspect there was more than a degree of homo-eroticism about it.

The school was not so much copying state grammar schools as aping the public school model. Its full prefects had tassels on their caps and wore distinctive undergraduate gowns. Sub-prefects, limited to the fifth form, had vertical stripes running down their caps. This elaborate uniform was provided by Kinch & Lack of Buckingham Palace Road. Full prefects were allowed to put their initials before their names, e.g. P. G. Salway, who was Head of School and later became a fellow of Sidney Sussex College, Cambridge, All Souls, Oxford and afterwards a professor at the Open University. He wrote *Roman Britain* (1981) part of the definitive Oxford History of England. Full prefects had a distinctive tie. Sub-prefects also had a special tie but one which indicated they were not quite so superior. The school had three Houses named after famous inter-war cricketers: Jack Hobbs, Maurice Tate, Wilfrid Rhodes. Wednesday afternoons were reserved for sports which consisted of cricket and athletics in the summer and soccer in the winter. We played schools of similar standing in the west Middlesex area, including Ealing College and Fray's College at Uxbridge.

Norman Hindle urged parents not to allow their sons to listen to the BBC Radio Light Programme, do paper rounds and other part-time jobs, go to the films or read red top newspapers. His aim was academic excellence which he achieved by means of a type of Darwinian academic attrition. In the first form there were twenty-plus pupils. By the time I came to leave after the fifth form there were only fifteen or so left. Miscreants, dimwits and lazy boys had been expelled earlier. Indeed, just as we were due to take GCE 'O' Levels, one boy - the senior sub-prefect - was instantly dismissed by the head, for working out arithmetic problems backwards from the answers contained at the end of the textbook. I thought this an amazing feat as I could not work them out from either the front or the back.

The sixth form was even smaller. It offered a limited range of subjects: Latin, history, French, English and maths. Those who survived to enter the sixth form succeeded quite well with some going on to Oxford or Cambridge and a few others to London University. The fees in the sixth were reduced to encourage gifted boys to stay on. So the operational principle was not profit-maximising to put it mildly; it was the relentless pursuit of academic excellence and, as I have said, many fell by the wayside, including me, at the end of the fifth form having not being weeded out before.

The school aped the public school/Oxbridge model in other respects. Its sports and other activities were organised by a Union Society. This was run by a committee of three teachers who acted as trustees, the Head of School (the senior pupil), and three other pupil representatives elected following hustings. Candidates had to be in at least the third form or above. I was the first pupil ever to stand as a third-former. The hustings were my first taste of electoral politics. I made an impassioned speech imploring those in the more senior forms – whose votes counted for more at each stage (third-formers counted one, fourth-formers two and so on) – to be inclusive in their choice. I was duly elected and my form master, a very congenial English teacher called Frank Parrott, BA (Birmingham) who later taught at Kingston Grammar School, remarked to me afterwards that "I should consider taking up politics". He may well have been being ironic but in fact I had achieved an unprecedented result; as it turned out he was also accurately prescient as my lifelong political involvement with the Liberals illustrates.

The other aspect which I liked was the debating society which met at six o'clock on Friday evenings in winter. Two sixth formers would propose a motion and two oppose it. I remember one subject for debate was "This house prefers Beethoven to Be-bop". Sometimes the teachers also spoke but for the most part exercised restraint. The Headmaster was always present, taking notes of what the speakers contributed. Very few of my third form classmates attended. I was an avid supporter. The Headmaster predicted in one of my reports that I would "go a long way because of my interest in and contributions to the Debating Society". Although, he was later to revise this opinion of my abilities, I like to think it was a fair comment on my precocious oratory.

I said earlier that Norman Hindle was something of an enigma with his somewhat contradictory ideas and more particularly in view of his inflated academic achievements. It turns out that he was a fraud and his degrees were bogus. In 2011 I enquired of the academic records at the London University Senate House and there is no trace of a Norman Hindle except insofar as one who had matriculated at Birkbeck College, the University's night school – but there is no further record. Furthermore, the *Middlesex Chronicle* contained no obituaries of him when he died. This is remarkable given that he was Headmaster of a local school for more than fifty years. It may well be that the family declined to contribute to an obituary because they could not cite the evidence for his alleged qualifications. But there is no doubt he had harboured academic ambitions. In a letter to *The Times* that appeared on 19 April 1923, a one Norman Hindle responded to a letter from Sir Joseph Larmor, the Lucasian Professor of Maths at Cambridge, questioning his interpretation of aspects of Einstein's Theory of Relativity. This is as remarkable as it is difficult to explain. It could, of course, have been written by another with the name of Norman Hindle, though that would be an unlikely coincidence. But the letter does suggest a deep knowledge of the Theory because it was accepted by the newspaper. Where had he acquired this? He was only in his early twenties at the time. Was he a mathematical autodidact or had he attended Birkbeck for a while but left before graduating?

He seems to have been something of a fantasist and he was not the only one around for, in the 1950s, he had recruited to the staff a one Frederick Walker, who claimed to be an ordained Anglican priest and the possessor of both a BA and a BSc from London University. He went on to be Headmaster of The Mall School, Teddington, where later he was exposed as a fraud regarding both his prefix title of "Reverend" and his two degree suffixes. He was convicted and imprisoned for illegally conducting marriages. Con men, I have observed, frequently invoke strict conformity in others as an aid in camouflaging their own deviousness. Both Hindle and Walker are vivid examples of the genre, but Hindle succeeded in getting away with it for the whole of his lifetime which spanned some ninety-eight years. Hindle by name – Swindle by nature, or so it would seem.

Looking back, I suppose I can say, I managed to survive at Hounslow College. A narrow escape came when at a headmaster's detention, always held on Saturday mornings, a boy borrowed a French textbook from my desk. In its pages, I had sketched a number of nude female figures which the headmaster seized upon and interrogated me the following week. He particularly wanted to know whether the sketches of the back part of the body were of women or men. I suspect I may have disappointed him when I said they were women. I thought to myself, it was after all a French book.

On another occasion, a boy, with whom I had been friendly, had not been as academically successful as his potential and past achievements would have predicted. He was an only child, and his excuse was that I had bullied him. This was complete nonsense, I had thought we were friends. His mother had seen the headmaster, reporting this to him and he called me in. Again, another fierce interrogation. The mother had claimed that I had shouted insults at him at their garden gate which was near the athletics ground we used occasionally in the summer term. Since I was a reluctant athlete I could prove that I had not regularly passed by his house.

The third occasion was when the headmaster called my parents in – I don't know what the precipitating cause was – but he did say to them, "Of course you do know that he is a socialist?" This did not alarm my mother who held to the ideals of George Lansbury's Labour Party. His evidence for this came, I think, from the current affairs meetings the fifth form had to which were invited representatives of the main political parties and others. I enjoyed these immensely. We even had a member of the Communist Party come to speak to us – which was a very liberal thing to do in those early Cold War days. Because of the various books on Marxism and Socialism my father had brought home during his flirtation with the Left in the early 'forties, I was able to provide Lenin's real name (Vladimir Ilyich Ulyanov) and talk about the main elements of the Communist Manifesto. I didn't have much detailed knowledge but it certainly was in stark contrast to the total political ignorance of my fellow pupils. All of them would have been unthinking Conservatives at the very best, having imbibed these views from their parents. I have to admit I was prompted to exhibit my knowledge of the Left in order to stand out and cut a dash and frankly show my superiority. My contemporaries much resented this and one invented a ditty which went:

> "Smith's a little Communist,
> His favourite colour's red
> And if I ever get the chance
> I'll shoot the bugger dead".

I took this to be a badge of honour, given the near-total political illiteracy of my fellow pupils.

Although I left Hounslow College with a motley collection of GCE 'O' Levels, I had acquired nevertheless some worthwhile skills. I had been form prefect for three years and a sub-prefect during my final year when I was also made captain of Rhodes House. I had gained oratorical skills in both the debating society and in standing in the hustings for the Union Society to which I had been successfully elected. As a result I had no fear of public speaking which was to hold me in good stead throughout my life.

In retrospect, however, I have very mixed feelings towards Hounslow College. The main impression I have of it, which stemmed directly from Hindle (I almost never saw him smile), was one of "seriousness". The elaborate system of hierarchical punishments was a major factor – it inspired fear in all of us. The relentless application of attrition in the form of academic Darwinism added to it as was vividly illustrated by the numbers of those who were required to leave and others who were expelled. The lack of any prizes for good academic achievement added to this: the only prizes were for athletics in the summer and there were House and School colours for cricket and soccer. Apart from school camps in the summer and Easter holidays there were absolutely no outings to theatres or music centres at all. At least at Rutland House we had been taken to the "Britain Can Make It" exhibition at the Olympia, Earls Court in 1948 and to a film about Christ's Crucifixion at the local fleapit cinema. There was nothing analogous available at Hounslow College.

One of the redeeming features that made life agreeable were my daily cycle trips to school. On the way, I would stop and chat with a number of attractive girls. Anne Davies was one who especially appealed to me. I asked her to play tennis one Saturday evening. I dressed in a blazer and crisply ironed shorts, carrying my racket in a sports case. I had prepared my introduction to her parents and duly knocked on their front door. It was opened by her father who roared at me. I fled down the path back to the gate. He was joking but I had difficulty in regaining my composure. We remained friendly but, a couple of kisses apart, nothing came of it romantically. To my chagrin, she later had a longer relationship with one of my contemporaries at the London School of Economics (LSE), ditching him and marrying one of his fellow National Service lieutenants in the Royal Army Engineering Corps (RAEC).

I recall, too, her close friend, Anna Karpinska, who attended St Anne's Covent School with her. There were also the Rudderham sisters, Rosemary and Susan who went to Gumley House, a rather better Catholic girls' school in Isleworth. At the time their uncle was a bishop in the Bristol area.

My ever-observant father had noticed my early female liaisons. He always slept late on Sunday mornings. Calling me to his bedside, he said he had noticed my interest in girls and explained that "he didn't want a pregnant girl sobbing on his front porch". He told me "I would have no excuse as" – pointing to the chest of drawers – "I always keep a gross box of Durex sheaths there, and you can always help yourself". Aware of this imperative, I collected "a packet of three" and put them in my wallet. Three years on, when I had need of them, they had perished. But the lesson was not lost on me and I was grateful for it and to my father's very liberal attitude towards teenage sex which was quite remarkable for the time.

These very innocent relationships made for pleasant distractions from the more disagreeable, and totally male, atmosphere of Hounslow College. The curriculum at Hounslow College was very circumscribed. It consisted of the Englishes, maths, French, Latin, history, geography, physics and divinity. This last one was on the syllabus because it was compulsory but there were no religious assemblies of any kind ever. There was no chemistry or biology nor indeed any laboratories at all and physics was taught simply from a textbook and blackboard.

The vacation camps were a regular feature at Hounslow College. I attended those at Burton Bradstock in Dorset, Flackwell Heath in Buckinghamshire and one at Battle near Hastings in East Sussex. We took the train to the distant sites though we cycled to Flackwell Heath. The bell tents and various cooking utensils followed in a lorry. I quite enjoyed these camps.

Seriousness – A Hallmark

But I revert to the overall and rather intimidating atmosphere of "seriousness". For me it was quite congenial since I myself was a very serious young boy. Hounslow College reinforced that trait in me. Why was I so serious? – The war years, in short. I had endured the Blitz in both Gosport and London in all its forms. I had lived in the utmost intimacy with my parents in billets and air raid shelters. I was privy to many adult conversations about the war and what might follow it. I had been lightly exposed to left-wing literature and my bosom pal, Michael Parsons, who lived a few yards from me, was of a very scholarly natural disposition. By the time we were fourteen he had introduced me to the thoughts of Spinoza, the Dutch philosopher. We had many discussions between us about the obligations of the citizen to the state and vice-versa and other such momentous issues. We both thought we were pacifists and he indeed registered as a conscientious objector when called-up for National Service. Contributing to all this was the general atmosphere of the times post-1945. The First World War had promised the building of "a land fit for heroes" which subsequent events leading to the inter-war Depression, rendered a hollow undertaking. Following the Labour landslide of 1945, however, and despite the continuation of rationing and other deprivations, including the very cold winter of 1947, the coming of peace created an optimistic Zeitgeist: there was a sense of social reform and renewal with the creation of such things as the National Health Service (NHS) in 1948 and the reforms in education following the earlier 1944 Act. Furthermore, the creation of the United Nations in 1945 promised greater world peace. The fact is that the advent of the Cold War between the West and Soviet Russia that led to the Berlin airlift and later became fully manifest in the Korean War, dashed many of these earlier optimistic hopes. By the same token they elevated political issues both at home and abroad to a higher level of consciousness. These created very serious concerns for my friend Michael and me. He had not been evacuated and so wasn't subject to the sort of experience I had had in Gosport and Scotland. So, in contrast to our age group peers, we were "little old men", infused with the secret not of youth but rather of "eternal old age". We had been rendered old before our time. This affected us differently. He became absorbed in classical music and scholarship for its own sake and went up to Pembroke College Oxford to read Philosophy, Politics and Economics (PPE). He became a school teacher and did a tour of duty in Zambia. The result of that was to disabuse him of his idealism and he became very reactionary in his views and we lost touch until more recently when he had regained some of his former liberalism.

CHAPTER 4

A DOUBLE LIFE: SUBURBIA AND FITZROVIA IN THE 1940s

Returning from the brief stay in Edinburgh in early 1944 meant another great change in my life-style similar to the geographical mobility that would mark me out from most of my age cohort. I was to lead something of a double life. On the one hand, I would spend most of the week as a suburban schoolboy, while on the other I would regularly spend Friday evenings and some Saturdays living it up in the West End. I dwelt, so to speak, in two quite distinct parallel universes moving seamlessly between them, or so I fondly like to think. The reason for this was my father's new career.

Thus, my alter ego resulted from my increasing involvement in Fitzrovia. After demobilisation in 1942 my father had to find work. I think he went back to Mayfair for a short while but my mother had always objected to Raymond's influence on him. Being under contract, which Raymond would most certainly have enforced, he could not leave and work in hairdressing at least for a specified minimum period. A new business venture, therefore, had to be launched.

Coincidental with my father's departure from the army was the release from directed labour of Danny Ginsberg. Danny and his wife Kitty had been our neighbours in Gosport. He was a skilled carpenter and had been deployed in the dockyards, building and repairing ships. My parents, both being Londoners and the same age, had become firm friends not least during the nights spent in air raid shelters. Another coincidence was that he, too, suffered with a back problem – in his case a curvature of the spine. It was this which led to his release from the docks and they had returned to London and Danny did not wish to return to carpentry which would have exacerbated his condition.

Toys

For different reasons, then, the two men wished to change careers. They decided to team up in partnership, making toys and later dolls. They saw a gap in the market: the large toy firms like Tri-ang had their factories transformed over to the production of munitions and other war necessities. Food and clothes rationing also meant that there was a degree of surplus income among much of the population at large.

Their first "factory" was our garage in Boston Vale. They bought up hundreds of redundant date boxes from, I think, Clarnico's, which were no longer required given that dates would not be imported and seen in the shops of Britain until after the war. The tops and bottoms of these boxes made excellent toy airplane wings. They also bought up a whole load of timber offcuts and produced toy aircraft. My father designed these and his partner built the planes. They acquired a spray gun by which the toys could be painted in sky grey and affixed with red, white and blue roundel transfers, simulating the RAF identification marks on their wings and fuselages. Small nails were deftly tapped in to act as aircraft guns. They sold like hot cakes.

Fitzrovia

It was probably a combination of the supply of redundant date boxes running out and the need to expand both premises and their product range that Ginsberg & Smith (as their partnership was called – or G &S for short) moved to a unit in Tottenham Mews in Fitzrovia. Tottenham Mews consisted of a nineteenth century series of artisan buildings that included a foundry and a number of other trades. Alf Graber, a cousin of Danny's and also a trained carpenter with his own furniture workshop there, had found the vacant accommodation for them. Toy aircraft were abandoned and it was decided instead to produce dolls. My father's move to working in Fitzrovia would open up – for me especially – a new, very cosmopolitan world of sophisticated delights largely absent in the suburbs.

Before the mass immigration from overseas into Britain which started in the mid-nineteen fifties and has continued unabated, isolated migrant communities had established themselves in Liverpool, Cardiff's Tiger Bay, Chinatown near the London docks, the Jewish ghettoes of the East End and the Irish in Kilburn. These were all relatively segregated communities. In London's West End, by contrast, were two very cosmopolitan districts living cheek by jowl and divided by Oxford Street. To the south was Soho with its strip and clip joints and a whole variety of restaurants and cafes, of mainly continental, European derivations. The French and Italians were the most conspicuous foreigners while in Shaftesbury Avenue the first Chinese restaurant appeared.

North of Oxford Street was Fitzrovia. It is an area bounded by Marylebone Road to the north, Tottenham Court Road to the east and Great Portland Street to the west. The spine of Fitzrovia was and is Charlotte Street running from north to south.

To my young eyes, at least, Fitzrovia seemed to have a greater mixture of nationalities than Soho. There were far fewer French with the exception of the fashionable L'Etoile restaurant. Hungarians, Czechs, Italians, Germans, Swiss and most noticeably Greek and Turkish Cypriots interacted with each other as well as a small contingent of Jews and, of course, the native English.

Fitzrovia was something of a cultural and artisanal area. The performing arts were represented by the Scala Theatre which stood at the corner of Charlotte Street and Tottenham Street. Slightly "off Broadway" so to speak, it put on drama – both professional and amateur, pantomimes at Christmas, musicals and conventional plays at other times in the year. The plastic arts were represented by Tiranti's, one of the leading art book sellers and retailers of artists' tools and equipment which included paints, brushes and sculptors' spatulas, chisels and other modelling tools. Tiranti's attracted many artists among its customers. Years later it moved its headquarters to Reading.

My father readily took to the bohemian character of Fitzrovia. In addition to its mixture of foreign nationals and vocations, it was more political than Soho. Its southern neighbour Soho had Collets, the Communist bookshop. Not to be left out, Fitzrovia had a small, almost clandestine Marxist bookseller housed in a Dickensian shop in Tottenham Street. The greater mix of eastern Europeans also contributed to the political atmosphere. Freed from the constraints of army life, and the equally restrictive obsequiousness that was a necessary part of the stock-in-trade of a Mayfair stylist catering to the whims of his expensive clientele, my father went to the opposite extreme. He grew a beard and long hair, wore a camel overcoat and open toed sandals. He was, as it were, a trailer for the "hippies" of the 1960s. He saw himself as a "Left Bank" artist of the kind he had seen in pre-war Paris. This was not altogether a conceit for he had enrolled part-time at the Ealing School of Art to learn the techniques of sculpting. He swiftly acquired modelling skills, working in both clay and plasticine, as well as the casting of moulds. He sculpted a very good bust of my mother which is now in the possession of my brother.

In his flirtation with Communism he bought a number of Marxist and socialist tracts, including some by George Bernard Shaw and Friedrich Engels, as well as Robert Tressell's working-class classic *The Ragged Trousered Philanthropists*. He sported a Red Star lapel badge with its Hammer and Sickle motif. His then politics would have been a culmination of resentment of his childhood life in the workhouse, the recollection of Oswald Mosley's British Union of Fascists raids in the East End, the differential treatment meted out to officer cadets and other ranks in the army, together with his ambivalence towards his Mayfair clients. It was also fuelled by the contemporary Zeitgeist: the entry into the war of Soviet Russia, the siege of Stalingrad and the popular portrayal of Joseph Stalin as "Uncle Joe" encouraged him in adopting such a stance. I do not think he formally joined the Communist Party but flirted as a "fellow traveller", and in any case his outlook changed swiftly as a result of the embourgeoisement occasioned by accelerated earnings.

His Left Bank attire was swapped for Saville Row bespoke suits (I still have his dinner suit made by Kilgour & French) as he became the model of a successful businessman. But in all the roles he assumed, they were carried off with great aplomb and style – he could be a true chameleon.

The skilled trades in Fitzrovia were clustered, for the most part, in Tottenham Mews. This cul-de-sac contained a whole series of artisanal units on the north side and at the end, but the south side was dominated by a very large foundry. The latter catered for both artists and industrial clients. For their part, various cabinet makers catered for the needs of the nearby up-market furniture stores like Heals and Maples.

The European continental flavour of Charlotte Street could be seen in the Swiss Club next to Tiranti's which catered for a number of rather elderly Swiss where they could eat, drink and play snooker or billiards. It allowed non-Swiss to join and both Danny and my father became members. I remember it was always infused with very heavy cigar smoke.

Charlotte Street abounded with restaurants providing a variety of international cuisines. In addition to L'Etoile there was Schmidt's, the famous German restaurant and Bertorelli's, the equally famous Italian one which later spawned a chain of such eating houses. The rest, and altogether rather more modest, comprised a number of Greek and Turkish Cypriot dining establishments. The Scala Restaurant, directly opposite the theatre of the same Italian name, was in fact run by Greek Cypriots and it was there that I experienced my first homemade yoghurt prepared on the premises; henceforth yoghurt became an addiction. At an angle across the road was Barba Yanni's, a

Turkish Cypriot kebab house. There were one or two Cypriot men's tailors and a continental pharmacy, displaying a Green Cross sign, on the junction of Goodge Street and Charlotte Street. The Green Cross, common enough in Europe was not generally adopted in the UK until the end of the twentieth century and is now as ubiquitous here as in the rest of Europe.

Tottenham Court Road was dominated by Heals and Maples, two famous furnishing stores, at the bottom end was the large Odeon cinema – and until fairly recently, mid-way along stood the formidable police station which was a grimly fortified Soviet-style fortress; it was regularly used to interrogate major criminal suspects. Another of the features of the street that attracted me was the existence of Shearns' vegetarian shop and restaurant. I was taken there quite often.

Dolls

Ginsberg & Smith started to increase the range of products they made. My father modelled them and cast the plaster of Paris moulds which would be replicated and multiplied in alloy necessary for mass production at the Tottenham Mews foundry. He took over our dining room as a studio, and I would watch fascinated as he designed and sculpted different objects. These ranged from pet rabbits and other ornaments to baby dolls. I saw him start with the requisite armature supports for the clay or plasticine materials, through to designing and fitting the "keys" that would secure the two halves of the plaster moulds. Toy guns and airplanes came to an end as the production of dolls and other more profitable products took over.

My father was essentially at the creative and production end of G&S while Danny looked after marketing and accounts. The two of them collaborated in the design of the various machines they needed to produce the dolls and other products.

The dolls were made of what would now be called polymers. The development of such plastics was then at a very rudimentary stage and consisted of a silica gel base. This was rationed and in very short supply. They managed to get regular supplies by bribing the lady official from the Board of Trade who was responsible for rationing the essential gel. They would entertain her to lunch at L'Etoile and would almost certainly have paid her cash bribes.

The plastic material was boiled in steel vats and poured into the alloy moulds. These were then placed on a bed of ice to congeal and later transferred to hot air driven ovens (essentially wind tunnels) until they were baked hard. Limbs, heads and bodies were all manufactured separately. They were sprayed with flesh colour paint and assembled by means of a series of internal elastic bands. Later on, the plastic moulded hair gave way to real wigs. My father taught the increasing number of female staff to make these and fix to the skulls along with opening and closing eyes, painted rosy lips and cheeks and clothed in sumptuous dresses.

Such was the latent potential demand for these dolls that G&S had to move again to even larger premises around the corner at 99 Charlotte Street ('phone number: *Museum 2896*). This was just next to the Middlesex Hospital and at the end of a terrace of nineteenth century villas. It consisted of a basement, ground floor, two upper floors and an attic, all of which were utilised for different stages of production. It was later demolished to make room for better hospital access but the rest of the terrace is still intact. Staffing was a problem and they could not always choose whom they would have wished. The men working in the basement, filling up the moulds and freezing them, were as often as not ex-Borstal boys from Kentish Town who were rejected for military service as unsuitable because of their criminal records. The young women, who were employed in assembling, dressing and packing were from similar backgrounds. G&S employed a manager, a foreman and a forewoman who were more reliable. As mentioned previously, they also hired a technical expert, a one Martin Ratzer who was a chemical engineer employed full-time by Pyrene's on the Great West Road. He was a necessary consultant to advise on combating what were endemic problems of instability in the new silica gel polymer composition. Often batches of the plastic became adulterated and quite useless and the vats in which they were prepared had to be thoroughly cleaned and the contents destroyed.

Rationing and full employment in wartime meant that there was a good deal of personal disposable income that could not readily be spent. The demand for dolls, particularly at Christmas time, could hardly be satisfied. The firm employed Messrs Cohen and Randell as part-time salesmen. They had been commercial travellers for Clarnico's but sweet rationing had restricted their activities. Doubtless they had met at the start when the date boxes had been purchased from Clarnico's. As a Jewish and Gentile team they felicitously mirrored Ginsberg and Smith.

I remember, too, that G&S would regularly attend the annual Harrogate Toy Fair to display and promote their dolls. At the height of their fortunes G&S dolls would retail at around £45 each. This was a colossal sum of money for those days. As a consequence both families achieved their maximum life-time personal earning power. Both had cars. I remember our first one was a rickety three-wheeler van. This was swiftly replaced by a pre-war Opel followed by a second-hand Ford V8 and then a Vauxhall saloon whose registration, I recall, was CKY 152. Each one was an improvement on the other. My father usually drove from Boston Manor to Charlotte Street via Acton and Hammersmith rather than take the Tube as he had previously.

Food was in plentiful supply. In addition to its other features, Charlotte Street was one of the main centres of the black market although the two main histories of the topic make no reference to this. The probable reason for the lacuna is that the authors relied heavily on court records of prosecutions of those black marketeers who operated mainly in the suburbs and provinces where their nefarious activities could be more easily spotted both by envious neighbours and government officials. The heterogeneous nature of life in Fitzrovia may well have helped conceal the subterranean activities of its many spivs, and in any case, a sort of omerta - or code of silence - was observed there.

Along the same terrace as G&S, in the basement below Louis' Italian restaurant, you could buy as much tea, cheese, butter, ham and bacon as you could pay for at the inflated prices demanded. Some of these items would be bartered with Bib Parsons in return for weekly joints of beef or lamb which he brought back with him from Allen & Co, the Mayfair butchers that he managed.

While doll manufacturing was the mainstay of G&S they

also branched out into producing various ornaments, including a "Squander Bug" money box emblazoned with Nazi swastikas. The Ministry of Information had invented the Squander Bug as a satanic cartoon character to discourage waste in war-time. Adapting the Squander Bug as a money box was intended to encourage thrift but the authorities banned it because it publicised the insignia of the foe.

In the years 1943-44 I would go up most Friday evenings with my mother to meet my father after work. Taking the Piccadilly Line from Boston Manor to Leicester Square we would change onto the Northern Line and go two stops up to Goodge Street. These Underground stations served as air raid shelters and were fitted with hundreds of steel bunks catering for sleepers seeking protection from the incessant bombing forays of the Luftwaffe.

On these Friday excursions we would take in a film at one of the cinemas in Tottenham Court Road or Leicester Square. Not being very religiously observant or *frum* Jews, the Ginsbergs would often join us. We would then eat at Lyon's Corner House or one of the restaurants in Fitzrovia. Occasionally, I would be taken to Veeraswamy's in Regent Street which was one of the first Indian restaurants to open in London. We would also regularly frequent the Chinese Hong Kong restaurant in Shaftesbury Avenue which was overwhelmingly patronised by American GIs. They were invariably accompanied by their current English pick-ups, who were game for a night out and a new pair of nylon stockings purchased from the US army's PX stores. Nylons were highly-prized in a time of acute clothes rationing and shortages.

From 1947 onwards, I would spend my summer holidays from

school working at G&S for quite a good wage, usually operating the ovens which baked the dolls. Accordingly, I acquired regular experience of Fitzrovia and its environs. This was before the Fitzroy Tavern had become the favourite haunt of such literary luminaries as Anthony Burgess, Dylan Thomas and Brendan Behan. Unlike these heavy imbibers I saw the Fitzrovia of the period through the eyes of a sober young boy. One of the most dramatic incidents was the murder that occurred in a botched robbery at Jay's Jewellery between Charlotte Street and Tottenham Mews. It hit the national headlines.

There were also one or two brothels in the area. I recall Bill Neale, a sculptor originally from Loughborough, who occasionally helped my father, pointing out to me a bedroom across from G&S with open windows in the summer where one of the locals plying the streets had taken her client back. It was all part of my education that the conditions of war had induced. Relative to my school fellows, then, I was a "man of the world" long before my time regarding both sexual matters as well as the very wide range of cuisines and nationalities to which I had been introduced.

The fortunes of G&S did not last as the established toy manufactures returned to their original trade. In any case, the durability of the silica gel dolls was relatively short-lived and that is why none exist today. They tended to turn mouldy after about a couple of years. Had they been wise, Messrs Ginsberg & Smith would have diversified their newly gained wealth into other activities. Many more financially adroit people became wealthier by investing their fortunes made in war in buying up disused bomb sites for later commercial redevelopment. G&S

did not have that foresight and spent their money as fast as they earned it. By 1951 the bubble had burst. G&S was liquidated and my father returned to hairdressing, his contractual obligations to Raymond having long since expired.

Jews & Israel

Danny Ginsberg then ran a model agency and later specialised in providing animal turns for film and stage productions. I liked him very much. He had given me my first cricket bat and indeed would call upon me to make up a team for the Jewish Maccabi Club cricket eleven. They played every Sunday on my school sports ground in Boston Manor. He was the wicket-keeper and quite a good batsman. It always amused me how the cricketers were accompanied on alternate Sundays: one week the wives came along and the next one the mistresses.

The Ginsbergs introduced me to Anglo-Jewry, its culture and that of the wider diaspora. It has remained a fascination throughout my life. I attended Jewish weddings and bar mitzvahs and acquired a smattering of Yiddish which later came in handy. In his autobiography, John Gross details a hundred or so Yiddish phrases he had picked up from his East End relatives which, I was gratified to discover, were almost identical to those I had learned.

In the 1940s, it was impossible for any sentient being not to be aware of the plight of the Jews. We learnt of the Holocaust through the BBC radio broadcasts of Richard Dimbleby, the cinema newsreels, newspapers and magazines that had reported in great detail the liberation of the Nazi concentration camps. The emaciated, dying and dead victims were seen alongside the trains, huts and gas chambers that had transported, housed and destroyed so many. Most vividly, I recall welcoming the repatriation of Kitty's mother, always known as "Buba" (Grandma), who had survived Auschwitz. My father rolled up the sleeve of her blouse to reveal the tattooed individual number given to all inmates as part of the methodical recording that typified the Nazi war apparatus.

Much publicity was also accorded to the attempts of surviving European Jews to migrate to Palestine which the mandated British authorities tried to stop. In 1948 the State of Israel was created following a successful war of independence. I followed these developments and the different role played by the Haganah (the "regular" army) and the terrorist groups like the Irgun Zvei Leumi and the notorious Stern Gang.

In the 1980s I went to Israel for the first time along with a group of British academics at the invitation of the Zionist Federation. The main purpose was to meet our Israeli counterparts and their universities. We also went to Yad Vasheim – the memorial to the Holocaust, attended the Knesset and viewed most of the main Jewish, Muslim and Christian sites.

It was usual to take turns thanking our Israeli hosts. When it came to me, I could not forbear but to include a smattering of Yiddish. This somewhat surprised the tour organisers as they intended our group to consist exclusively of *goyim* (non-Jews). Anti-Semitism is all too common, but there is also what one might call Semitism by which Jews recognise other Jews even when strangers. My use of Yiddish caused some bafflement in this regard and the inevitable and anxious enquiry came "are you Jewish?" This had happened to me before in London. My stock reply is: "Ah, Cain and Abel – the hands and the voice. It's your problem, you decide." I always enjoy teasing my interrogators.

Shortly afterwards, I was to serve briefly as an international governor of Haifa University. Traditionally, and long before the creation of Israel in 1948, the City of Haifa had been among the most secular in the region, enjoying good inter-communal relations between Palestinians and Jews. The University had been established in 1972, had gained a good academic reputation, occupied a delightful site on Mount Carmel and had the most pluralistic student composition in Israel.

During the 1980s, however, inter-communal relations had deteriorated very badly on campus. At the time, the Israeli students were being manipulated by Rabbi Meir Kahane, who originally hailed from New York, and was a militant, very vociferous ultra-Zionist. He served jail terms in both the USA and Israel for spreading hatred. He managed to form his own political party and even got himself elected to the Knesset. He was assassinated in New York in 1990 by an Egyptian-American. For their part, the Palestinian undergraduates were being organised by the Israeli Communist Party which took its instructions directly from Moscow.

The position was almost a stand-off. One result was that the Palestinian students were regarded as security risks and could not apply for any government jobs. The State of Israel being the main employer of graduates meant suitable employment was denied them which further inflamed feelings. I was able to secure funds from the Joseph Rowntree Reform Trust (JRRT) to appoint a careers adviser for the Palestinian students who comprised nearly half of the University's output.

Among the international governors I was by far the poorest as the rest comprised multi-millionaires from America and South Africa. Waiting to be invited in to meet the domestic governors, I ventured to say to my colleagues as an amusing conversation point: "I have long pondered the origins of Jewish genius and my empirical researches have established beyond peradventure it is not due to the workings of the Darwinian Law of 'the survival of the fittest' following two thousand years of persecution; rather, it results from the wearing of the *yomulka* (skull cap) which heats the brain to the optimum working temperature." One of them, not appreciating my attempt at humour, retorted: "I'm a self-made millionaire, president of my Reform *schul* in Philadelphia, and I've never worn a *yomulka*!" I retorted: "But think how more money you'd have made if you'd worn one!"

Someone who did appreciate my humour, introducing me to one of the domestic governors, an ex-head of Mossad, said: "General, this is Professor Trevor Smith. My God, he don't look like a Jew, but he certainly sounds like one!" Again, I took this as a compliment.

On another trip to Israel, I fortuitously met a group of the "old guard" who had served in the Haganah, including Dr Zez Vilnay who had been its map compiler and who presented me with a signed copy of his *Israel Guide* that had gone into over twenty editions. These men had subsequently held high State positions, such as running the nationalised industries. They were part of the old Ben Gurion Labour Party establishment that governed the State until ousted by the Likud. They were mainly Ashkanazim from pre-WWII Eastern Europe whose ranks were swelled by post-1948 refugees. The right wing Likud Party gained power with the later influx of Sephardim from Morocco, Iraq and other parts of Africa and Asia along with those who managed to flee from the Soviet Empire. Like many, I found it easier to support the earlier Israel rather than the subsequent one.

The present situation in the Middle East is as untenable as it has ever been and, despite the many and continuing diplomatic efforts initiated by the USA and the European Union (EU). It seems as intractable as ever and far from any peaceful resolution. Two states, one Israel and the other Palestine, is the only practical way forward but remains an elusive goal.

CHAPTER 5

FURTHER & HIGHER EDUCATION: CHISWICK POLYTECHNIC AND THE LONDON SCHOOL OF ECONOMICS & POLITICAL SCIENCE (LSE)

On leaving school at the age of sixteen in 1953 I had to find employment. Influenced by my mother's preference for a career in insurance, I entered the City. The manager who recruited me at Sun Alliance instructed me to enrol for evening classes to take the appropriate Institute of Chartered Insurance examinations in order to qualify professionally. I discovered these were available at Chiswick Polytechnic which, despite later connotations, was simply a further education college built on the same site as the Chiswick School of Music and Drama which my maternal grandmother had attended decades earlier.

The general prospectus included the insurance exams but also GCE 'A' level courses which caught my eye. I discovered that formally I only needed to acquire two 'A' levels in order to gain matriculation at London University. Something stirred inside me. I talked to my father. Although the family fortunes had nose-dived with the demise of Ginsberg & Smith, my father had always instilled in me the need to acquire a university education. As he said: "The letter B something after your name is the hallmark of a gentleman so long as it's not BF!" I asked him if it was possible for me to enrol as a full- time student to take 'A' levels. I said I would take them as quickly as I could, working as a temporary postman at Christmas and temporary jobs in factories during other holidays. Without hesitation, he agreed. I shall always be in his total debt and have utter admiration for him. My mother, by contrast, was horrified. I had anticipated her reaction accurately. I had enjoyed a good schooling in her eyes but the reduction in our family fortunes meant she wanted to see money coming into the house and for me to embark on a steady professional career in insurance. Anyway the dice were cast and her objections ignored. Like many parents she had aspirations for her offspring to advance, but even so, in her view, these had their own upper limits. Later, she tried to resist my brother going up to university while my sister had to wait many years to enter higher education.

Chiswick Polytechnic

I enrolled at Chiswick Polytechnic being accepted by the Head of the Department of Commerce and Languages, a Mr R S Ashworth. I always thought his initials RSA were particularly fitting as many of the examinations taken by his students were set by the Royal Society of Arts (RSA).

Chiswick Polytechnic was a complete eye-opener. It made me realise what education should really seek to be. It was democratic with mutual respect between staff and students and everyone was treated as an adult. Some of the lecturers even called me Mr Smith. There was an excellent library and librarian. The staff were all competent and some quite excellent.

There was a Day Students' Union with a parallel one for evening students. When the time for the nomination of office holders came round I stood successfully and was elected President of the Day Students' Union. In that capacity I was meant to make representations to staff in the case of student complaints but, not surprisingly, there were none. It arranged socials such as dances, then very much in fashion, and amateur dramatics. One of the girls taking a senior secretarial course was a very attractive medal-winning ballroom dancer. Students wanted ballroom dancing lessons but there was no male who could reach her standard and provide these lessons. I had recently taken a twelve week introductory course in the three main ballroom dances – viz waltz, foxtrot and quickstep. I volunteered to partner her and instruct some two hundred of our fellow students in the techniques of ballroom dancing so long as she agreed to take the lead. She was more than happy and I successfully hid any anxieties on my part. It was all good skills training for me as well as for the fledgling dancers.

Initially, I opted to take French, English Literature and Political History at 'A' level. They were taught respectively by Mr L V Hebblewhite, Mr Fisher and Dr M J Sydenham. I continued with these courses during the first two terms of 1954. However, I learned that Economics, about which I was fairly ignorant, was also available - a subject which sounded terribly relevant to public affairs and contemporary issues. Accordingly, I abandoned English and French and in the September I chose to take Economics, continue with Political History and add to it Economic History. To take two Histories was something of a cheat and would not be allowed today. However, the selection suited me perfectly.

Dr Sydenham continued to be an outstanding teacher. I

still have the first essay I wrote for him on the Greek War of Independence. He used the then 'A' level marking scheme which was up to 20 marks per essay/answer. He awarded me 2/20. I was shattered. I had sweated over that essay in order to impress him. His laconic comment was "It is at least good to see that you can write good English but you failed to answer the question". Not only did he teach me modern political history but, more importantly, examination technique.

Bert Whelan, another lecturer, had studied PPE at Oxford. He had married well, and rumour had it that he had extensive property holdings where he personally collected the rents. He would appear down the long corridor smoking a cigarette and stubbing it out before he entered our small classroom. He was very laid back and not the most assiduous of teachers. Nevertheless, after some weeks he suggested to me that I should try for a place at Oxford University. I replied that I did not have Latin or Greek, either of which was a pre-requisite at the time for matriculation to Oxford. He said I should wait a year and take 'O' level Latin. I said I couldn't afford another year.

Economic History was taught by David Kitchen and I owe him a great debt of gratitude. He was a graduate of the University of Manchester and had had a career in banking. He was a Gilchrist Medalist. He taught part-time and led the amateur dramatic society. He was in his element there. He agreed to teach Economic History to me and another student, Richard Brown. We did not comprise a quorum sufficient for him to be paid so he taught us voluntarily in his spare time.

Dr Sydenham went on to become a University professor at Carleton University, Ottawa and established himself as a major expert on the history of the French Revolution. He was succeeded by Dr Andrews, a Tudor historian, who later became a colleague of mine in the University of Hull and ultimately a professor there. Until the Robbins expansion of universities there were few academic vacancies in the UK of the 1950s which resulted in the high academic quality of the teaching that we received, enjoyed and from which we greatly benefitted.

The extra curricula student activity was supervised by Marjorie Leslie. I came to know her in my capacity as Day Students' Union President. She was the wife of Robert F Leslie who was an eastern European historian teaching at Queen Mary College, London. I became a colleague of his when I joined the staff there some thirteen or fourteen years later. At the time they were both paid-up members of the Communist Party but left following the invasion of Hungary in 1956 along with so many others. Marjorie Leslie later became Principal of Richmond College of Higher Education and was a justly famous pioneer and promoter of further education. She was awarded the OBE.

So I was committed to studying for Political History in a year and a half while taking on Economics and Economic History in a year that effectively meant nine months to which I enthusiastically and assiduously applied myself. There were the distractions of the Day Students' Union Presidency but also the fact that I had fallen seriously in love for the first time. One of the liberating features of Chiswick Polytechnic was that it contained a majority of female students. Hitherto I had been subjected, for the most part, to all-boys schooling.

In September 1954 I became enraptured with a very

attractive girl both physically and in terms of her very engaging personality. She was the only child of a local GP from South Ealing and both parents were of Anglo-Irish Protestant origin; he was a graduate of Trinity College, Dublin. We spent a great deal of time every day literally in each other's arms. Her father, an avid Tory who spent most evenings in the local Conservative Club, insisted at the end of our courses that we broke up as she was destined to marry the son of her parents' close friends in Dunmore East, County Waterford.

I was to learn the hard lesson that at the end of most romances, you leave something of yourself behind and this endures long after the affair comes to an end. I also learned to associate a particular song with each girlfriend. In this case it was Ivor Novello's *This is my lovely day,* it is the day I shall remember the day I'm dying. She had a delightful voice and we performed as a reasonably harmonious duet. Thus, for me, the academic year 1954-5 was both intellectually, emotionally and physically very demanding.

As I have retailed it, I had a varied experience of schooling. Rutland House was quite a good prep school by the standards of the time where I learnt well. Lammas Primary School could also have been good for me had I spent more time there. Hounslow College was pretty dire as I have explained. Chiswick Polytechnic, as I hope I have indicated, was a quite outstanding and maturing educational experience which provided a brilliant bridge to university. Chiswick Polytechnic had liberated me and, in so extending me, I had matured a good deal in the eighteen months I spent there. It had also enabled me to feel educationally 'normal' in the sense it was part of the state system and, as such, a common experience for most of my age group. Nearly all of my schooling up to then had been, in one way or another, freakish.

London School of Economics

I wanted to become a barrister, which I fondly thought would engage my oratorical gifts, and so toyed with the prospect of reading Law at one of the London University colleges. But the world generally counselled against this: "read law by all means and then qualify as a solicitor, as your family does not have the means to support you as you try to establish yourself in the senior branch of the legal profession, and besides, you lack any influential contacts." For the first and, I think, the only time in my life (so far as my career direction was concerned), I yielded to the advice of others.

I think it not fanciful to believe I could have had a successful career at the Bar. In 1995 I represented my younger son at an industrial tribunal. Gideon had worked his way up to become deputy general manager of a small waste disposal firm. The owner sold it and it became a subsidiary of the giant Thames Water Company who appointed a chief executive from another waste disposal firm. In his turn he immediately recruited two of his colleagues, without advertising the jobs. Soon after in 1994 Gideon was summarily dismissed on a trumped-up charge of mis-conduct. He brought a claim for wrongful dismissal. I represented my son. One of my degree subjects had been Administrative Law so I had a rough idea of the work of employment tribunals.

Thames Water was represented by a solicitor from the

Employers' Federation (EEF). I cross-examined the new chief executive and his two cronies. Among the points I raised was that he sported the suffix indicating he was a Fellow of the Institute of Waste Management. That came with a subscription to the trade journal and was not therefore in any sense a professional qualification he purported it to be. Thames Water had seconded part-time a human resources manager. I asked her if her professional association would agree that appointments to senior posts should be made only after advertisement and interview. I also said that in a very multi-ethnic community like Slough was it acceptable all the employees were white males. She had to agree that both questions revealed bad, unacceptable practices.

In true Perry Mason style, I denounced the management as "a bunch of cowboys". At the chair's request, of course, I had to withdraw that description but the point had been made. My son won his appeal, received the fullest compensation available, and the solicitor later lost his job at the EEF.

It was very gratifying that Gideon had been vindicated and recompensed, I enjoyed a buzz and another stain had been inflicted on Thames Water's tarnished corporate reputation.

Since I was not to be a barrister, and had positively no intention of becoming a solicitor, my second choice was to become a professional economist. I made application, therefore, to both University College, London, and the London School of Economics to read for a BSc (Econ), they being at the time the only two London colleges to offer economics degrees. I was interviewed by Dr Stonier at UCL and by Professor Ben Roberts and Dr Vera Anstey at LSE. I was agreeably surprised to be accepted for admission to both and opted for LSE. As it turned out, this was a wise, or more truthfully, lucky choice for it quickly became apparent that my maths was not good enough for me to do well specialising in economics, and I switched rapidly to Government as my final year special subject.

The London School of Economics was a fortunate choice in another respect, though one not without risk, for a young student in the circumstances of the time could have been overwhelmed. All university education, of course, is intended to aid the maturation of students, but LSE in the mid-fifties was something of a hothouse in this respect – at least for those of us who entered its portals straight from secondary schooling. Those of us who had sought deferment from National Service call-up until we had completed our studies, formed a very small minority of the intake. The vast majority of males (and there were relatively few women students in any case) had completed their military obligations and had seen service in all sorts of seemingly exotic theatres: Egypt, Cyprus, Yemen and beyond. The reality, they informed us, was rather more tedious, full of deprivation (particularly a lack of company with the opposite sex) and generally a fatuous waste of time, at least for the generality of conscripts. Some, of course, had 'a good war' especially those selected like Michael Frayn to learn Russian at Cambridge, which took up most of their service time.

Whatever their military experience, however, they appeared a good deal more senior to us than two years' mere chronology would suggest. And, to accentuate this already palpable age gap, there was a significant sprinkling of even more mature students who had come via Ruskin and similar adult colleges.

My particular age cohort, I was just eighteen, might well have felt intimidated by this overwhelming phalanx of 'old soldiers': if so, few showed it and many of us thrived on the challenge of living up to the task of being seen as an equal, perhaps, because by some form of osmosis we ingested the experiences of our older, more worldly contemporaries.

There was another factor at work and one that has been a distinguishing and enduring feature of LSE throughout its existence. Unlike most other British universities, it is essentially a single faculty institution. The disadvantage for the undergraduate is that he or she will not rub shoulders daily with scientists, engineers, or law, medical and humanities students as would have been possible in multi-faculty institutions. These days, however, this is becoming ever less likely as degree syllabuses become increasingly narrower and vocationally demanding. The advantage, if such it was, is that a concentration of students studying the social sciences makes for a confidence - justified or not - that they know more about the realities of how humanity actually ticks than the rest. However much this is a false conceit, as it undoubtedly is, it was nevertheless a reality as a self-perception - and there are not many shrinking violets in the social sciences. Thus, the impact of former National Servicemen and the artificial confidence the social sciences induced, combined to provide a forcing ground for maturation amongst the younger members of the class of 1955.

Intellectual giants like Lionel Robbins, Richard Titmus, James Meade, Michael Oakeshott, Karl Popper, Morris Ginsberg, Raymond Firth, Otto Kahn-Freund, S A de Smith and T H Marshall stalked the corridors. Even the second eleven, so to speak, was star-studded, while among the junior ranks of academic staff the signs of future brilliance were already manifest – at least in their own eyes. International reputations, then, were a dime a dozen and it was intoxicating for a young person with intellectual pretensions to bathe in their reflected glory.

Another benefit of LSE was its proud tradition of internationalism with a very cosmopolitan student community. The two largest blocs came from the continents of Asia and Africa; the latter's university provision at the time was too sparse and patchy to cater for the demands and expectations of the youth of those British colonies that were on the verge of gaining national independence. The presence of East and particularly West African students made the contemporary struggles for de-colonisation all the more immediate and poignant for British students like me. One's studies apart, LSE was a ferment of political ideas and activism if one chose to be involved which many did, including me.

Student Politics

There was a wide variety of political societies. Most, one way or another, catered for those on the Left and mirrored its fractured nature in the world outside. The largest, not surprisingly, was the Labour Society, which was officially accredited to the National Association of Labour Student Organisations, to which belonged those who harboured parliamentary careers – of which there was a surprising number.

Then there was the Socialist Society, smaller but more cerebral, which endeavoured to provide an intellectual 'Popular

Front' for the Left, where Labour Party members could meet with Communists without transgressing the rules of the Labour Party. These rules forbade formal contacts with the Communist Party, which was designated as a proscribed organisation. It should be recalled that the mid-fifties were the height of the Cold War (Stalin had only recently died in 1953), and Labour, therefore, was at great pains to distance itself from the Communist Party of Great Britain which was thought to receive its money and instructions from Moscow.

While insignificant in parliamentary terms, the Communist Party had secured many strongholds in the trade union movement from which it fomented a good deal of industrial unrest through both official and 'wild cat' strikes. Various Trotskyite factions also found the Socialist Society a convenient forum. The Communist Society, though smaller than the other Left wing societies, was nevertheless still quite large. It punched much above its weight, being more dedicated and better organised - with considerable assistance and advice from King Street, the Communist Party HQ in Covent Garden and a mere stone's throw away from LSE.

There was a smaller, but vociferous Conservative Society, that was continuously advised on tactics by Conservative Central Office through its very efficient subsidiary, the Federation of Conservative University Associations. It ran debating classes and its members, along with some of the Communists, were among the leading orators in the LSE Students' Union.

International Affairs

Because of their numbers and the particular international geo-political constellation at the time, the Africa Society and the Asia Society were very politically influential. The Korean War and the Malayan Emergency were of very recent memory, while the UK was still struggling to contain nationalist uprisings in Africa and, closer to home, Cyprus. At the time, the role of the United Nations loomed large in our consciences; its failure to achieve a defined and authoritative role for itself in the years since then, has dashed the earlier optimism and has encouraged a corrosive cynicism. But the 'fifties were a time when the myriad of young nations, emerging, or about to emerge, from colonial domination saw in the United Nations a possibility to assert themselves alone, or mostly likely in combination, against the two major power blocs in the Cold War.

Remarkably Yugoslavia managed to detach itself from the Soviets and this, and other straws in the wind, were sowing the seeds of what later was to become a grouping of young, uncommitted nations that came together at the Bandung Conference in 1955. This grouping was an attempt to provide a coherent and unified 'third' force' in world affairs which also encouraged an internationalist optimism.

There was also much excited debate about the prospects of Pan-Africanism. The fact that in the event the aspirations unleashed by the Bandung experiment and Pan-Africanism came to nothing is beside the point; they were both manifestations of an international Zeitgeist that held sway at the time and it was one of hope that ideas could make for a more civilised and mature world order – everywhere would be like Scandinavian social democracy.

The fact that the course of African history in the intervening years makes such idealism now seem naïve and unwarranted is undoubtedly if sadly true. As V S Naipaul was later to remark: "The African continent from Cairo to the Cape has been raped by both white and black alike." Such internationalist naivety, however, in no way validates the tough-minded Cold War attitudes then in currency.

If optimism comprised the main "pull" factors that many of us fondly hoped would mould the international future, there were also major "push" factors that impelled our thoughts in the same direction. Most starkly among them was the move to consolidate the institutionalised racism of Apartheid in South Africa. To this was added the frequently bungled actions of the British Government in futile attempts to constrain, if not actually reverse, the forces of nationalism in what remained of its colonial Empire. Whatever the atrocities committed in the name of freedom perpetrated by nationalist guerrillas or freedom fighters, the reaction of the UK government seemed to us somehow worse, compounded by the fact it never learned from its mistakes.

The Hola Camp massacres of 1959 encapsulated all that was wrong with British policy as further recent evidence illustrates: brutally over-reactive, criminal and not in the UK's longer term interests, it was totally anachronistic.

The dénouement, of course, came with the ill-fated Anglo-French invasion of Egypt in 1956, in collusion with Israel. To the younger generation such sabre-rattling and recourse to arms should have been consigned to history long before, and it evoked widespread and public, especially student, amazement and condemnation.

Events in 1956 were momentous. The ham-fisted attempt to recapture the Suez Canal which had been recently nationalised by the Egyptian dictator, Colonel Abdul Nasser, gave Soviet Russia the pretext for invading Hungary, to put down ruthlessly the embryonic and modest attempts being made to create a slightly more democratic society. If Britain and France could flout international law so blatantly why, by the same token, could not the USSR use its military might to expeditiously snuff out the Hungarian uprising?

During these dramatic events academic activities at the LSE were put on hold as an almost continuous series of prominent opinion formers, MPs, journalists, staff and others came to address thronging audiences in the Old Theatre, then the largest lecture venue at LSE. There was near total hostility expressed to the Suez venture on two main grounds: it was illegal in that it broke the rules of the UN Charter, and many thought it immoral as well; while in terms of practicality and prudence it was ill-judged, triggering as it did immediate US condemnation. It was also ill-prepared as its abject failure proved within days, leading to an ignominious withdrawal from Egypt. Added to these errors was exasperation that the USSR had been given the excuse and the opportunity to invade Hungary when the world's attention was distracted from the dynamics of the Cold War and fixated on the unbelievable Suez outrage.

Suez provoked public protests that culminated in the famous Trafalgar Square rally at which the oratory of Nye Bevan, then Shadow Labour Foreign Secretary, was at its most eloquent. We crammed into the Square, which was overflowing with banners proclaiming "Law Not War". It was an impressive occasion and one which cathartically released the pent up emotions of those of us who opposed the atavistic folly of the Eden government. I have never witnessed the like before nor since. Inevitably, it ended in trouble as some of the crowd, urged on by extreme Left- wing factions, tried to march down Whitehall. There were major scuffles, involving attacks on the police and the inevitable counter attacks by the forces of law and order. I took part in none of this, believing that such conflict was irrelevant to, and indeed detracted from, the legitimate opposition to the Suez crisis. In the event Suez turned out to be a short-lived affair, but one which had shattered the illusions of the idealistic young.

The Hungarian escapade, though equally short-lived, also had long term consequences. Coming so soon after Nikita Khrushchev had denounced Stalin's crimes and excesses to both a surprised Soviet Russia and Communist Parties world-wide, the determined and swift re-imposition of Soviet hegemony in Budapest starkly illustrated that post-Stalinist Russia intended to be as totalitarian as the previous regime. This bald fact led to significant resignations from Communist Parties in the West, including Britain, and the loss of many leading intellectuals. *Darkness at Noon* after all, had not just been a literary contrivance of Arthur Koestler but a portent as to the future. Committed Socialists and ex-Communists regrouped, uniting under the banner of the 'New Left'. This spawned its own intellectual magazine that survives to this day as the New Left Review, a successful but more transitory club and coffee shop in Soho, and later, an influential publishing house Verso. The value of emphasising novelty and the re-birth connotations of the 'New' was not lost on Tony Blair and Peter Mandelson when they successfully reburnished the image of the Labour Party in the 1990s.

The Hungarian invasion also had its hilarious side. Some Conservative students, in an attempt to distract opposition to the Tory government's Suez excursion, called for volunteers to assist the democrats in Hungary. Sending a lorry or two with food and clothes was estimable and symbolic in its own way, even though ultimately a futile gesture. What was utterly fatuous, however, was calling for volunteers to join the armed struggle. A few adventurers were attracted to the resurrection of the 'International Brigade' idea and actually went for a weekend's manoeuvres on Dartmoor.

South Africa and its repulsive Apartheid regime was of more lasting concern to us and, of course, to many successor generations. In my time at LSE, it was the subject of many debates in the Students' Union and at the annual conferences of the National Union of Students. A major demonstration was organised by LSE to march on South Africa House in Trafalgar Square to hand in a petition calling for an end to segregation.

Joining the Liberal Party

On enrolling at LSE, I had immediately joined the Liberal Society – by far the smallest political grouping, making it relatively easy for me to be elected its chairman and in quick order at that. It also made me a target for the Communists who, as usual, had effectively taken over control of the anti-apartheid march. It was their normal cunning tactics to nominate a non-

Communist as a "fall guy" to be formally in charge of such events and, therefore, if things got out of hand, (as was frequently the case if they had anything to do with it), the one who would be held accountable by the Metropolitan Police and very likely arrested. I, of course, was named as the official organiser who had to seek permission and guarantee the march would be properly stewarded, stick to its prescribed route from Hyde Park, and cause no civil disturbance. I could hardly object to the position as the Liberal Society had agreed to join with the more Left-wing societies to sponsor the march, though I fully realised I had been bounced into assuming formal responsibility for it. To say I was very anxious would be a massive understatement. If my name had not been on MI5's list of agitators before, it most certainly would be now. In fact, it was probably already on it by virtue of merely being an active student politician. The paranoid political psychology of Senator Joseph McCarthy and John Foster Dulles (the long-serving FBI Director) had also infected the British secret services. As it was, my entreaties to my hard Left colleagues were heeded and, to my amazement, it was agreed that any more militant action would have been counter-productive and detracted from the central purpose of the march.

The Students' Union at LSE was the main focal point of student life, to an extent I have never found elsewhere in any other university, and it was very political, especially during its regular general meetings. It also undertook a good deal of other business arranging dance hops, the occasional ball at the Royal Festival Hall, other related social activities, while also catering for the welfare needs of the student body.

My first introduction to the Union was the Freshers' debate that featured as the leading protagonists two famous journalists, Kingsley Martin, the long serving editor of *The New Statesman* and Malcolm Muggeridge, then editor of Punch and at his iconoclastic best, long before his mawkish and final religious phase. It was one of the finest debates I have ever heard, being a perfect presentational blend of wit and seriousness.

To stand any chance of being elected to Union office one needed the backing of a political coalition. I could count on the support of the small, but reasonably active Liberal Society, which numerically was not enough, so that it was necessary to solicit support from more powerful groups. There was also little point from such a fragile power-base contesting the vice-presidencies covering the higher profile, and therefore much sought after, portfolios of Social or External Affairs. With these tactical considerations in mind, I duly opted to go for the Welfare vice-presidency and, with the support of the Asia and African Societies that I had assiduously canvassed, I was duly elected.

The Executive of the Students' Union handled a good deal of money which it doled out to a multiplicity of social and political societies that made up the rich tapestry of student activity. A separate Athletics Union handled the sporting side of LSE. The Students' Union could influence the pattern of non-sporting activity for either good or ill and, for the most part, it was for the good. However, one serious case arose when the external auditors discovered that the Treasurer, who had served in the previous year, had funnelled off a significant amount of Union money for his own purposes. He was an overseas post-graduate, who had taken a Master's degree in Accounting, appropriately or not depending on one's viewpoint, and had since returned to his own country. There had not been a (discovered) fraud in the Union's accounts since some time in the 1930s. The LSE Director, Sir Sydney Caine, called the Executive in for high level talks with the auditors and also, I recall, with Huw (later Sir) Weldon, the well-known broadcaster. Weldon had been the last President of the Union when embezzlement had been revealed and who had had to tighten up its financial procedures.

In the long vacation of 1957, with the rest of the Executive dispersed far and wide, I was effectively put in charge of all the Union's affairs, including its finances, with plenary powers to act. I spent most of the time checking and re-checking the daily accounts for fear that any of the funds would go missing. The exposure of the fraud had a searing and salutary effect that has profoundly shaped my subsequent career. While I have doubtless been guilty of many sins, I have always brought Gladstonian rectitude to bear whenever corporate money is involved.

Being chair of the Liberal Society, which was complemented by being vice-president of the Student's Union, was to lead to the twin careers I have pursued almost equally in the ensuing years. University Liberals were organised nationally in a loose confederation called the Union of University Liberal Societies (UULS) which unlike Labour, the Communists or the Conservatives, had goodwill but virtually no practical or financial assistance from the party HQ – the Liberal Party Organisation then housed in Victoria Street. The post-war years had seen the Liberal Party reach its parliamentary nadir.

No sane young person with political interests, let alone seeking elective office, would have entertained joining them. Yet a small number did. In recent years the leadership of UULS had come mainly from Cambridge, while young Liberals in the country organised under the National League of Young Liberals (NLYL) whose main support was then centred in the north-west around Manchester, Liverpool and the Wirral. I became Secretary of UULS in 1957 and, towards the end of my final year at LSE, I was elected its chairman with an ex-officio place on the national executive of the Liberal Party Organisation.

Final Year

In those days the BSc (Econ) degree, for which I was studying, was split into two parts. Part I, which took two years, covered eight subjects, which gave a soundly based introduction to the main social sciences. Part II, taken in the final year, consisted of a special subject, in my case Government, that covered five courses selected from a range of compulsory and optional programmes. I worked extremely hard, aiming to secure a good Upper Second degree, a First being highly unlikely given my heavy involvement in the affairs of the Students' Union (annual paid sabbatical leave for Union officials, long a commonplace in all UK Universities, was then unheard of) and the Liberal Students nationally. In the compulsory Comparative Government paper the most popular option to take was "The Politics and Government of the Soviet Union", which was taught by the redoubtable Sovietologist, Leonard Shapiro. Although later promoted to professor, he was then a lecturer in the process of establishing a formidable international reputation. He had taken my British Government tutorial class in the first year. A kindly man, who espoused liberal values then, but like so many academics (particularly at LSE) turned turtle and fell under the spell of Margaret Thatcher, becoming a right-wing ideologue. Although always strongly opposed to the antics of the Soviet Union, the later course of the Cold War hardened his attitude. I later overheard him in conversation, les évènements of 1968 – the year of student rebellious outbreaks – which had their own version at LSE, had further cemented his shift to the Right. "They actually occupied our Senior Common Room!" he exclaimed.

Though seriously tempted, I chose not to take his course, opting instead for one on "Colonial Administration and the Process of De-Colonisation" offered by the well-known anthropologist, Dr Lucy Mair. I was the only white student in the class. The topic had always held a particular fascination for me and I secured a First class mark, as I did in some other papers, but not enough to be awarded a First classification overall. Dr Mair's course gave me a good grounding for when I was to work in Northern Ireland, towards the end of my career, as I had already gained a knowledge of the problems thrown up by tribalism thanks to Dr Mair which I was to witness at first hand in Ulster.

Of my particular LSE cohort few were later to become publicly prominent: it was not a good vintage from that point of view. Of those still known to me, most have had successful careers. One who gained international professional recognition was John Williamson. I had defeated him for the chair of the Liberal Society, but who compensated for the loss by becoming chair of the University of London Liberal Federation. He was to become one of the leading international economists of his generation, based in Washington DC, working for the World Bank and major international think tanks. A *Festschrift* written in his honour stated he was the most cited international economist of his day. Although meeting only intermittently, we remain firm friends.

The other success was Jean Moss, who chaired the Conservative Society. She became a well-known rally driver and businesswoman. As Baroness Denton of Wakefield, she served as a junior minister, first in the Department of Trade and Industry (DTI), and secondly as Minister for Industry in Northern Ireland where we met up again well over thirty years later. She was subsequently struck down by cancer and died all too early in 2001.

Jean Denton's published recollections of LSE record she was unhappy there; my views are to the contrary. It really did "train me on", as the racing fraternity put it, intellectually, politically and in terms of the competences (in the current argot) I was able to acquire. As an earnest of my appreciation, immediately upon graduation, I took out life membership of the LSE Society for £5, the cost of the subscription I could ill afford at the time. In reciprocity, LSE reneged and unilaterally revoked the deal two decades later.

CHAPTER 6

A GAP YEAR AND A HALF, INCLUDING THE 1959 GENERAL ELECTION

Call-Up

After graduation I received my call-up papers for National Service which had been deferred during my university studies. Conscription was coming to an end but a shortfall in regular recruitment meant the last cohort would have to serve beyond the normal two years. In addition to that, the Cyprus Emergency was raging as the British army endeavoured by whatever means to defeat Colonel Georgios Grivas and his pro-Greek unification EOKA force. Not a propitious time to serve I thought, if, indeed, there ever is one.

I was (and remain) essentially a pragmatic pacifist, bolstered in my belief by the sheer folly of the Suez adventure – the possible exception being WWII. As the former Labour Defence Secretary, the late Dennis Healey remarked, almost every war in the twentieth century could have been avoided with better diplomacy. I would agree with that assessment but equally I did not fancy being enlisted if I could avoid it. In his autobiography, Sir Roy Strong, in spite of him being a monarchist, loyal patriot and Tory, writes that he, too, successfully contrived to fail his National Service medical.

My friend, Michael Parsons, and I had endlessly discussed the pros and cons of pacifism in our mid-teens. He was conscripted at eighteen. He was a principled pacifist – at the time at least – and opted for conscientious objection. I attended the tribunal to which he was summoned, testifying on his behalf as to the sincerity of his beliefs. He was minded to apply for unconditional objector status recognition and be excused military service. Tribunals rarely granted this and it was likely he would have had to serve time in prison. I successfully urged him to accept conditional recognition and be prepared to serve in the army as a non-combatant; he had poor eyesight and would probably fail the medical, which he duly did.

I decided not to apply for registration as a 'Conchie' and accordingly I attended for my medical in a church hall in Acton. A motley collection of retired GPs apportioned the various medical tests between themselves: hearing, eyesight, bronchial, cardiac and so on. They had no specialist expertise and what little they did have would have been very outdated.

Again, I adopted the two-fold approach utilised by my father. I would accentuate my myopia but seek to pass all the other tests. I decided not to sleep the night before, smoked cigarettes (which otherwise, I never did) and presented myself with two very blood-shot eyes. The examiner asked if this condition was usual. I replied only when I read intensively as I had done before Finals. He referred me to an ophthalmic consultant.

My second ploy came into force when I went immediately following the medical to be cursorily interviewed by a retired colonel. I recognised the insignia on his uniform and knew correctly to call him "Colonel" rather than "Sir" as in the case of all other commissioned ranks. This was so rare among would-be recruits he took a greater interest in me. I enquired if one of his chest medal ribbons was the Military Cross? I had correctly identified it. I was the sort of nerd who took an interest in such baubles. He showed an even greater interest in me when I asked very much with tongue in cheek: "Colonel, this job must be a tedious duty for a man of action such as yourself?"

By this time, I had relieved the boredom for him of such mornings, which he doubtless himself relieved by sending lorry drivers to the Army Catering Corps and chefs to the Royal Corps of Transport or some such game. We engaged in seriously discussing my likely military career. I indicated a preference for the Royal Army Educational Corps. While saying he would recommend me for that, he also said I would have to do basic training in either an infantry or artillery regiment. Having assiduously studied recent troop movements, I noticed the Middlesex Regiment had just moved from Cyprus to the British Army on the Rhine (BAOR) in West Germany. Having no desire to engage with the fighters of EOKA, I opted for the Middlesex on grounds of geographical affinity and the fact my father had served in the Regiment. If the Educational Corps had refused me, I would at least be safer in Germany. The Colonel also designated me as a POM - "potential officer material".

The excruciating combination of medical examination and army interview I experienced was precisely as Richard Vinen describes in his *National Service*: Conscription in Britain 1945-63 (2014).

I was later referred to a relatively young and newly appointed Ophthalmic Consultant at West Middlesex Hospital. I had slept soundly the night before, did not smoke and presented two clear eyes. Having examined me he adjudged

I had straightforward myopia. I said my own consultant, a Mr Triesman from Harley Street, had forbidden me to do weight-training in my adolescence because of the possibility of causing detached retinas. I had asked him to confirm this in writing but he said the risk only applied in adolescence. I cited Triesman's name to the Consultant who would have known of his professional pre-eminence, though I did not mention the teenage qualification. It was enough and I was rated Class Four and unfit for service, although as Vinen observes, as the end of conscription approached the bar in the medical tests was raised as fewer soldiers were needed. Be that as it may, the main thing was I was free.

Again, as Vinen establishes, National Service was boring, often cruel and unnecessary. It hampered the post-war economic recovery, gave free rein to brutish NCOs, officered by the dimmer products of the minor public schools, motivated by the outdated nostalgia for a rapidly disappearing Imperial age – the residues of which, amazingly enough, I find are still operative to this day. Moreover, the conscripts were often ordered to commit atrocities against indigenous populations in Malaya, Kenya, Cyprus and other colonial theatres. It must have been a hellish nightmare and one well avoided and hardly character-forming as is so often misguidedly claimed to this day by Conservative xenophobes. The only certain outcome of sending British troops abroad at any one time is that Aldershot becomes a safer place on Saturday nights.

Interlude

Nowadays, of course, it is a commonplace for students to take a year off either after school prior to entering university or after graduation before seeking a full-time career. I decided on the latter.

I had been elected chair of UULS in the Easter of 1958, shortly before I was to graduate. The position would last a year and I needed to be fairly free and flexible with my time until the following Easter. I had succeeded Roger Straker from Cambridge, a scion of the well-established printing and stationery firm, who was ultimately to become Director of Human Resources at London Transport. I was succeeded in that post by David Lea, also from Cambridge, who later worked for the Trade Union Congress (TUC), rising to become Assistant Secretary, and ultimately a Labour working peer. My vice-chair was Stephen Jakobi, a Cambridge law student, who later formed Victims Abroad, a pressure group aimed at promoting the rights of Britons charged and/or jailed in foreign jurisdictions.

In order to be master of my own time, I worked, for the first nine months after leaving LSE, as a supply teacher with the (then) London County Council, and mainly at Hay Currie Secondary Modern School in Poplar. It was a pretty desperate educational establishment, and even worse than the one - Bordeston - I had briefly attended at the age of eleven. At Hay Currie, Michael Hanley, one of the few permanent members of staff, had taught me for a year at Hounslow College. A jovial Irishman, he was rather embarrassed when I produced one of my school reports and read out the comments he had written about me. I was paid on a daily basis and could take the odd day off when student Liberal politics called. I was returning to my roots in East London, having been born in Clapton and baptised in Stepney. I was later to return to the area when I joined the academic staff of Queen Mary College in 1967 where I was to remain during twenty-three very eventful years.

As chair of UULS, I was determined on modernisation. I had its constitution changed from its loose confederal basis to a unitary one, renamed as the Union of Liberal Students (ULS). Change was in the air for the Liberal Party. In 1956 the charismatic Jo Grimond had succeeded Clement Davies as its Leader. And his brother-in-law Mark Bonham-Carter had won a spectacular by-election at Torrington in May 1958, the first such Liberal win since the war. Liberal youth was more than ready to play its part.

New Orbits

The ULS and the National League of Young Liberals formed a Joint Political Committee (JPC), which had the services of a National Youth Officer based in the Party's Victoria Street HQ. At first it was Anthea Grant who was succeeded by Rosemary (Ro) Chester, later to become the wife of Archy Kirkwood MP, later a colleague both on the Joseph Rowntree Reform Trust and in the House of Lords; we became firm friends.

The formation of the JPC was timely in view of the appallingly organised annual Party Assembly held at Torquay in 1958. The Party president, Sir Arthur Comyns-Carr QC, who had distinguished himself as a prosecutor at the Japanese war crimes tribunal in Tokyo, appeared, Emperor Hirohito-like, in winged collar and morning suit, and insisted on delivering his address without the aid of a microphone. The speech was a shambles and but for a rousing Leader's speech by Jo Grimond, the popular image presented by the Liberals would have been a near-total catastrophe.

Never again should this be allowed to happen, vowed the youth wings of the Party, which immediately set about remedying the situation. Proposals were made to reform arrangements for the Assembly and steps were taken to modernise the Party's policy which, until then, consisted largely of advocating the five cardinal principles of: Free Trade, Proportional Representation, Land Value Taxation, Co-ownership in Industry and a UN Peace Force. There had really been no policy development since Lloyd George's famous *Yellow Book* of 1928, though Liberals claimed credit for the fact that the post-war managed economy and the welfare state had been based on the ideas of Keynes and Beveridge respectively, both long-standing Liberals.

Clearly more was needed, as Grimond appreciated when he mobilised members of the Unservile State Group to advise him that included leading academic economists such as Alan Peacock, Peter Wiles and Nancy Seear.

Similarly, the Liberal youth wings had become impatient with the slow pace of reform within the Party which is why they had formed a JPC in order to combine and thus maximise their influence. In the immediate aftermath of Torquay, they realised the task was all the more urgent. They redoubled their efforts and the JPC launched, what it called, "Operation Manifesto" to beef up preparations for the forthcoming General Election. As we later wrote: "The first stage was the setting up of study groups among Young Liberal branches and university societies throughout the country during the autumn of 1958".

The reports of these groups were then analysed by the JPC,

which wrote a consolidated pamphlet which "sought to integrate the different strands of Liberalism into a coherent whole, so that we were able to project a clear image to the public. Rather than merely list Liberal policies the aim is to show how a Liberal thinks and reacts, and to illustrate basic principles in terms of specific policies."

The third stage was to present the pamphlet to a specially convened joint Congress of Young Liberals and Liberal Students in Manchester on 18 and 19 April 1959. By then the JPC was slightly worried it was over-stepping itself constitutionally. The NLYL and ULS were, after all, separately constituted formal organisations within the Liberal Party; the JPC was not, and had merely been adopted as a convenient device to facilitate joint action. At this point, therefore, we decided to play down the existence of the JPC, while heavily promoting the pamphlet under the title that I suggested of New Orbits, which we hoped would capture the innovative spirit of the times: the USSR had just pioneered flights into outer space with the launch of its Sputnik rocket.

The Manchester Congress was carefully planned and was a huge success. Grimond attended and gave the keynote address. The event occasioned a first leader in the *Manchester Guardian*, whose editor sent a fledgling journalist called Anthony Howard to report on the proceedings. I suspect, being a staunch Labour party member, he was somewhat reluctant to undertake the assignment.

After the Congress and the attendant publicity it had received, we decided to wind down the JPC as such and put in its place the New Orbits Group, along the lines of the highly successful Bow Group of "One Nation" Tories and, so constituted, it would be formally autonomous and freer to act as a ginger group around and within the Liberal Party.

The New Orbits Group was established in early 1960, just after the General Election held in the previous September, "..... to act as a focal point for creative policy work by younger Liberals throughout the country." We proudly proclaimed "Its work has only just begun, but, with the reputation of New Orbits itself behind it, there is every reason to suppose that it will play an extremely influential part in future developments of a live Liberal policy." Thus the scene was set and the mission proclaimed.

The Group was launched with a second, collectively written pamphlet, entitled *High Time for Radicals*, which sought to capture the mood of the moment that had been deeply affected by the recent Labour defeat at the polls in 1959, despite Hugh Gaitskill's revisionist style. The 'morning after' had a very sobering effect on non-Conservatives, be they Labour or Liberal. Three successive Tory election victories in a row were difficult to stomach, and this reaction gave rise to a large wave of intellectual activity seeking to explain the causes of the apparent continuing Conservative hegemony and how it might be reversed. Mark Abrahams and Richard Rose asked *Must Labour Lose?* Their book identified the growing embourgeoisement of the working class as the main reason for the Tories' victory.

Anthony Crosland and Richard Crossman (in my later experience, their near similar surnames were to be a source of confusion among less diligent students taking courses on British Government) rushed out Fabian pamphlets. These were from differing perspectives, revisionist and fundamentalist respectively, that analysed the reasons for Labour's electoral predicament.

A whole series of Pelican Specials was launched, beginning with Michael Shanks' *The Stagnant Society: A Warning* to address that issue while John Goldthorpe and David Lockwood were prompted to begin their important sociological survey of *The Affluent Worker*.

The distinctive call of *High Time for Radicals* was for a realignment of the left in Britain, echoing and reinforcing the post-election reflections of Grimond. Like New Orbits, it was authored collectively, although subsequent pamphlets were either jointly or singly written. Among the topics they dealt with were the farce of the Central African Federation, the role of international trade and aid in promoting a 'welfare world' (to which my LSE friend John Williamson contributed), a five year plan dealing with social objectives, economic growth and tax reform, and *New Unions for Old*, to which I contributed, that made a sympathetic argument for the reform of the trade union movement and industrial relations. Others dealt with schools and higher education.

The founders of the New Orbits Group were the leading lights of the younger Liberal generation of the time. They embraced a formidable set of talents. Barbara Burwell, ex-chair of NLYL, was a research chemist and an inspired amateur typographer. She was to become the first wife of Timothy Joyce, who was her successor at NLYL, and who had just completed a Cambridge Doctorate in philosophy. He had recently joined the British Market Research Bureau, then a subsidiary of J

Walter Thompson. He later organised a management buy-out of the parent company, becoming head of the famous American advertising agency. He was probably the brightest of us and died prematurely in 1998.

Frank Ware, another Cambridge product, was then head of research at Liberal HQ and later became a partner in a leading firm of city accountants. Sarah Myers, from Oxford, had been chair of UULS, after which she joined the journalist staff on the *Times Educational Supplement*.

One of our more colourful members, and slightly older than the rest of us, was Ronnie Fraser, an agricultural economist who had trained at both Glasgow and Newcastle universities. While at Glasgow, he sallied forth with some like-minded students successfully to retrieve the Stone of Scone from Westminster Abbey just before the coronation of Elizabeth II or so it was claimed. By tradition, it was placed under the throne but was absent on this occasion. It remained hidden in Scotland for many years before it was returned to the Abbey. Michael Forsyth, when Secretary of State for Scotland, in the run-up to the 1997 General Election, ceremoniously repatriated the Stone in a futile attempt to counter the ever-increasing popular demands for a Scottish parliament; this belated ploy did nothing to stop the complete rout of the Conservatives, who lost all their Scottish seats at Westminster. Ronnie later became a much respected editor of one of Scotland's leading farming journals. I, as chair of ULS, made up the Committee, serving as its vice-chair.

The New Orbits Group continued for a while after the 1959 election until a newer and more radical generation of officers took control of ULS and NLYL. The so-called "Red Guards" were much more impatient for change, both within the Party itself and the world outside. They were to form part of the phalanx of student protest that culminated in events throughout Europe and the US in 1968. These protests were the radical political face of the "swinging sixties"; a counterculture that challenged most aspects of the established order. It had its roots in the anti-Vietnam war protests and race riots that characterised America during that decade. These forms of direct action, tailored to local needs, were copied in Europe, often leading to forms of extreme terrorism, as in the case of the Baader-Meinhof group in West Germany.

In England, the manifestations of protest were of an altogether lower order. There were occupations and "sit-ins" in some universities, most notably Essex and LSE, but even the major anti-Vietnam demonstration outside the US Embassy in Grosvenor Square was not so different from the anti-Suez one in Trafalgar Square of a decade earlier. In its turn the Red Guard cohort of young Liberals were to yield to another generation who focussed very single-mindedly on South Africa. Peter Hain, the chair of NLYL, led the successful "Stop the Seventy Tour" campaign that resulted in the South African cricket team being banned from all Test matches worldwide. Though I took no part in the activities of the campaign, I observed it indirectly as he was, at the time, my personal tutee at Queen Mary College from which he graduated with a brilliant First. He later switched to the Labour Party, becoming MP for Neath and holding three posts in the Cabinets of Tony Blair and Gordon Brown. We were to meet again in Northern Ireland when he was its Secretary of State.

It is true that those of us who clustered around the New Orbits Group, and they included Richard Holme and William Wallace whom, much later, I was to join in the House of Lords, were a good deal more staid, less radical and had much less overt impact than those who succeeded us; that doubtless explains why contemporary historians of the Liberal Party have highlighted the Red Guards and Peter Hain.

By contrast, very little attention has been paid to the New Orbits Group. I suppose I would say that, but, even allowing for my inevitably biased viewpoint, I would assert we played a not insignificant part, to put it at its least, in preventing the Liberal Party disappearing from British politics altogether. We helped in its refurbishment which was taken forward, albeit ever so slowly by Jo Grimond, Jeremy Thorpe and David Steel and much more dramatically by Paddy Ashdown and Charles Kennedy. At the time the founders of the New Orbits Group, and in their capacities of leaders of the NLYL and ULS, were among the most powerful forces for modernisation within the Liberal party. Admittedly, it was a small pond, but it is equally true they were big fish in it. (Cf my article in *The Journal of Liberal History*, Summer 2017).

My year of office as chair of ULS ended at Easter 1959, so that I was free to seek out what I thought might be a suitable career. I knew, particularly after Hay Currie School, I did not want to be a school teacher, although I think I was pretty good at it. After I left, I had a letter from one of my former pupils urging me to return. He was semi-literate and the son of a prostitute and on both counts was the subject of consistent bullying by his fellow pupils, especially the girls. I had taken him under my wing, offering what encouragement, support and protection I could. His heartfelt plea asking me to come back was deeply moving; seemingly he had told his mother what he wanted to say and she had written the letter in pencil which he traced over with a ball pen. It was the best reference regarding my teaching abilities I have ever had.

Seeking a Career

The Careers Adviser at LSE, Lt Cmdr D Warren-Evans RN (retd.) was, I discovered, a cousin of my first real girlfriend's family. That may well have prejudiced him in my eyes, I admit, though his daily garb of bowler hat, striped suit and rolled umbrella seemed altogether out of place at LSE. He was one of those many people I have come across in life whose main achievement was to turn innate laziness into an art form. Fellow students, who had consulted him, reported that he only ever had two suggestions to make – either join the Inland Revenue or else become a Cost and Works Accountant, neither of which held the slightest appeal for me. I imagine he thought his stereotypical, regular uniform acted as a camouflage, evoking the image of an assiduous, on-parade and at-the-ready officer and gentleman, while actually disguising a professional idler who, I noted, took very long lunch hours at his Club some distance away from the premises of LSE.

The central University of London Careers Service, for which I opted, was an altogether more efficient source of vocational advice. The economic climate of the late 1950s exuded optimism that was reflected in Harold Macmillan's boast,

"You've Never Had It So Good", during the 1959 election campaign. The nature of American capitalism was being proclaimed and imitated where possible. William F Whyte's best-selling *The Organisation Man* (1956), although intended as an Orwellian-type parody of the way big business was being conducted in the US, actually induced envy in the UK. The Brits would have welcomed the chance to sell themselves body and soul for such salaries. In similar vein, Anthony Crosland, in his hugely influential revisionist work, *The Future of Socialism*, re-packaged for a British audience Adolf Berle and Gardiner Means' thesis that the divorce between ownership and control in industry had produced a new breed of professional managers who put corporate responsibility above a relentless drive for profit maximisation. The old, red-in-tooth-and-claw owner-manager, the creature of the first Industrial Revolution, had been overtaken by a quite different class of competent technocrats – characteristic of the second Industrial Revolution – who, Crosland claimed, were much more benign and conducive to the public good. The example of such firms as Marks & Spencer were singled out by Crosland as demonstrating that their better customer service and products were superior to those provided by the state-owned public utilities, and hence there was no need for further nationalisation.

The first stirrings among the British firms towards becoming more like US corporations were taking place. They were reflecting the changing intellectual outlook that was to lead to what we now call, "globalisation".

While no one could foresee how the future would evolve, there was a sense of transition in the air, and a corresponding sense of excitement. It was also a graduate "seller's market". With only five per cent of school leavers entering the universities there was a chronic shortage of graduates, with demand greatly outstripping supply. Almost any graduate, however inferior his or her degree, could pick and choose which job to accept.

The Careers Service got me shortlisted for a traineeship with the steel brokers, Coutinho Caro, in the City. I was wined and dined by the chairman and his managing director, more than once, and finally offered the job which attracted a relatively large salary and perks. To their annoyance, I turned it down. On reflection, I could not see myself buying and selling, at very small margins, quantities of rusting steel of varying tensile strengths from all corners of the world on a continuous daily basis. Fascinating for a week, perhaps, but a boring (and continually nerve-wracking) prospect in the longer term.

The second attempt proved a little more alluring and enduring. I was employed as a media executive with the S T Garland Advertising Service, based in their Mount Street, Mayfair, offices. By the standards of the day, it was a medium-sized advertising agency. The structure of the firm was an accurate microcosm of the changes then occurring in British business: it was at a halfway stage between the traditional owner-manager set-up and the rapidly emerging professional management model. In a manner evoked in the TV comedy serial, *Are You Being Served?*, the founder was the very part-time non-executive chairman; S T Garland must have been a successful entrepreneur in his time, but by now his position was almost honorary. His son, "young Mr Garland", was formally the managing director but seemed content to play second fiddle to Dick Desborough, the media director, who provided the agency's real leadership, together with Barry On as media manager. Desborough was a jolly, rotund man who had the habit of pulling down on his jacket's side vents to prevent its collar rising up. His physique was hardly that of a tailor's dummy. He had a very sharp commercial brain and a stunning and charming PA, whom he allowed to run two or three of the smaller accounts on her own. He had recruited an excellent design team, dextrous at film, animation and straightforward graphic design.

Among Garland's prestige clients were Parker Pens, Rowntree's Fruit Pastilles and British Overseas Airways Corporation (BOAC) the main forerunner of British Airways). Sometime after I had left, it became Garland Compton which later was absorbed by the internationally renowned agency Saatchi & Saatchi.

This was more like it, I thought; advertising, a thoroughly modern, twentieth century industry. Drafted into the ranks of *The Hidden Persuaders*, Vance Packard (1957), I thought "Madison Avenue, here I come!"

The reality, for me, turned out to be somewhat different. I was not an account executive, glad-handing clients hither and yon, making presentations and clinching new commissions which would have been much more my forte. Rather, I was a back room boy, providing background data for my front-line colleagues. My working week was split up between Mondays and the remainder. Every Monday morning, accompanied by a shorthand typist, I descended into a darkened basement to watch *Monday Morning Newcomers*. This programme consisted of showing all the new advertisements that had appeared on ITV in the preceding week. There seemed to be hundreds. Video recorders not having been invented, we had to sit through the lot, noting those of all our clients' competitors, giving a detailed description of each relevant "commercial", including its storyboard and jingle. It was as painstaking as it was mind numbing. The afternoon would be taken writing-up the results of my reconnaissance and swiftly despatching it to all parts of the agency.

For the rest of the week, I was engaged in endless 'cost per thousand' calculations. This amounted to working out the comparative value for money data of the different media, viz newspapers, magazines, television, cinemas and posters. In other words, I had to demonstrate what the cheapest medium was for a particular product to reach its largest target audience. While this was intellectually fascinating for a week or two, it swiftly palled as it became routine.

I sought relief from the sheer boredom of the job in two ways. I escaped, as often as I could, to have diverting conversations of a more intellectual kind with the agency's chief copywriter, John Bowen, who later became a well-known novelist. Like so many budding authors, I suspect, he was earning a crust and biding his time until he could make a satisfactory income as a full-time writer. One of his novels, *Storyboard*, revolves around the operations of an advertising agency.

1959 General Election

My second, and main escape, came from my increasing pre-occupation with the pending General Election. I had been adopted as Prospective Parliamentary Liberal candidate for the West Lewisham constituency in south-east London. Campaigning was gruelling in the long, hot summer of 1959 and I used as much time as I could get away with, using my employer's telephone to orchestrate my campaign, which was conducted on the spot most weekends and evenings. At twenty-two I was the youngest candidate of any party in the Election. I managed to double the Liberal vote to 4721 but narrowly lost my deposit; I got 11% of the total vote, whereas 12% was needed to save the deposit. I had improved, almost doubling, the Liberal performance from the previous General Election which was creditable, given how badly the Party did in the rest of Greater London.

I remained an active Liberal Party member. I was adopted as a prospective candidate for West Ham South which I relinquished on moving to East Yorkshire where I was invited to stand for York which I decided to decline. However, I invariably attended the annual Liberal Assemblies which gave me a lasting nightmare. I dreamt of being shot by Major Oliver Smedley MC and being treated by Dr Michael Winstanley. If the first man didn't kill me the second assuredly would have. Smedley, a prominent Free Trader and parliamentary candidate, worked in the City and owned an off-shore pirate radio station. A rival pirate station owner visited him and was instantly shot dead by the Major. He was tried for murder but acquitted as having acted in self-defence. Winstanley, a Manchester GP, and later an MP and Liberal peer, presented a Granada TV medical programme and hadn't seen a patient for years. In reality it couldn't have happened as Smedley was active in the party in the 1950s and early '60s, while Winstanley came later to Liberal politics.

The year 1959 was not to be a good one for the Liberal Party generally, especially in London and its environs. It was time for me to seek out new pastures.

CHAPTER 7

LUCKY JIM: TEACHING AT PROVINCIAL UNIVERSITIES – EXETER, HULL, YORK

Having decided to quit advertising, I wrote to one of my former tutors at the LSE asking if he would referee me for a PhD in the USA. To my very great surprise, Professor Kingsley Smellie 'phoned the next day to say there was a vacancy for a nine month temporary assistant lectureship in political thought at Exeter University starting in January 1960. The interviews for the post were scheduled in a day or two in his office and, as far as he was aware, I was the only candidate.

I dashed round to the Economist Bookshop and hastily read the flap blurbs on the dust jackets of those books that had been published on the subject in the two years since I had graduated. Thus scantily equipped, I attended the interview with Professor Smellie and William Steer who was in charge of politics at Exeter. The following week I went down to meet the Vice-Chancellor, Sir James Cook.

Exeter

I was duly appointed to fill in for Derek Crabtree who was teaching for two terms at the Nigerian University of Ife (now renamed the Obafemi Awolowo University). Nor had my luck run out with the new job. I had been offered a pro-rata salary at a rate of £600 per annum. In December 1959 university salaries were enhanced as never before nor since and the annual rate went up to £900.

I rented a bed-sit in Vellwell Road close to the newly opened campus at Streatham Park – a wonderful estate consisting of a mixture of handsome detached large Victorian houses and new purpose-built, well designed academic teaching and research facilities. The University's origins went back to the mid-nineteenth century but it was designated the University College of the South-West in 1922, teaching external London University degrees. It became a fully-fledged university in its own right in 1955. This route was one taken by many English provincial universities and, for that matter, ones in the colonies of Malaya, Ceylon, Africa and the Caribbean.

Again, as was the case in many UK universities, Politics was taught initially within Economics which traditionally had been termed 'Political Economy' and that was still true at Exeter when I arrived. There were five political scientists: Bill Steer, the senior lecturer, Andrew Dunsire, later professor at York, Peter Fletcher, a former president of the students union during my time at LSE, and Maurice Vile, later professor and pro-vice chancellor at Kent. I shared an office with Maurice, taking over Crabtree's desk. Like me, he had been born in Hackney and was in the process of becoming one of the foremost British interpreters of the US constitution.

I was responsible for three courses: the history of political thought from Plato onwards to first year students; social and political theory to the second year; and modern English political thought from the nineteenth century Idealists to the present day as a special option in the third year. I also had to conduct weekly seminars for all three courses. This would have been a very arduous teaching load for an established academic, let alone a rookie like me. I struggled to keep a chapter ahead of the students. Many of these were the same age as me or slightly older having done National Service. But it was heaven compared to the banal world of advertising.

I took to the multi-faculty character of the university having only experienced the mono-faculty atmosphere of LSE and also enjoyed my first real taste of English provincial life. In addition to my teaching, I joined the staff cricket team. It was called, quite accurately, "The Erratics" and had been founded in 1934. It always played away and seemed to bat and bowl according to academic rank. Being a temporary assistant lecturer, the lowest of the low, I batted at number eleven, fielded deep in the field and never bowled. Professor Joe Sykes, my head of department, insisted on exercising his seigneurial rights as first change bowler against the Royal Marines at Lympstone. He was in his sixties at the time and his first ball bounced two or three times in front of a burly Master-Sergeant-at-Arms who whacked the ball past me, with Sykes shouting "If you can't stop a simple ball like that Smith, you'll never get tenure here!"

What the team lacked in cricketing prowess, however, it made up for intellectually, containing a number of future professors. These included Robin Fox, who had been a year my senior at LSE, and was to become an internationally recognised anthropologist, settling finally at Rutgers University in New Jersey. Alan Williams, the wicket-keeper, was then a public finance specialist but later became a professor at York and a very innovative health economist and was elected a Fellow of the British Academy.

Bill Steer, my immediate line-manager, was a very kindly man who had come up the hard way in academia. While a career local government officer he had taken a diploma in public administration followed by a law degree. He began teaching public administration and particularly local government at the University College and rose to become senior lecturer-in-charge of the politics side of the Economics department. He was evidently impressed with the way I tackled the teaching at such short notice and he asked me to stay on as a research fellow in local government. I appreciated this but felt I should get on and take a PhD in America.

Princeton

I had been accepted as a post-graduate at Princeton University - a top Ivy League institution. I had married in the February of 1960. Brenda, my wife and I set sail for New York from Southampton in the by now very dilapidated *SS Mauretania.* It had been a famous Cunard liner between the wars and had served as a hospital ship during WWII. Transatlantic air travel was still very expensive and Fulbright scholars, such as me, were packed off into steerage in one of the ageing liners. En route we called in at Cobh where hordes of young Irish men and women joined us. They were all destined to enter seminaries and convents in the United States. It was my second direct contact with Irish culture. They sung traditional Irish songs which are melancholy enough, particularly so when sung by those young novitiates who thought they would never see their native land again.

Arriving at Princeton, it was soon apparent that my meagre stipend would not be enough to keep us. Also, my wife thought she was pregnant and would not have been able to work. We decided to return to England.

Acton Society Trust

I could not retrieve the offer of a research fellowship at Exeter which had been already filled. Also, at the beginning of the academic year there would be no vacancies to apply for but I noticed a job for a researcher at the Acton Society Trust in Welbeck Street, London. The Acton Society was what would now be called a 'think tank'. It had been set up by the Joseph

Rowntree Social Service Trust Ltd (JRSST) as a research facility for the Liberal Party in a way similar to the role performed by the Fabian Society for the Labour Party. Created in 1945, a succession of directors determined that it should be a politically independent research agency, rather along the lines of Political and Economic Planning (PEP), which had been set up in the 1930s.

Its first reports dealt with the public corporations which had been formed under the Attlee government to run the nationalised industries. These were followed by a series of reports on the creation of the National Health Service (NHS). The third director, Rosemary Stewart, was particularly interested in matters of business administration and management. She hired me to work on a project dealing with management training. I did most of the research and writing up under the guidance of Michael Argyle, a social psychologist at Oxford University. He was an excellent mentor and later became quite well-known as a broadcaster on radio and television, interpreting human behaviour and body language.

Training Managers was published in 1962. It covered the mushroom growth in general management training courses in the two decades after 1945. These were mainly put on by management consultants' firms, together with the one established institution, the Henley Staff College. This patchwork quilt of provision reflected the very haphazard approach adopted by British industry to the mid-career training of its managers. The report served as a prelude to the later Franks Report which recommended the formation of the London Business School and the Manchester Business School to provide systematic

MBA education. This, in turn, prompted the epidemic in business courses throughout the United Kingdom's further and higher education sectors. Even Cambridge, with the formation of its Judge School, and later Oxford, with its Said School, succumbed to the virulent infection.

Interesting though management research was, I was more anxious to return to political science. I proposed that the Acton Society should undertake a study of councillors in local government. This would improve my political science credentials and the possibility of gaining another university post. It was also a fertile time as it was at the start of a new wave of interest and research into local government and it was very likely the system of local government would be reformed in the near future. The Institute of Local Government Studies had been founded at Birmingham University and Anthony H Birch's pioneering *Small Town Politics: A Study of Political Life in Glossop* had sparked off a number of similar studies of which the Acton Society's *Town Councillors: A Study of Barking* was an early example. Written by Anthony Rees and myself it was published in 1964, being generally well received.

The Acton Society was also to provide me with further opportunities for career advancement. At the time it had a very prestigious group of trustees including Walter James, then editor of the *Times Educational Supplement*, Sir Jock Campbell, Peter (later Sir) Masefield, Sir Walter Warboys and four who were also Trustees of the Joseph Rowntree Social Service Trust Ltd which, later, was to prove incredibly important to me.

Hull & York

I was to continue my close contact with the Acton Society for more than a decade. *Town Councillors* helped secure me a tenured post at the University of Hull. The foundation professor of Politics was one Anthony Birch. As at Exeter, the Politics department had grown recently out of Economics and, also like Exeter, Hull had become a fully-fledged University in its own right in 1954. It had been created as a university college in 1927 on the initiative of Thomas Ferens, then head of Reckitt & Colman Ltd. His firm made the famous Colman's mustard and Reckitt's equally popular blue laundry whitener. Accordingly, Hull adopted motto was Lampeda Ferens ("The Light of Ferens") and its colours were mustard and blue.

The move to Hull in October 1962 was the beginning of my lifelong romance with Yorkshire and I can well understand how the East Riding inspired both the poetry of Philip Larkin and the landscape painting of David Hockney: its Wolds and plains are very engaging.

Arriving in Hull, my wife and I lived first above a grocer's shop in Cottingham Road, close to the University, where my first son, Adam, was born in 1964. The impending birth of my second son, Gideon, made us look for larger premises and we went from the sublime to the ridiculous. We moved to Winestead, a hamlet about halfway between Hull and Spurn Point. The White Hall was being restored and refurbished by an early-retired army captain. He was doing this largely by himself with his wife's assistance. He was Nicholas Hilliyard and was related to the famous sixteenth century miniaturist portrait painter of the same name on his mother's side. He had changed his surname by deed poll. His wife was the daughter of Mr Justice Salmon, the judge who had handed out exemplary four year jail sentences to the 1958 Notting Hill race rioters. Having completed the renovation of the west wing he had to let it out in order to generate income and we took it for a year. Architecturally it was the finest home I ever had until I occupied the Vice-Chancellor's lodge at Coleraine some thirty years later.

I taught British government and public administration at the University of Hull for the next five years. Two colleagues, already in post, were W H Greenleaf, a noted historian of political ideas and later author of a prodigious four volume analysis of *The British Political Tradition* and Robert E Dowse, a political sociologist, who had been in the year above me at LSE. I constituted the fourth member of staff and was Birch's first appointment.

Tony came out of the illustrious Government Department created by William J M Mackenzie at Manchester University that provided so many professors for the burgeoning numbers of Politics Departments in provincial universities. Birch was one its finest exports. He had wide-ranging research interests. He was undoubtedly one of the most successful political scientists to interpret the inter-relationship between thought and action in modern British politics. He was also a recognised authority on federalism in Canada and Australia. For all his scholarly attributes, however, he was a poor manager. He was a rather indifferent head of department and as a faculty dean lasted for only one year. His management style was a compound of bouts of hypochondria and throwing tantrums. Birch was also particularly secretive so that to find out what was going on in the department a number of us would repair to his secretary's office in the evening where my wife, Brenda, would re-read the shorthand notes.

Be that as it may, his other undoubted quality was his ability to attract first-rate staff. Building on the foundations he laid, the Hull Department of Politics has invariably been amongst the best performers in the subject ever since his time. Almost all of those he recruited subsequently became professors. These included Bob Benewick (Sussex), Michael Leifer (LSE), Dennis Kavanagh (Nottingham and Liverpool), Paul Taylor (LSE) and David Coombes (Loughborough and Limerick). The most brilliant, undoubtedly, was Bhikhu Parekh FBA who stayed at Hull, retiring as a professor and later joining me in the Lords – though taking the Labour whip. Overall Birch's many virtues far redeemed his inadequacy as a manager.

As at Exeter, I enjoyed the multi-faculty nature of the institution. Jacob Bronowski had been a maths lecturer before the war. It was the custom in those days in provincial university colleges for a department to consist of a professor with permanent tenure and an assistant lecturer who had a limited four-year contract before he or she usually went into school teaching and another temporary assistant was recruited. At the advent of war, legislation was introduced to guarantee people's positions for when they returned. To the relief of senior colleagues, Bronowski did not exercise his right of return, going instead to work as a statistician for the Coal Board before becoming a famous broadcaster. Nevertheless in the 1960s, there were still Hull academic wives of a certain age who recalled the young Lothario and would blush at the sound of his name.

The most famous person on the staff at Hull when I was there, of course, was its Librarian, the poet Philip Larkin. In the then still relatively small institution almost everybody knew everyone else on the staff. There was also a lively social life with parties on the go most Saturday evenings. The staff cricket club was an altogether more serious team than Exeter and I 'retired hurt' after a couple of seasons. As with all ardent Yorkshire cricketers they used to work out batting and bowling averages to three decimal points - much too keen for me.

The Faculty of Social Studies contained a number of leading left-wingers. They helped give Hull the sobriquet of being "the reddest of the red-bricks". *The New Reasoner*, later amalgamated with *The Universities & Left Review* and becoming the *New Left Review*, had been formed there. Peter Worsley, the sociologist and anthropologist, and John Saville, the economic historian, were nationally well- known as leading Marxists. Richard Hoggart, a traditional Labour supporter, had worked as an English tutor in the extra-mural department before being shot to fame as the author of *The Uses of Literacy* (1957). This book launched him as an academic celebrity that led to a professorship at Birmingham, then Assistant Secretary of UNESCO and later Warden of Goldsmiths College, London University. I was to get to know him well in this last role.

While it may have justly been termed "the reddest of the redbricks", the university's senior administration was right-wing, which accounts for the failure to promote both Hoggart and Worsley who had expressed a desire to stay at Hull. It was also very hierarchical and authoritarian. Sir Edward Boyle, then Tory Shadow Minister of Education, told me he would like to visit Hull and I passed this on to the vice-chancellor. Boyle was duly invited up to visit but I received no thanks or even a response for my go-between role.

I supplemented my stipend by teaching extra-mural classes. First, it was by ferry across the River Humber and then on to Grimsby Technical College to lecture on social policy to local government officers. This lasted a year. I risked often being stranded, mid-river on a winter's night, on *The Tattersall Castle* in the company of many drunken fishermen having landed at Grimsby but going home to Hull. The ferry is now a restaurant moored on the Thames Embankment which I pass when regularly attending the House of Lords, reviving as it does vivid memories of an earlier existence.

The following year I taught current affairs in the benighted seaside resort of Withernsea. Its railway had been cut off by Dr Richard Beeching as part of his notorious cull of the railway system. The course consisted of a dwindling band of evening class aficionados who had attended courses regularly for many decades. They welcomed me by saying "there's only thirteen of us left but when the 'flu comes in winter we'll drop to eight which means the class will be closed unless you tick us in as attending". They were the most critical class I ever taught as, over the years, they had covered the gamut of arts and social science subjects. At the conclusion, they half complimented me but said "You're not a patch on Mr 'oggart". They were referring, of course, to Hoggart.

In the academic year 1963-64, I also travelled to teach part-time at the newly- founded York University. Harry Rée had been appointed the foundation professor of education by Sir

Eric James, the first Vice-Chancellor and former High Master of Manchester Grammar School. Rée had had a heroic career in occupied France with the Special Operations Executive; he had been awarded both the OBE and the DSO for his services. He had written *The Essential Grammar School* when headmaster of Watford County High School for Boys. Eric James thus considered him a close ally and supporter of selective secondary education. Moving to York, however, Rée had experienced something akin to a Damascene conversion and became an ardent advocate of comprehensive schooling, then being introduced on a large scale throughout England and Wales. He was something of an innovator and wanted to incorporate teacher training into the undergraduate curriculum whereby students could opt for education alongside a traditional subject such as English, modern languages, history, etc. He wanted someone to teach educational sociology - a Department of Sociology was not due at York until the following year. John Vaizey, a noted educational economist, who had acted briefly as director of the Acton Society, and a friend of Rée's, suggested me to him, knowing that I was nearby in Hull. I taught again in 1965-66 at York as things had not worked out smoothly with the new Sociology Department. It was at York that I met a number of distinguished educators who visited, including Albert Rowe – a famous head teacher, poet, and broadcaster, who became a firm close friend.

During my time in Yorkshire I also moonlighted as a commentator on the BBC Home Service (North Region). I had done some radio work before but the knife-edge 1966 North Hull by-election would open up new horizons for me. Harold Wilson had a majority of two in the House of Commons following the 1964 general election. He had to rely on Woodrow Wyatt and Desmond Donnelly, both drunks and mavericks, in order to stay Prime Minster. The Labour MP for North Hull, an ex-Fulham local councillor, had lied about his age (claiming to be ten years younger) when being selected and soon dropped dead with a heart attack.

Not surprisingly, given the minute Parliamentary majority, the world's media descended on Hull. I wrote a description of the constituency for *New Society* with my colleague David Coombes. The visiting journalists used this as a main source for their reports but otherwise stayed boozing in the Paragon Station Hotel. I had ended the article by predicting that Labour would hold the seat but the then editor, a one Timothy Raison, later a Conservative MP, erased my conclusion. As I had predicted, against the flow of editorial opinion, the Labour candidate Kevin McNamara was elected. Raison had denied me the credit I warranted for my forecast.

Radio & Television

As a result of the article, Stephen Banerjee, one of the most senior political news producers in BBC radio, invited me to take part in the all-night Home Service programme analysing the result. In the run up to the by-election, Barbara Castle, the Minister for Transport, had attempted to bribe the electors of North Hull with the promise to build a bridge across the River Humber. The morning after the by-election I was on the BBC North Region with my colleague from the Economics Department, Dr Eric Evans. We were asked by the northern political editor what was the case for the Humber Bridge? To which Eric replied in his mellifluous Welsh accent, "if there was a case for the Humber Bridge, the Romans would have built it!" That comment should enter the Book of Quotations. A beautiful architectural construction, the bridge leads to nowhere and it remains very much a white elephant: it could not even pay the interest due on the sum borrowed to construct it, let alone the principal amount itself, because of the short-fall in toll income. A later government – the 2010 Coalition – had to write off the accrued debt.

There were other radio opportunities at the time. I was asked to present *Northern Campus* for the BBC North Region which went out on Sunday mornings opposite the highly popular *Family Favourites* presented by Cliff Michelmore and Jean Metcalfe. The programme aimed to describe current developments both in the new universities like Lancaster and the older ones like Sheffield, in the wake of the Robbins Report. I visited both institutions, lugging the heavy Ewer recording machine. Miniscule listening audiences, however, made for a short life for the programme.

More exciting was television. I contributed to the coverage of the 1966 General Election for Granada TV which at that time broadcast on both sides of the Pennines. David Plowright, one of its leading producers who had pioneered the award-winning *World in Action* programme, sought to utilise the newly available talent in the expanding universities in his region as a panel of academic commentators that could be called upon as necessary. Accordingly, Vanya Kewley, later a distinguished investigative broadcaster in her own right, was sent to scour academia in

Lancashire and Yorkshire for likely candidates. My friend Bob Chester, a sociologist, and I were selected for an audition at Granada's HQ in Manchester. I was interviewed by George Reid, Granada's political correspondent; I next saw him, as a Scottish National Party (SNP) MSP, when he was the second presiding officer of the Scottish Parliament. On first meeting him, I played the role of a taciturn introvert; I hoped he would feel no competition. He must have wondered what was in front of him so that he tried to relax and draw me out. I changed character when the cameras rolled and the interview proper began. Vanya told me I passed muster, as had my Hull colleague, and we would have been engaged but for the fact that the other academics from the region had been such poor performers that Plowright had abandoned his original idea.

Lucky Jimism

The early sixties were the most exciting times for British tertiary education. From 1961 to 1963 the Robbins Commission on Higher Education examined the system and recommended a vast expansion of the universities. The Hull Department of Political Studies was formed as a full department in 1961 in anticipation of this and York University was set up simultaneously with the publication of the Robbins recommendations. York had been particularly well prepared as it had a York Academic Trust, established by the Rowntree Social Service Trust Ltd, under the chairmanship of Dr Alan Milner, then Dean of York Minster, to promote the case for a university in that ancient city.

The potentialities of the times blessed me. I was straight out of Kingsley Amis's *Lucky Jim* a hilarious novel depicting the many absurdities of provincial university life. It later became a film, starring Ian Carmichael (who coincidently came from Hull) as the hapless junior lecturer. I, indeed, had been 'lucky'. Although lacking a doctorate, I had nevertheless been able to embark on an academic career, teaching a quite disparate range of subjects in three different institutions. Kingsley Smellie and his wife Stephanie acted as an employment agency and had helped launch a number of LSE graduates in our careers. I had the chance vacancy at Exeter crop up as had the part-time job with Harry Rée at York. Hull had been the one post I had got by a regular recruitment process.

I was very happy at Hull but feared that I would languish there and become part of the furniture if I did not move on in my career. Accordingly, I applied for two jobs that came up. One was at the newly created Brunel University which was moving from Acton to a new campus in Uxbridge in west Middlesex. Previously it had been designated as a College of Advanced Technology, being born out of Acton Technical College. Robbins had recommended that the half a dozen CATs, as they were termed, should become fully-fledged universities. A new Department of Social Sciences was being formed under the headship of Professor Eliot Jacques. He was a Harvard-trained psychoanalyst who had developed a very lucrative practice in Harley Street. He had also been concerned with industrial behaviour and was closely involved with Wilfred (later Lord) Brown at the Glacier Metal Company in West London. They had collaborated in writing an influential book, *The Changing Culture of a Factory* (1951). John Vaizey had been made the foundation professor of Economics at Brunel and citing him as a referee may well have helped my being interviewed.

I also applied to the Department of Economics which had just been formed in the East End constituent School of University of London in the Mile End Road. Queen Mary College (QMC) was a long-established institution with Arts, Science and Engineering faculties. In response to Robbins, QMC had added a Faculty of Laws and a Department of Economics to its repertoire. I applied for the one lone lectureship in political science at QMC. I was offered both posts but chose the latter. As with Hull, I had undergone a regular recruitment process but the QMC job, as I had hoped, was to afford me many more career opportunities.

CHAPTER 8

BACK TO THE EAST END OF LONDON: QUEEN MARY COLLEGE

I arrived at Queen Mary College in October 1967 and was destined to stay there for the next twenty-three years. It was to be my main career location. The College was firmly established as part of the East End. The Economics Department was a half mile away from the main campus, being housed in what had once been the offices of Spratt's dog biscuits.

The founding Head of the Department was Maurice Peston (father of the, to be, more famous business, economic and political journalist Robert Peston). Maurice had been a junior lecturer at LSE during my undergraduate years there but had gained rapid promotion and was a protégé of Lionel Robbins who had chaired the eponymous report. The federal University of London degree in economics required a compulsory two papers in politics which is why I was appointed. Maurice Peston had appointed some very bright young economists. As the lone political scientist, I regarded myself as being something of a 'remedial' teacher, offering a leavening to my economist colleagues.

In 1968 I was joined by Elizabeth Vallance who was followed by Judith Evans, Wayne Parsons and Raymond Kuhn. By 1970, following the precedents of both Exeter and Hull, I managed to contrive the creation of a Sub-Department of Politics within

Economics and two years later a fully-blown Department in its own right. It was an unprecedented academic development in that its advent had never appeared in any College plan. It was solely due to my opportunistically seizing the initiative at a propitious moment. The various authors of the College's history have declined to mention this or perhaps were prohibited from so doing: no institution likes to appear so informal in its decision-making as this admission would have revealed. The Department has now grown to some thirty staff.

This gave me greater freedom of action and enabled the development of a series of joint degrees with subjects other than economics, including history and geography. I was promoted to senior lecturer as well as being head of department. A Faculty of Social Studies had been created encompassing Economics, Geography as well as Politics. Heads of Economics and Geography served as its first two Deans and I put myself forward to be the third. There were some murmurings about my not being a professor. However, I ignored these, insisting I would stand for election and in the event I was not contested.

At Hull University my research had concentrated on four areas of public policy, viz local government, the civil service, economic planning and the future pattern of British politics. The last carried on over and pre-occupied my early years at Queen Mary. Two books resulted and in the first volume of his monumental survey of *The British Political Tradition* (1983), my former colleague, W H Greenleaf, observed:

> "What is required ... is two types of book. The first is the kind which aims precisely both to present a general view of institutions and to relate this to cognate developments in political thought. There are too few of these studies of recent note but they are admirable and point the way and .... I must acknowledge my very great indebtedness to them. I have in mind four particular works: A H Birch on *Representative and Responsible Government* (1964), S H Beer's *Modern British Politics* (1968) and T A Smith's analysis of *Anti-Politics* (1972) and his later *The Politics of the Corporate Economy* (1979). Like Bacon these serve the office of bell-ringers, first up to call others to church. Then there are the historical exercises ... (page 8)."

I was gratified to be included alongside such scholars as Birch and Beer and my two books no doubt contributed to later promotions in my career.

California State University, Los Angeles

In 1968 I met Dr Tom McEnroe who was enjoying a sabbatical year at London University. We became close friends and he managed to get me hired as a visiting associate professor at California State University (Cal State), Los Angeles, where he worked, for the summer quarter of the following year. It was a memorable experience for a number of reasons.

First, Cal State was a huge campus catering at peak quarters for over 30,000 students almost all of whom were part-time, working their way through university. To cater for their job needs teaching was confined to mornings and evenings, leaving afternoons free. The institution was one of a number scattered throughout California and was the middle element of the three-tier tertiary system devised by the ingenious Clark Kerr. It could offer bachelors' and masters' degrees. The smaller number of grander University of California institutions could offer all grades of degrees, including doctorates. This top tier included prestigious campuses at Berkeley, LA, Santa Cruz, Santa Barbara, San Diego and elsewhere. The bottom and larger third tier was composed of community colleges distributed throughout the State, offering diplomas and the first two years of the conventional four-year undergraduate degree. Students could progress through the system. It was a remarkable exercise in mass higher education. It was to hold me in good stead as a model I could adapt when later I was running the University of Ulster.

Secondly, in the year following the upheavals of the race riots in the Watts district of LA, tensions were still simmering on campus. Black Power was being employed to some effect in the reconstruction of parts of the curriculum. I addressed a gathering of students, being sympathetic towards some of their aims. I told them they had the political clout to force through syllabus changes but I urged restraint so that they maintained the academic integrity of degrees. Black Music, Black Literature were legitimate subjects, but not Black Sciences, Black Law or Black Engineering.

Thirdly, of course, my stay in Los Angeles coincided with the first moon landing. It concluded a memorable summer.

Faculty Dean

My term as Dean of Social Sciences at Queen Mary College coincided with the economic crisis occasioned by the OPEC (Organisation of the Petroleum Exporting Countries) oil price rise of the early 1970s. This had serious economic repercussions for the western world and retrenchment became the order of the day. For tertiary education, it was to be, in effect, the flip side of Robbins expansionism.

Expenditure cuts were announced for higher education and I and the four other Deans were in almost continuous session with the Principal and Bursar to work out how these cuts should be apportioned within QMC. The Science and Engineering Deans, of course, were most adept at analysing the mathematical data with which we were swamped. Holding their hand calculators they would work out the various financial algorithms, invariably to their own Faculty's advantage. I countered by randomly stabbing at numbers on my calculator and asking if their calculations were correct? This had a salutary effect as they often reworked their sums with less advantageous results for themselves.

My career advanced with promotion to a personal chair in 1983. The Principal, Sir James Menter, was a distinguished engineer but thought it prudent to consult Ralf Dahrendorf, the eminent sociologist, and then Director of LSE, as to my suitability. Helpfully, he responded affirmatively; I remain ever-grateful to both for their patronage. Two years later, I was transferred to the first established chair in politics at QMC. My Inaugural Lecture entitled British Politics in the Post-Keynesian Era was delivered on 7 November 1985. In the lecture I had presciently warned that "hooliganism in high places would be more subversive of the body politic than the hooliganism of the mob." The parliamentary expenses scandals, along with those in the financial sector – especially the banks – some thirty years on, vindicated my prediction. I enticed Jo Grimond (then Lord Grimond of Firth) to preside at the occasion which was a memorable event.

The following day Menter, invited me to become one of his two deputies with responsibility for the arts-based faculties and other ad hoc duties that would come my way. This was a full-time post and from then on I concentrated on a career in higher education management. I served as Pro-Principal and later Senior Pro-Principal for five years until 1990.

That five-year stint involved a good deal of time in committees. When not chairing them, they involved long periods doing little else and I interested myself in sketching the other participants. Actually, they invariably ended up as caricatures, reflecting my fairly twisted views on life. The art of caricature lies in representing the personalities in as minimalist a way as possible: this usually requires a series of revisions. I produced a tableaux of all the senior staff at QMC: Principal, the Deputies, Faculty Deans, and the top professional team. The Librarian was very taken with it and placed it in the archives. My best depiction was of the Principal.

I continued the practice at Joseph Rowntree Reform Trust board meetings prior to becoming Chair. My best one was of Jo Grimond – a sparse outline of the essential person.

Moonlighting

During my time at QMC I had continued to exercise my penchant for moonlighting or, as it is termed more fashionably these days, developing a broad portfolio of activities.

The first off-site activity was radio broadcasting. On returning to London I had contacted Stephen Banerjee, who had produced the Hull by-election broadcast I had contributed to, and he arranged for me to undertake a number of projects. I reported on the Liberal Party Conference held at Scarborough in 1971; I had a five night week-long spell presenting the *Talking Politics* programme, that included interviewing Tony Benn; and I regularly appeared on *The World Tonight* – the BBC Radio 4 news programme at 10 o'clock. At that time it was presented by Douglas Stewart, a veteran BBC stalwart. The BBC World Service also engaged me frequently as did the newly-formed LBC (London's commercial radio news station). Around Easter time I contrived to broadcast both on the World Service and on LBC in imitation of the Pope's traditional St Peter's message Urbe et Orbe - one of my little private conceits.

Another portfolio I gained was to run my old stamping ground - the Acton Society. I had maintained work with the Acton Society while at Hull, being commissioned to submit written evidence to the Mallaby Committee on staffing in local government and published as Town and County Hall (1966). Similarly, I had suggested the Acton Society should submit written evidence to the Commons' Estimates Committee enquiry into Recruitment to the Civil Service (1965). This was based on an attitude survey of students at Hull University with regard to the senior Civil Service as an employer. I was assisted in this by my former student Danny Lawrence who was later on the academic staff of Nottingham University. Dr Jeremy Bray, MP was chairman of the Estimates Sub-Committee which was examining Whitehall recruitment and the need to open it up to attract applicants beyond the traditional 'old boy' recruiting pools. He told me that it was the first time a Commons Committee had research undertaken specifically for a parliamentary inquiry. Our research added to the Report's impact which led to the appointment in 1966 of the Fulton Committee that proposed wide-ranging changes to the civil service.

As a result, I had been visited in Hull by three civil servants from Whitehall: one from the Civil Service Commission, one from the Ministry of Defence and one from the Foreign Office - Ewan Ferguson, an Oxford Rugby Blue and later HM Ambassador to France. They entertained me to dinner where copious amounts of alcohol were drunk. The man from the Civil Service Commission retired first, followed by the man from Defence. I stayed up with Ferguson getting much the worse for wear. He was a tall diplomat bred for the purpose of seeing off heavy vodka drinking bouts with Soviet diplomats while remaining sober himself.

My third preoccupation outside academia was as a director of the Joseph Rowntree Social Service Trust Ltd. I joined its board in 1975, having previously served as its research adviser from 1970. This extraordinary body gave me very wide access to contemporary developments in British politics as they occurred, because many sought finance from the Trust to initiate their aims. I will discuss these in a later chapter but suffice to say here the directorship enabled me to represent it on the boards of a number of companies. These included the magazine *New Society* which later merged with *The New Statesman.* I was to serve briefly as chair of the amalgamated weekly periodical in 1990-1991. That was a quite remarkable experience. My fellow directors preached fraternity but practised fratricide, so deep were the divisions between them. In the review of its centenary, *The New Statesman* (2013) makes no reference to this very difficult period when the Rowntree Trust saved it from financial extinction.

I became involved with another aspect of publishing when I joined the board of the left-wing Pluto Press book publishers. It was run by Michael and Nina Kidron whom I had first met at Hull University. Their young daughter, Beeban, became a successful film producer and later a crossbench peer.

I also became a director of Duckworth & Co, the well-established book publishers, having to contend with the remarkable, but equally exasperating, Colin Haycraft. His two main guiding principles were that only women could write fiction and rules only applied to other people. He had discovered, among others, the talents of the novelist Beryl Bainbridge. Duckworth's had a good back list of famous authors which helped keep the firm afloat as well as to purchase Bristol University Publishers' well-established Classics division. But, like *The New Statesman*, it fell on hard times.

I had been introduced to Haycraft by my colleague Bill Fishman. His books, including *East End Jewish Radicals 1875-1914*, had been published by Duckworth. The Rowntree Social

Service Trust Ltd had helped Victor Gollancz to get started in publishing in the 1930s, later producing his famous series with The Left Book Club. It had proved to be a very profitable investment when eventually sold to a US publishing house. With this precedent in mind, I suggested the Trust should also help finance Duckworth which it did. Colin Haycraft's irascibility, however, made it impossible to continue beyond a few years and the Trust ended its association while managing to get its money back.

I was also put on the board of Job Ownership Ltd (JOL), a company set up by Robert Oakeshott to promote the idea of industrial and commercial co-operatives. He was an engaging personality and a drinking partner of Jo Grimond. His father, Sir Walter, had been headmaster of Tonbridge School and later Rector of Lincoln College, Oxford. Robert, like Grimond, had been to Balliol and was the possessor of a cut glass accent which was in direct contrast to the shabbiness of his charity shop second-hand clothes. His accent appealed to businessmen but alienated the workers, while his attire would have had the reverse effect.

He had been a successful journalist on *The Financial Times* but gave it up to work as a schoolmaster in Botswana. On returning to Britain he founded Sunderlandia Ltd as a co-operative wholly owned by redundant building workers in the North-East. When given the opportunity, however, they voted him out as their chief executive. Undaunted, he set up JOL to preach the faith of what he called 'granulated capitalism'. He wrote a number of authoritative books on co-ownership and introduced the ideas behind Mondragon, the Spanish federation of industrial co-operatives, to Britain. Robert was a unique person who also opposed the regime of Mugabe in Zimbabwe with little success.

During these years I was also active in the Church of England. I served on my Parochial Church Council in Harrow and both the Area and Deanery Synods. I was also appointed to the London Diocesan Higher Education Committee whose duties included appointing chaplains to the various universities and then polytechnics around London. The general quality of the candidates was invariably extremely poor – almost unemployable. Being an ardent member of the Movement for the Ordination of Women (this was before woman could be made priests), I was not surprised. I amused myself by asking the candidates if they saw themselves as potentially either Deans or Bishops: priests I had noted tended to opt for one or the other if they gained preferment. Since women were admitted to the priesthood, and later to the house of bishops, there has been an enormous improvement in quality.

Finally, I served on the Tower Hamlets District Health Authority which was responsible for running the Royal London Hospital in Whitechapel, an institution made famous by receiving the victims of Jack the Ripper and also treating Joseph Merrick, the 'Elephant Man'. I later became its vice-chair.

The NHS at that time was undergoing one of its regular re-appraisals and the District Health Authority was quite chaotic. Tower Hamlets is a particularly difficult area in terms of medical provision. It had long been a receptor of waves of inward migration. The Huguenots were followed successively by the Irish, Chinese and Jews and now Bangladeshis and

Somalis. The Authority's publications were translated into over sixty languages. It also attracted an itinerant population which meant that GPs' patients' records had a rapid turnover and were always out-dated and therefore inaccurate. Tower Hamlets was attracting a good deal of the indigent, unemployed and homeless from all over the United Kingdom and hosted one of the two London Welfare Benefits Centres for the homeless. This had, amongst other things, a big impact on its mental health services. I also acted as a Mental Health Act Manager, adjudicating each Monday on the validity of Sectioning of patients at St Clement's mental hospital, Bow.

St Marylebone Grammar School for Boys

Added to these other activities beyond the confines of QMC, I had become chair of the parents' association of my elder son's school, St Marylebone Grammar School, famous for educating Jerome K Jerome, the author of *Three Men in a Boat*. Over the years it had catered for successive generations of Jewish and Irish bright young boys.

The School was under threat of closure by the Wilson government, dedicated as it was to the creation of a universal system of comprehensive secondary education. The Inner London Education Authority (ILEA) had packed the Governors with Labour Party activists of whom the chair, the Dowager Lady Lucan (Veronica Mary Duncan), was one. Alf Dubs, later MP for Battersea, life peer and a minister in Northern Ireland, was another. I led the minority of parent governors who decided to oppose the closure.

We raised enough money, including a subvention from the

Illustrations

Trevor aged six by Arnold Slack

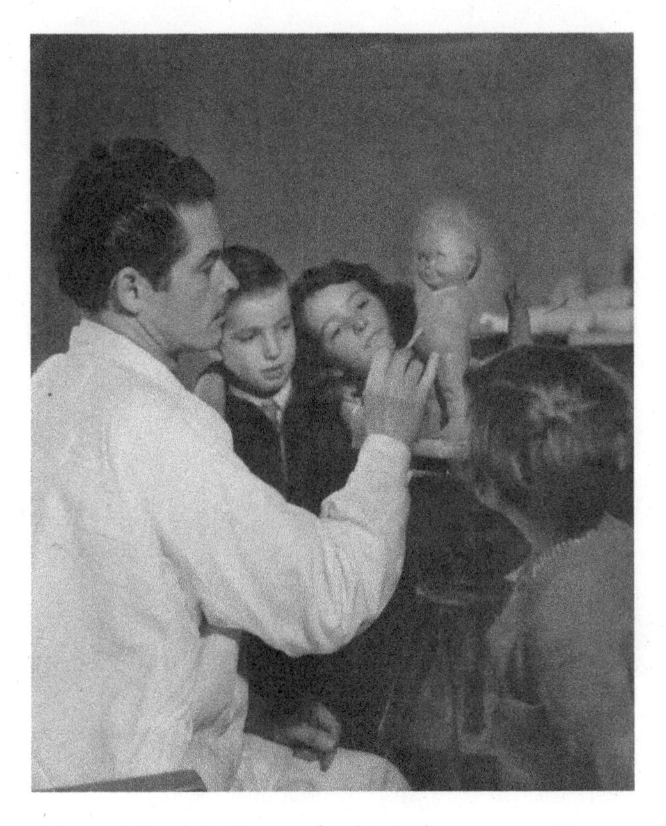

Father modelling doll with young fans, late 1940s

Trevor speaking when being adopted as Liberal candidate for West Lewisham 1959 with Manuela Sykes seated

1959 General Election poster

Illustrations

With President & Mrs Clinton, Derry 1995

With Prime Minister Tony Blair and Julia, Coleraine 1997

With Naomi, Adam and Gideon 2008

With Julia in 2014

Rowntree Social Service Trust, to engage Anthony Lincoln, QC to apply for an injunction. In the High Court, the Vice-Chancellor, Mr Justice Magarrey, found in our favour. The triumph was short-lived as the ILEA immediately appealed. Anthony Lincoln increased his fees which were unaffordable. Instead we would be represented by his junior, the Hon Michael Beloff, at the time an up and coming barrister himself, later to take silk and become Master of Trinity College, Oxford.

The appeal was heard before Lords Denning (Master of the Rolls), Brown and Lane over five days in July 1977. It attracted much publicity. Usually the Appeal Court deals with disputes between major corporations. In contrast, this was a band of little people fighting against a mighty state bureaucracy. The American Bar Association was meeting in London and Chief Justice Warren sat alongside Denning to observe the proceedings.

In the event we lost, though Denning would not award costs against us for which the ILEA had applied but the school's fate was sealed.

The parents had made it clear that it was not selection at 11+ they wanted to retain, but a school of its size in an inner-city environment. As reported at the time I said, "A boy living in a high-rise apartment block, going to a high-rise comprehensive school, would likely vandalise a telephone box on his way because he found its human scale alien". The poor performance of most London comprehensives over the next fifteen years or so, until massive new funds were forthcoming, bore this out.

Shirley Williams was the Secretary of State for Education at this time. I would later join her as a Lib Dem peer and she was my leader for a time. I greatly respected her but not uncritically so. Her daughter was attending Latymer Godolphin, a fee-paying girls' day public school in West London. She was transferred to Camden School for Girls for her Sixth Form. It had been a very acceptable state grammar school and this was its first year as a comprehensive. Her daughter then, in some formal sense, received comprehensive schooling - but in a sixth form still to all intents and purposes being that of a selective grammar. As I said in the press at the time: "St Marylebone Parents believe in standards – not double standards!"

Thus, in the course of my twenty-three years at QMC, I experienced a broad range of activities in a number of walks of life. Most of these were unpaid to my wife Julia's annoyance (I had married for a second time in 1979) but I explained they would hold me in good stead for the last stage of my university career.

A Merger Maniac

Back at QMC, my tasks as Deputy Principal included interviewing vast numbers of staff inducing them to take early retirement on quite favourable terms as we sought to reduce staff costs.

The federal University of London was also rationalising its wide spread of academic activities in order to cut costs. Accordingly, its Senate decided to reduce the number of biology departments and each school of the University had to compete and make its case for retaining the subject. To my surprise and alarm, the Principal asked me to compose the case for QMC. By nature I am essentially a broad-based policy-maker but this task obliged me to go into very great detail if the case was to be convincing. I presented my lengthy submission to Sir James Menter and the head of biology, Professor Alun Bevan. They were very agreeably taken with my endeavours. Sir James said it would go ahead under my name but I insisted that he authored it. Bevan said he was amazed a non-biologist could have written such an authoritative and convincing document. As a result, the Senate decided QMC should be one of its schools to retain biology. This was gratifying both for QMC and myself, not least because it showed me I could amass, distil and convincingly present a case. Again, it showed I could have been a competent barrister. I asked Menter, why had he given me the task? He replied because he thought I was a master word-smith. Anyway, my document had served its purpose.

Another cost-cutting exercise involved the rationalisation and closure of small colleges in London University. This was proceeding apace. The Science Faculty of Westfield College in the salubrious environs of Hampstead had already migrated to QMC. Its Arts Faculty was playing hard to get and flirted with a number of options. I organised QMC's tactics. I knew that we were addressing not just the staff, who were generally opposed to moving to the East End from their leafy surroundings, but also Westfield's Governors. I suggested we offer them the title of Queen Mary & Westfield College. That was a clincher and it secured the merger under the nose of King's College, London. King's had already absorbed a number of smaller colleges but had made no provision for maintaining their identities.

The other merger I was involved with was that of Bart's Medical School and the London Hospital Medical College.

In 1968 a Royal Commission report on the future of medical education (the Todd Report) had recommended that individual medical schools should be combined with multi-faculty university campuses. This was achieved for the most part in London but Bart's held out to maintain its own independence: it was said, "you can always tell a Bart's man, but you can't tell him very much!" The diehards were very proud of the fact that Bart's was the oldest hospital in Britain, having been founded in 1123, whereas the London had only appeared in 1740. Against this, however, was the counter fact that the London had formed the first medical school in 1785, while one had only been set up at Bart's a century later in 1882. Since the Todd Report, successive medical statesman and scientists had sought over nineteen years to bring the two medical schools together but to no avail.

In 1987 Bart's was threatening action in the High Court against both the Universities Funding Council and London University. Dr Ian Kelsey-Fry, the Dean of Bart's and a noted radiologist, was anxious to avoid this confrontation but had great difficulty in view of his medical staff's firm opposition. He made overtures to QMC and I and my fellow Pro-Principal, Professor Michael Laughton, were deputed to meet with two senior pre-clinical medics from Bart's to discuss the possibilities of a solution to the impasse.

After many evening meetings we jointly proposed that a small top-level working party be created to try to devise a thirteenth-hour resolution to the deadlock. It should consist of the Deans of Bart's and the London Hospital, the Principal of QMC, together with one other representative from each of the three institutions. Professor Roy Duckworth, head of dentistry and later Dean, was the London Hospital's representative. Professor Antony Allott, a lay member of the Council of Bart's and Professor of African Law at SOAS supported Kelsey-Fry while I joined to make up the QMC team.

After a preliminary meeting I suggested that Professor Allott and I go away and attempt to compose a broad "heads of agreement" working document as a basis for consideration. The combination of a specialist in the customary laws of Africa and a political scientist was just the sort of skill-set required - why hadn't it been tried before? We swiftly drew up a set of draft proposals for further consideration. It recommended that there should be an initial pre-clinical merger of the two medical schools, conjoined with QMC, but without prejudice to any full merger of the clinical departments of the two hospitals. This proved acceptable to all parties. It was a successful ploy rather like retaining the Westfield College identity in the earlier merger.

An academic committee of the three institutions was set up to devise a common pre-clinical syllabus and one was thrashed out. But, of course, it would merely be a prelude to the full merger which inevitably occurred in 1985. The real hero of the saga was Kelsey-Fry. His prescience and guile throughout was crucial to the ultimate success of the exercise; he proved to be the real saviour of Bart's.

I had played a major part in amalgamating the magazines *New Society* and *The New Statesman* at around the same time. *The Times Higher Educational Supplement* heralded me as a "merger maniac".

A Disaster

Earlier in my career I had benefited from the expansionary policies in higher education; towards the end of it I would experience the opposite extreme of managing rationalisation and decline.

The then Principal of QMC, Professor Ian Butterworth, had been Head of Physics at Imperial College and an associate director at CERN. Apart from that he had little or no managerial experience. He much enjoyed taking foreign trips to China and he got a reputation as a champion dim sum eater. The finances of QMC were deteriorating rather rapidly. I suggested to him that he could be 'prime minister and foreign secretary or prime minister and chancellor of the exchequer' but not all three which was beyond the abilities of any one person. He replied, "I can't delegate" to which I responded, "that's a problem between you and your psychiatrist and should have nothing to do with the College".

From early on, he had wanted rid of me so he could promote John Charap in my place. Charap had worked in concert with Lord Brian Flowers, the vice-chancellor of the University and Butterworth's former lecturer at Manchester, to secure Butterworth the Principal post. It was a physicists' coup. Butterworth suggested I should become Dean of a proposed QMC Business School. I refused the offer despite the urgings to accept by Lady Falkender – an alumna and a Governor of QMC who became a good friend of mine.

The financial situation continued to worsen. I approached the chairman of the QMC governors, Sir Arthur Drew, a former second permanent secretary at the Ministry of Defence (MoD), to explain my concerns for the College's future. He replied this was "treasonable talk". He was a classic 'conflict avoider' whose reluctance to take decisive action would have led to disaster in times of international crisis. I needed to go to a higher authority but could not approach Lord Flowers, due to his ties to Butterworth. Through the good offices of my friend Professor Geoffrey Alderman, I made contact with Sir Peter Swinnerton-Dyer, then Chairman of the Universities Funding Council (UFC).

My concerns received a much more sympathetic attention though events were not to proceed smoothly from then on. Sir Peter informed the new chairman, Martin Harris – a prominent City chartered accountant – and vice-chairman, Sir Norman Lindop, of the QMC Governing Body of the situation and demanded that action be taken. They felt obliged to inform Lord Flowers who promptly warned his protégé of what was afoot. Butterworth, not a decisive person, informed John Charap one of my junior Pro-Principal colleagues. The Science Faculty mobilised into a staff meeting in support of Butterworth and critical of me. It was like a Nuremberg rally.

Butterworth called me in and asked me to resign. I declined, saying I would take legal advice. My colleague Professor Ross Cranston, later Solicitor General in the Blair government (and subsequently a High Court judge) suggested I consulted Cyril Glasser. He was a genius legal practitioner in the mould of Arnold Goodman and he gave me very wise counsel for which I remain very grateful.

Butterworth, in the midst of these troubles, succumbed to

a stroke and retired from the Principalship. Technically, as the Senior Vice-Principal, I should have been appointed Acting-Principal pro tem. This was clearly not possible because I had been instrumental in reporting Butterworth to Swinnerton-Dyer who had then taken further action to have him removed. My junior colleague, Michael Laughton, had collaborated with John Charap to lead the defence within the College of Butterworth. Neither of us, therefore, could be Acting-Principal. The third Vice-Principal was John Chalker, a recent import from Westfield College, who would have had some difficulty in mobilising enough internal support.

The upshot was that the chairman, Martin Harris, persuaded the Governors to make him Acting-Principal. He had never been to university himself but hankered after some sort of academic recognition. It was a preposterous decision. Chalker remained Vice-Principal while Laughton, Charap and I were retired from our offices. I was given a year's sabbatical leave – the first I had ever received in my academic career.

The whole Butterworth saga would have taxed the descriptive powers of a C P Snow to do justice to the machinations of academic politics that were pursued at QMC. In the event I came out of it exhausted, stressed but ultimately unscathed with another academic post ahead of me.

A New Career Opportunity Beckons

In 1987 I had become chair of the board of the Joseph Rowntree Social Service Trust, a name which I persuaded my colleagues to change to the Joseph Rowntree Reform Trust Ltd three years later on the grounds that its core business was political reform rather than social services. Throughout my sabbatical, I busied myself with the Trust and being vice-chair of the District Health Authority. The chair of the District Health Authority had resigned and the executive members together with the officials at Region suggested I should succeed her. I would have welcomed the job but unfortunately Kenneth Clarke was Secretary of State for Health at the time and would not countenance appointing a long-time card-carrying Liberal Party member. He later stuck to his guns when I was recommended for another post.

While being Deputy Principal at QMC I had applied for three headships of London colleges and always been shortlisted but had not succeeded. The arrangement I now had with QMC was that I would have a year's sabbatical leave and return for three years on a third pay although having formally retired.

Another option was to apply for vacant vice-chancellorships and three were to come up while I was on leave: Ulster, Hull and Newcastle. I applied for the first two although I had some reservations about Hull, having enjoyed my previous incarnation there and being a believer in not returning to old pastures. Swinnerton-Dyer warned me that the Ulster post would likely go to an internal candidate.

I learned later that the outgoing Vice-Chancellor, Sir Derek Birley, had told all of his top team that any one of them would be a good and worthy successor to him. Birley was not anxious to retire and was seeking an extension of his term of office. His tactic was to encourage his staff to think they had his support were he to go but in the meantime he sought their support for his continuation. Swinnerton-Dyer would doubtless have heard about these machinations. Nevertheless I pursued with my application for the job which was offered and accepted by me. I think it had helped that I had visited all four campuses during my sabbatical year. I had got my own ship at last.

The selection process was more prolonged because of 'The Troubles' that, in the years 1990-91, were still raging. Clearance had to be sought and consultations made beyond the referees I had cited. Among those approached was Swinnerton-Dyer who told me that when presented with the final short list of three he had blue-pencilled the other two out; my handling of QMC's impending financial crisis had clearly impressed him and so played out in my favour.

On the day of the announcement of my appointment in *The Times* my wife Julia received two telephone calls. The first in a deep Ulster brogue asked if I was at home. When she said, "No", they replied, "Tell him we'll be looking after him" to which my wife replied, "Thank you very much". The Ulster nuance had escaped her – they were not enquiring after my wellbeing but rather that they were "on the look-out for me!" They 'phoned again soon after and said, "Tell him not to come over" just to make it quite clear.

We reported this to the Metropolitan Police who sent a sergeant and a constable round two days later who clearly didn't understand the difference between a Vice-Chancellor and a janitor. I telephoned John Hunter, the Secretary of Ulster University (UU), and he referred it to the chair of Council, Sir Robert Carswell. He was a High Court Judge who himself had recently escaped a would-be assassination attempt when a bomb was placed under his car. He later become Lord Chief Justice of

Northern Ireland and then a Law Lord. He alerted the Royal Ulster Constabulary (RUC) who made their own investigations. Although my politics were such that I had doubts about the role and performance of the RUC, its efficiency on this and other occasions regarding myself was exemplary. They concluded it was "armchair terrorists" and I should not be unduly worried. "If people were intent on murder they would not usually forewarn their subjects", I was told. They also said, "We don't care if you are murdered, but we don't want it on our patch!" Charming of them.

It turned out later that these telephone calls had actually come from members of staff who were pro-Birleyites. Such was my introduction to Northern Ireland.

CHAPTER 9

NORTHERN IRELAND

I had made two trips to the island of Ireland prior to 1991. The first had been to the Republic in 1955 which turned out to be a rather dramatic experience. I went for a fortnight's holiday with a Hounslow College school chum, Ian Davey, to Dunmore East in County Waterford. It was a popular seaside resort later made famous as the setting for some of Maeve Binchey's novels. The vacation had been arranged earlier that year when I was still involved with my girlfriend; she always went there for a month as it was the hometown of her parents. They had all gone ahead two weeks before during which time she thought she was pregnant. Her father took her to see a gynaecologist friend in Dublin. Tests proved negative but she had had to admit we had been intimate. Her father was furious and wrote demanding I did not come and he also wrote to my mother. I replied saying I could not cancel my holiday which had been booked long since with my school friend.

Soon after our arrival at Willie Lawler's pub where we were staying, he burst into our bedroom and angrily demanded I avoided meeting his daughter. My friend, Ian, had the presence of mind to ask him to leave as it was also his room. Thereafter, the father spent his time patrolling the resort endeavouring, but failing, to prevent my covert meetings with his daughter.

At that time the Republic was Eamon de Valera's dream: a priest-ridden, impoverished rural economy dependent on agriculture and little else. I recall a crowded Friday night dinner in the pub. The parish priest entered the door of the dining room and waited expectantly. The local diners vied with each other for him to join them as their guest. The competition for his favours was intense. He took his time in deigning to make his choice. It was vivid testimony of the powerful hold the Catholic Church exercised at the time over the faithful. Five years later sailing to the US, my ship called into Cobh to collect a multitude of Irish youngsters destined for American seminaries and convents which indicated that nothing had changed in the meantime. These shipments had been going on since the Famine which had blighted Ireland in the mid-nineteenth century, when it was forced to export masses of migrants for whom it could not provide employment.

On the following Sunday, Davey and I were having a lunch time drink in the bar. In those days pubs were forbidden to serve alcohol on the Sabbath except to foreign tourists. It was hot and the place was heaving with standing room only. The window blinds were closed and the door firmly locked. Suddenly, silence was called for as the local policeman was seen coming to the pub. The Garda knocked loudly on the door saying, "Open up Willie, this is an unofficial visit, I'm parched and dying for a drink." He was promptly admitted as was regularly the case. As I was to learn later, laws on both sides of the Border in Ireland, had something of a flexibility in their enforcement.

Ulster

My next trip, this time to the North, was in 1990 when I toured the campuses of the University of Ulster. Ireland, and the Republic in particular, had undergone profound economic change especially since joining the EU. It was well on its way to becoming the "Celtic Tiger".

My move to Coleraine in September 1991, perhaps, had something inevitable about it. My great grandmother had hailed from Ballywillan, close by where I was to live and maybe the residues of her genes were still active in my DNA. Then, again, my childhood experiences of the war served as a good trailer for The Troubles that had been going on for nearly thirty years. These reflected a divided society that was centuries old but which had erupted into a more extreme form with terrorism on both sides and military intervention by the British government. The terror tactics, particularly of the Irish Republican Army (IRA), had spilled over into mainland England for the past few years.

Northern Ireland also gave me the opportunity to live, for the first time in my life, in a single universe. It enabled me to bring into better balance my twin activities of a university administrator and political scientist on the one hand, and as a very active chair of the Rowntree Reform Trust on the other. I don't believe in pre-destination but if I did this would have confirmed me in my faith.

The University of Ulster (UU) of which, technically, I was the second Vice-Chancellor had had a chequered history from the start. The New University of Ulster (NUU) was based at Coleraine and was the last in the line of new universities created as a result of the Robbins Report. It also included the Magee College campus in Derry. The decision to site the NUU in Coleraine sparked long protests in Derry which, as the 'Second City', felt it should have been given the new higher education institution. The resentment it engendered both contributed to the civil rights movement there and fed further the extensive para-military activity in Derry. There was no doubt about it that choosing Coleraine was a blatant political gerrymander, pandering to political Unionism by siting it on the eastern shore of the River Bann – the border that is traditionally regarded as separating the predominantly Catholic western area of Northern Ireland from the predominantly Protestant eastern one. There could be no other explanation for, by any objective criteria, Derry should have been chosen.

At the outset NUU managed to attract some students from Great Britain in its first year or so but this source soon dried up as the momentum of The Troubles gathered apace. As an institution it was fast becoming non-viable.

Ulster Polytechnic had been created in 1971 on the shores of Belfast Lough at Jordanstown and it also incorporated the famous, long-established Belfast School of Art in the city itself. It was a rather more successful educational innovation than NUU. In 1984 the Government took the decision to force the merger of NUU and Ulster Polytechnic as the first trans-binary amalgamation in the UK. This meant that the University of Ulster (UU), as it was called after the merger, had four campuses seventy miles apart, stretching from Jordanstown to Magee College. It was the first example of such a far-flung multi-campus university in the UK, while the other six universities on the island of Ireland remained single-site campus universities.

The decision was taken at the outset that the academic staff of UU would be required to travel between campuses as necessary rather than to move vast swathes of students. Many of the disciplines offered were on more than one campus. Thus, UU became the largest university by far on the island of Ireland which is not always appreciated as it is disaggregated on to four campuses.

The Character of Northern Ireland

Northern Ireland has a somewhat ambiguous reputation in the UK. On the one hand, holiday visitors often remark on the warmth of the welcome they receive. On the other hand, the average Briton wanted rid of it. So far as The Troubles were concerned opinion polls revealed, especially when they spilt over as terrorist attacks on the mainland, that Britons were indifferent as between the two options - a united Ireland or an independent Northern Ireland; British citizens just wanted rid of it.

Generally speaking, the residents of Northern Ireland from both Catholic and Protestant communities are warm in their welcome but don't try testing this by taking a job there. You would be regarded as a "blow in" stealing a local's job and therefore most unwelcome. It is alright for the two communities to compete fiercely with each other for jobs but altogether quite different when an outsider seeks work on their patch.

There was a further complicating factor in the structure of its internal labour market. Since the partition of Ireland in 1926 and the formation of Northern Ireland with its own devolved Parliament and Government at Stormont, the momentum of the so-called "Protestant Ascendancy" ensured the perpetuation of institutional discrimination in employment. This was to the detriment of the Roman Catholic community which made up about half the population. The one advantage for the Catholics was that they were given a near-monopoly of owning public houses and bookmakers' shops. This was because Ulster Protestantism observed, outwardly at least, its doctrinaire disdain for booze and betting. Otherwise, in almost all walks of life from top to bottom in Northern Ireland society, there was massive anti-Catholic discrimination. This could be seen in the Belfast shipyards, which provided considerable employment of a manual kind, and continued right up the society to the senior ranks of the judiciary and civil service. Simmering Catholic resentment at being denied employment in so many walks of life was a main cause of The Troubles and fed Irish nationalism. In an attempt to remedy and defuse this blatant bias in the labour market, the Fair Employment Act was enacted in 1989. It was a draconian, but very necessary and long overdue, piece of legislation that effectively destroyed discrimination in the workplace. However, long residues remained for some time. In the Royal Ulster Constabulary (RUC), for example, it took the deliberations of the Patten Report following the Belfast Agreement to propose positive discrimination in favour of Catholic police recruits. Interestingly, this succeeded well before the ten year period allocated for the purpose of increasing the number of Catholic police officers.

The thirty years of The Troubles had essentially cantonised the population into distinct monoglot areas. The Housing Executive, a Government body especially appointed to ensure that the allocation of council housing was non-discriminatory, abandoned early on any attempts at creating cross-community estates. This exacerbated the problem. Portstewart on County

Londonderry's Atlantic coast close to Coleraine, remained a mixed community thanks largely, I believe, to it being a dormitory town for the university. But only a few miles away in the small town of Bushmills, home of the famous whiskey blenders, the census records ninety-eight per cent of the population as being Protestant and the reason it fell short of a total majority, I believe, was because of the existence of a Chinese take-away. Bushmills was not untypical.

The boundaries of such enclaves were as often as not demarcated by the pavement kerbsides. Protestant/Unionist ghettos would display red, white and blue markings, while Catholic/Nationalist/Republican enclaves would be painted with green, white and orange strips. It paid to keep your eyes down.

The campuses of UU being so geographically dispersed required me to have a team of three drivers. One night, returning very late from an event in Enniskillen, I was listening to the BBC World Radio. The main news item was an up-date of the ferocious battles between the Serbians and the Croatians. My driver belonged to the Orange Order, the Apprentice Boys of Derry, the Black Preceptory, the Freemasons and the Royal British Legion so there could be no doubting his political and religious affiliations. I remarked on how awful the situation in the Balkans was. To my utter astonishment he replied: "We're on the side of the Serbs – the Catholic Croats collaborated with the Nazis, but the Serbs ran the underground movement against the Germans." He would have had difficulty in pin-pointing Calais on a map of Europe so I asked him for the source of his (admittedly mainly true) information. He said it was told to his Orange Lodge. On the principle of "My enemy's enemy is my friend", I suppose, he would have suppressed any objections he and his fellows may have had to the creed and liturgy of the Serbian Orthodox Church. It is an illustration of how deeply runs prejudice in Northern Ireland, particularly at the working class level.

The Markets Area in central Belfast corroborates these ingrained attitudes based, as they are, on a bizarre sense of geo-politics. Strictly bifurcated between the two communities, the Catholic/Nationalist/Republican half of the Area sports the flags of the PLA – making it a sort of Gaza Strip in the rain. For its part, the ultra-Protestant/Unionist side flies the Israeli flag. To put it in an Islamic context, it reflects the mutual and intense hatred Sunni followers of the Prophet have for their Shia co-religionists which is fully reciprocated. By their intolerance, the Muslims of the Middle East and the Christians of Northern Ireland could not try harder to promote atheism among impartial onlookers or so it seemed to me.

The middle classes do not escape from their politico-religious backgrounds very much either. Prejudicial talk is more muted for the most part, but still very obvious. The only time the bourgeoisie from both sides mix socially is at charitable fund-raising events. Otherwise people keep pretty close to their respective tribes.

An intriguing take on the strong sectarian divide, is that whenever natives of the two Northern Ireland communities meet in England, or elsewhere no doubt, their common birthplace binds them together strongly and erstwhile sectarian differences fade away. Perhaps Stalin's internal deportations had something going for them after all in forging a common Soviet identity.

Moving to Northern Ireland

In the 1990s, Northern Ireland was also a very sexist society. It was the worst male chauvinist place I had experienced. This was reinforced in both communities by the fact that in the Catholic Church the priesthood was all-male, while among Presbyterians the elders in each parish were almost invariably male. An early illustration of this was when my wife and I attended a tea party put on by the University Secretary to introduce us to senior members of staff and their wives. On arrival, we recognised the usual pattern of behaviour whereby the men were all congregated in one part of the garden with the wives in another. My wife went towards the men while I mixed with their spouses. Having introduced themselves to me the wives said, "Vice-Chancellor, we were just discussing the relative merits of butter and margarine." I replied, "Oh, you must be thinking of the 1971 film *Last Tango in Paris* starring Marlon Brando. Rather than butter or margarine, I prefer KY Jelly myself." Some burst into giggles which, as their innate Presbyterianism kicked-in, they strangulated by raising their hands to their mouths. Others were simply appalled. The segregation of the sexes and the repressed self-censorship is an indelibly etched vignette in my memory.

This experience ran counter to my interpretation of Ruby Murray's signature song. She hailed from Belfast and had a hit which ascended to the top of the charts entitled *I'll Come When You Call*. I took this to be the height of auto-eroticism.

At her insistence, we took our ten year old daughter, Naomi, with us to Northern Ireland. She asked me "What church will you go to here?" I replied, "Over here to a Catholic we'd be Prods and to a Protestant we would be Taigs". I had been in the habit of attending an Anglo-Catholic shrine, St Mary the Virgin in Harrow where we lived. I am a sucker for high churchmanship and its 'smells and bells' drama, although my theology is essentially universalist in outlook. I added, "While we are in Northern Ireland we will pretend to be Jews or Quakers".

In fact, I chose not to attend religious services in Northern Ireland except for staff funerals. I knew only too well that I would be carefully watched to see if I was pro-Protestant or pro-Catholic. However, I broke this practice on the Saturday after my father died. Being aware of my High Church predilection, one of my senior colleagues invited me to a requiem mass which his church held every week to pray for the souls of the recently departed. I said I would go provided that my name was not mentioned and no reference made to me; I would simply attend but not receive the sacraments. I was assured my wish for anonymity would be fully respected. At the opening of the mass, the parish priest welcomed me by name and expressed commiserations for the loss of my father. He couldn't resist it and I should have known better.

Another senior colleague, himself a Catholic from the Falls Road, observing me after three years at UU, said he judged me to be pro-Catholic. I vehemently denied this saying, "I am neither pro- nor anti-; I'm for fairness." When similarly challenged as to my politics, I insisted, in the context of Northern Ireland,

I was neither pro-Unionist nor pro-Nationalist, but was an unswerving democrat. When he first met me, Sir David Fell, later head of the Northern Ireland Civil Service, warned me it would be very difficult to be a Liberal in Northern Ireland. At my retirement dinner eight years later, I reminded him of his all too accurate prediction.

Soon after my arrival, I invited to dinner Edward Daly, the iconic Catholic Bishop of Derry who had appeared on television screens waving a white handkerchief endeavouring to take the injured to safety during the Bloody Sunday outrage, and James Mahaffey, the Anglican Church of Ireland Bishop of Derry and Raphoe. They were both splendid examples of pastoral leadership in their respective dioceses and were great advocates of peace. During the meal they showed signs of agitation when, speaking about the church I attended in England, they assumed I was a Catholic and were worried that their offices had not apprised them of this fact. I said, "Your Graces, I must put you at ease. I am something neither of you have much experience of; I am an Anglo-Catholic". Even had I wished, it would have been impossible for me to attend an Anglo-Catholic church in Northern Ireland as there were none. I was told St George's in Belfast was liturgically "very High" but, by English standards, was very middle of the road. Depending on location, the Anglican Communion tends to adopt a churchmanship opposite to what it perceives as its main Christian rival. Thus, in Scotland, Wales and the United States it is High Church because its competitors are seen as the Protestant denominations of Methodists, Baptists and Presbyterians and other such free-thinking sects. On the island of Ireland, however, the Church of

Ireland is very Low Church because it sees its main opposition as the Roman Catholics.

In Northern Ireland the Presbyterian Church of Ireland has a far larger membership than its Anglican counterpart. Also, the Presbyterian Church of Ireland is altogether quite different from its co-religionists in Scotland. The latter are relatively liberal both in the practice of their faith and in the political outlook they adopt. The Irish Presbyterian Church, by contrast, is religiously and politically very conservative. It put itself out on a limb, as the only church in the British Isles that withdrew from the World Council of Churches in Geneva because it thought it was too full of 'pinkos'.

Schooling

Topographically, Northern Ireland is essentially one great farmyard which both Protestant and Catholic farmers cultivate. They had two different unions to promote their interests. Similarly, of course, schooling still remains almost completely segregated. That is something to which the Catholic hierarchy clings tenaciously. Catholic schools are voluntary-aided, and traditionally were staffed by priests and nuns. The steep decline in religious vocations, however, has meant that policy was no longer sustainable. The state schools, by default, are essentially Protestant in character. There were two teachers' training colleges: Stranmillis, which catered for the training of Protestant teachers and St Mary's which performed the same function for Catholics. Recently the two have been assimilated by Queen's University, Belfast (QUB). Ulster University, to its credit, was the only teacher training facility that accepted students from both faiths and trained them in an avowedly non-sectarian context.

There were other features of schooling in Northern Ireland – some good, some bad. In the same way that the Thatcherite anti-trade union policies were never exported across the Irish Sea so, too, the adoption of comprehensive education did not occur. The traditional system of secondary selection at 11+, allocating the brighter pupils to grammar schools and the rest to secondary ones persisted. The latter of both faiths were invariably single-sex, separating boys from girls. A positive feature of maintaining grammar schools was that Northern Ireland had the best exam results at both sixteen and eighteen. As a region it outperformed all the others in England & Wales (Scotland is not so easily comparable). The success of the grammars also ensured the absence of public schools, although such was their excellence some grammar heads were given membership of the Headmasters' and Headmistresses' Conference (HMC), the representative body of the public school heads in Great Britain. Invited to dinner by the heads of the half dozen top grammars, three Catholic and three Protestant, their competence in Latin was impressive and the sextet would not have been matched easily by their counterparts anywhere in Great Britain.

There were two drawbacks to the system. First, those pupils not in grammar schools lost out. The educational achievements of these secondary modern schools did not compare at all favourably with those of the generality of comprehensive schools in England & Wales. Secondly, falling school rolls, due to lower birth rates, also meant that to maintain income the grammars often accepted pupils who were not best served by them.

Just before I arrived, an integrated schools movement had got underway. This had been funded by the Joseph Rowntree Charitable Trust (JRCT) (essentially Quaker) and the Nuffield Foundation. A few integrated schools had been created at primary and secondary level admitting both Catholic and Protestants in equal numbers, although there was under-representation of Catholics. This movement should have been strongly encouraged by the Government on two grounds. One, the maintenance of two separate systems for Catholic and Protestant meant there was an over-supply of schools and a positive move towards integration would have brought about significant savings to the public purse (that is, to the UK taxpayer). Two, more importantly, there was a need to attempt to break down the strong, very negative sectarian feelings by promoting secular schooling. Governments in London, however, were not prepared to take on the might of either the Catholic hierarchy or that of Protestants. This failure of political will is a shocking indictment of past UK governments of all political stripes and of the successor power-sharing devolved Northern Ireland Executive that allows the situation to perpetuate. Sir George Bain was asked to investigate some of the resource implications of the pattern of schooling but his recommendations still await implementation - not surprisingly.

Corruption

Corruption in Northern Ireland is also financial as well as sectarian. The UU I inherited from Derek Birley was characterised by elements of corruption. Birley had been the Principal of Ulster Polytechnic and had beaten Sir William

Cockroft, the Vice-Chancellor of NUU, to be the first Vice-Chancellor of UU. Cockroft had been a professor of maths at the University of Hull when I was there as a lecturer and in the meantime had written a major report on mathematical education for the UK government. Birley had created a strong institution at Jordanstown and Belfast. Rivals for the new head post they may have been but they shared a common dependence on alcohol. I confess to imbibing myself but I am not yet in their league. Indeed, it was common knowledge that Birley was never sober after 11 am. He was also a womaniser, a bully and cultivated favourites among the staff. There were other petty examples of corruption. Quite wrongly, he subsumed his entertainment allowance into his salary thereby enhancing his pension. Then again, when he left he used three vans from the University to transport his effects back to England so that he did not have to pay for a pantechnicon himself.

A more serious charge of corruption was the composition of his top team. Almost all of its members had been in post for a number of years and exhibited an excessively strong sense of entitlement to stay where they were. There were only two professionals – the Secretary and the Finance Officer.

Staffing and Estates were run by two Pro-Vice-Chancellors in a very amateurish way. Of course, as I have said, they were all men – and mostly heavy smokers at that – and of the two Catholics one was a Scot. Three of the senior team had applied to succeed Birley and, as a courtesy had been long-listed, but they did not make the final shortlist of three. Nor did any of them go on to become Vice-Chancellors themselves or even apply for such posts elsewhere so they avoided testing the academic labour market.

The difficult problems that confronted me as Vice-Chancellor, however, were made endurable by having an excellent office head in Margaret Connolly. In her long time at UU she served four V-Cs in all and I have no doubt they would acknowledge the debt of gratitude they owe her.

Political Transformation

When I accepted the Vice-Chancellorship of UU many English colleagues thought I had got the 'gulag' appointment, equivalent to being exiled to run a Mongolian power station which was the lesser of the two fates that could befall a disgraced member of the Soviet politburo. Actually, I saw it as a great opportunity, given the prevailing nature of the geo-politics of Northern Ireland, though I must admit I did not anticipate quite how dramatic would be the impending changes that were about to happen.

The Troubles were still raging but Margaret Thatcher and her successor, John Major, had initiated clandestine exploratory talks with the IRA. Peter Brooke was Secretary of State for Northern Ireland at the time and he had continued to move things along. The United States Consulate was one place where you could meet politicians from all parties, including Sinn Fein, on Independence Day every 4th July. Successive US Consuls played a very important part in trying to bring about some form of reconciliation. There was also the Anglo-Irish Secretariat at Holywood in the Belfast suburbs. This was a sort of political Noah's Ark where the staff at all levels consisted of co-equals recruited from London and Dublin. The basic tasks were allocated differently so that, for example, catering was undertaken by staff from Dublin which made it a very good place to dine and, more especially, drink wine. I remember being entertained for a very drunken lunch there where I spoke freely and candidly only to be told at the end by my Irish host that the conversation would have been recorded and transmitted simultaneously to the Government Communications Headquarters (GCHQ) at Cheltenham.

Apart from the oases of neutrality provided by the US Consulate and the Anglo-Irish Secretariat, Northern Ireland was very much a relic of Empire. It reeked of colonialism. At the top of the governing hierarchy was the Secretary of State who had taken over from the Governor in 1971 when direct rule was imposed and both chambers of the Stormont Parliament suspended. Beneath him came the RUC Chief Constable and the General Officer Commanding British Forces. They were followed by the Anglican and Catholic Archbishops of Armagh and then came the Vice-Chancellors of QUB and UU.

Richard Rose had written an interesting book about Northern Ireland entitled *Governing Without Consensus* (1971). The Government that faced me in Northern Ireland twenty years later could more aptly have been described as "*Consensus Without Government*". Security matters apart, Northern Ireland was effectively governed by a coalition comprising the Northern Ireland Civil Service and a myriad of extremely strong and well-entrenched voluntary groups who were far more influential in determining public policy than their counterparts in Great Britain. As I was to write later, "In 1991 I found Northern Ireland more collectivist than Joe Stalin's Russia, more corporatist than

Benito Mussolini's Italy and more quangoised than the Britain of the two Harolds (Macmillan and Wilson)." I wrote this as the Introduction to Seamus Dunn and Helen Dawson's *An Alphabetical Listing of Word, Name and Place in Northern Ireland and the Living Language of Conflict* (2000). Politically, it was hermetically sealed, almost impervious to the outside. As I have noted, even Thatcher's radical approach to the reform of trade union power could not extend to Northern Ireland – it didn't even reach the ferry at Stranraer; the unions remained firmly entrenched in Northern Ireland.

Thus, in so many respects, Northern Ireland was a completely different entity to anything I had previously encountered and presented both a challenge and an opportunity. After my appointment, but before arriving, in the six months available, I began to make an inventory of the potentialities I could perceive for UU within the context it operated.

The International Conflict Resolution Institute (INCORE) – a New Initiative

My first thoughts focussed on the strong reputation UU had for the study of cross-community conflict, but these endeavours had been confined almost solely to Northern Ireland. At the time, the world's leading conflict resolution centres were located in cities like Geneva, Oslo, Helsinki and other such safe havens that hadn't experienced physical unrest for centuries – if at all. It struck me that the UU Magee campus in Derry, a city that had suffered from civil strife and terrorism for three decades, was uniquely situated to host a think tank with a remit to look at conflict and its resolution from a world-wide perspective. War-torn Derry and the well-recognised academic expertise available in UU would be a perfect combination for a new facility analysing communal conflict and civil war that was, and remains, a growth industry. Ideally, it would need an international imprimatur.

I consulted a former QMC colleague and friend, John Belcher, who was then on the staff of the United Nations University (UNU) in Tokyo. All of its outreach centres were in relatively congenial places. I asked Belcher if he thought UNU would be interested in sponsoring, jointly with UU, a conflict resolution centre in Derry. He thought it a real possibility. I then put my idea to Dr John Darby, one of the two leading UU specialists in the subject, who expressed enthusiasm for such a project. The rest is history and INCORE (the International Centre for Conflict Resolution) was set up at Magee in 1993 as the first UN sponsored institution in the UK with Darby as its first Director. It now houses the largest database on conflict in the world for which it enjoys an international reputation. With the extreme financial cutbacks in 2015 INCORE was put at great risk and I fervently hope it will survive. Very sadly, its activities were transferred to the Belfast campus in 2017.

Other Initiatives

There were two pressing problems I perceived in UU in 1991. One was the vast plethora of academic departments spread across the University. They numbered over thirty-five. Over the course of the next year they were reduced and merged into just over twenty schools. All new Vice-Chancellors are prone to make these kinds of administrative changes because of the need somehow to put their own personal stamp on things. Whether the purported efficiency gains are commensurate with the costs of overhaul is highly questionable. But the new breed of managerialist Vice-Chancellors were meant to demonstrate a more business-like approach to the running of universities.

One of the most depressing aspects of meeting one's colleagues monthly at the Committee of Vice-Chancellors & Principals (CCVP), as the overall body was then called, was to see them in London en bloc. Not an inspiring sight collectively, they seemed so anaemic and weak that one was prompted to donate more blood. When the polytechnics became universities the CCVP could not cope with the institutional diversity and remain an umbrella, representative body. It split into a variety of associations reflecting the heterogeneous missions of the different higher education institutions.

Reforming the UU academic structures simplified the organisation, but my main task was to deal with the composition of the senior management team in terms of both functions and existing personnel. At my interview for the Vice-Chancellorship, I had been asked to deal sensitively with senior colleagues who had also applied for the post. Birley had intimated to all his close colleagues he thought they were all capable of succeeding him. Patently, they were not and as noted none ever tested the wider market, a fact which speaks for itself. But, as I have said, this did not inhibit a deep sense in them of incumbency entitlement. They would be difficult to shift – as I intended to do - but the process had to be started however gradual its implementation may be.

I introduced a systematic review that included personal

appraisal. The review, as intended, recommended the professionalisation of the Estates and Staffing functions. The appraisals determined the four Pro Vice-Chancellors would serve terms respectively of six months, two, three and four years. The most pleasant one was also the least effective and he got the period of six months. Those getting three and four year extensions were the most resistant. However, as luck would have it, illness, a resignation and an early retirement enabled me to re-jig the personnel of the entire top team within three years.

The posts of Estates, Staffing (to be re-named Human Resources), and Corporate Affairs (combining Finance and Secretary) were professionalised as planned. The salaries offered were good and attracted many applicants but, with one outstanding exception, the quality was not as high as I would have liked. But this was Northern Ireland still in the midst of The Troubles and one had to cope with what was available.

Another retirement offered the opportunity to amalgamate the post of University Librarian with that of Director of Computer Services. Most UK universities have now adopted this rationalisation, made inevitable by the technological revolution in communications, but UU was in the vanguard.

As senior posts became available, I had also to ensure the advancement of women and Catholics into the top positions. In the three professional posts, I had managed to recruit two Catholics; amongst the new wave of four Pro Vice-Chancellors, two Catholics and a woman, (Glory Be!) were appointed. The top team had a much improved confessional balance and a modest improvement in its gender balance. It was gratifying that Dr Ann Tate went on to become a successful Vice-Chancellor of Northampton University.

This breakthrough in the top of the team subsequently facilitated the advancement of women to senior posts as Faculty Deans and Heads of Schools, at the next levels down in the hierarchy.

The Peaceline Campus

Of all the projects I undertook the most ambitious was for a new UU campus on the peace line in Belfast. Wallace Ewart had become a Pro Vice-Chancellor and Provost of the Jordanstown and Belfast campuses. As such, he sat on an economic and community council covering north Belfast. Sir David Fell asked him if there was any possibility of building a UU presence in the area. Wallace relayed Fell's message to me. Its source meant that there would likely be a lot of strong encouragement for the idea, though I think Fell was free-lancing and floating the idea on his own initiative.

The project immediately appealed to me and I suggested to Ewart we should plan for a fully-fledged multi-faculty campus in the north of the city. A disused former factory site was vacant at Springvale, situated exactly between the Catholic Falls Road and the Protestant Shankill Road, the two thoroughfares that delineated the peace line and of deeply iconic world-wide status. I could see it as a symbol of reconciliation, having separate entrances for each of the two neighbouring communities. I also imagined the campus containing both a primary and secondary school run under the auspices of UU teaching on an integrated basis.

Great secrecy had to be maintained. Fell agreed to a

preliminary scoping study but insisted the project should be seen to come entirely from UU; he could not be seen to be involved. This was high stakes and, indeed, high politics. The scoping study proved positive but revealed deep amounts of acidic toxicity in the ground which would be costly to clean up. We secured a massive financial commitment from the International Fund for Ireland that had been set up by the extraordinary Irish-American Chuck Feeney out of the millions he had made inventing duty-free shops at Shannon and later other international airports around the world. At that stage I had to involve both my senior team and the Chair, Vice-Chair of the UU Council and the Treasurer. Many of whom were instinctively hostile to the idea – especially the Protestants. But, of course, they could not express their opposition overtly, precisely because it was so blatantly sectarian. It was agreed I could put the Springvale project to the UU Senate for formal approval to proceed further.

It was a difficult meeting, not least because the agenda had been leaked to BBC Northern Ireland TV which had devoted a full half-hour programme to it just before the Senate met. The editorial decision to do this, particularly in the context of 1994, was extremely irresponsible. It added to the difficulties of progressing Springvale and might easily have scuppered it. Nevertheless, in spite of this, the Senate gave its approval.

I had to go frequently to the US and to Boston in particular to secure maximum American political support. I made similar excursions to the EU Commission in Brussels. Very strong support was mobilised in the US culminating with Vice-Presidential endorsement. At the Northern Ireland Investment

Conference in May 1995 Bill Clinton had invited all the major political and commercial players. Two days before the formal opening, my brilliant young colleague, John McCaffrey, who was accompanying me, contrived to get us in to meet Al Gore's chief of staff, Jack Quinn, in the White House. We inquired if reference could be made to Springvale in Gore's welcoming address. It was asking the impossible as the speech had long since been put to bed. John persisted and suggested a form of words. Miraculously, Gore repeated them at the beginning in their entirety. It was worth being there to see the shock on Ian Paisley's face and feel a ripple of unease among a number of delegates, including Paddy Mayhew, Secretary of State, and indeed all the Unionists present.

A full-blown feasibility study was drawn up and formally presented to the Government, in effect Whitehall because of direct rule. Michael Ancram MP was the minister responsible for education. He went through the motions of considering the project but would not sanction its going forward. He had to play the "Orange Card" for narrow political House of Commons reasons.

Ancram, was heir to a Marquis, and in every sense a "Castle Catholic" with knobs on. He had married into the Norfolk family, the Duke of which was not only the hereditary Earl Marshall of England but also the acknowledged leading Roman Catholic layman; not too much empathy with his co-religionists in Northern Ireland, then, was to be expected. A further complication at the time was that the Conservative government of John Major had lost its slender majority in the Commons and was reliant on the support of the Ulster MPs.

They were bitterly opposed to any developments in North and West Belfast. Because West Belfast was a Republican stronghold, the official Ulster Unionist Party (UUP) had long abandoned Protestant North Belfast, ceding it to the very militant Progressive Unionist Party (PUP).

After the interview I had with Ancram, I wrote him a condemnatory letter in terms so strong his civil servants had never previously witnessed. That was quite something in the context of Northern Ireland but I felt I had no option.

The Government was fully aware of the massive US support Springvale had received, that local civil servants supported it and, above all, that it would have the potential of being the biggest ever "confidence restoring measure", as officialese puts it. As nearly always in such cases, however, immediate party political concerns took precedence. As consolation prizes, and possibly to assuage guilt feelings, Ewart was awarded an OBE and I a knighthood in 1996 for services to higher education.

Things took a tremendous turn for the better with the election of Labour in 1997. The new Secretary of State, Dr Mo Mowlam, I had known for years, first as a politics lecturer at Newcastle University and therefore an academic colleague and also as a recipient of a Joseph Rowntree Reform Trust grant which funded research assistance when she was Shadow Chief Secretary in the Treasury after becoming an MP. Also, I had met Jonathan Powell when he became Blair's chief of staff. He had heard of me first in connection with the Springvale project when working in the British Embassy in Washington. Things were looking up.

Mowlam had been shadowing the Northern Ireland portfolio

for some time before she assumed the substantive Cabinet rank. She was very supportive from the outset but with one proviso – Springvale should be a joint venture between UU and the Belfast Institute of Further & Higher Education (BIFHE). This complicated things and would set the project back as it would involve lengthy detailed negotiations with our new partners. Agreement was eventually reached and approved by Government. To cap it all the first sod at Springvale would be turned at a ceremony attended by Bill Clinton, Tony Blair and their wives. Where else in the entire world of tertiary education has that top political level of engagement ever happened? The veteran and authoritative journalist David Mackitterick, writing in *The Independent*, had described UU as "audacious" for its Springvale initiative. We had persevered and succeeded against very heavy odds.

But it was to prove a pyrrhic victory. I retired from UU in 1999. My successor, although he had sworn publicly to continue with Springvale, pulled the plug on it. It was aborted, despite protests from the Blair government. The Springvale campus' demise has been the bitterest sadness of my academic career.

Conclusion

I describe my time in Northern Ireland as being one of alternating 'highs' and 'lows', and such was the velocity of oscillation between the two there was never an 'average' day. I was there at an extraordinary and eventful time which was not confined to educational business but, as I describe later, extended into independent, non-partisan involvement with the local political parties.

I had been made a Liberal Democrat life peer in 1997 and it was now time to become fully engaged in politics and Parliament and we returned to live in our beloved and adopted county of Yorkshire. My involvement with Northern Ireland was to continue when I was made the Lib Dem spokesperson for it in the Lords for some eleven years.

The year 2017 saw the return of direct rule as the main Stormont parties could not agree on a new power-sharing formula. This prolonged impasse is bad enough in itself for the peaceful future of Northern Ireland but the Brexit issue will greatly exacerbate its politics. Brexit will have profound consequences for Northern Ireland. As the only land border between the EU and the UK the re-imposition of customs checks would have deleterious effects for both parts of the island of Ireland, leaving aside the dangerous political repercussions for the future of the peace that had ensued after the Belfast Agreement. It is little wonder the EU has made the border issue one of its major Brexit negotiating priorities.

It will require a bespoke solution if it is to be resolved. I had suggested a condominium arrangement during the five year suspension of Stormont whereby the monitoring of the border would be a responsibility shared between Dublin and London. Ulster unionism would dislike intensely such a proposal fearing, as well it might, that this could lead to a united Ireland. On the other hand, Northern Ireland had voted against Brexit in the referendum. It will require political skill and imagination of a very high order to come up with a working solution.

CHAPTER 10

THE HOUSE OF LORDS: PARLIAMENTART POLITICS

The House of Lords is, of course, the Second Chamber or Upper House of the UK Parliament. Apart from this formal position it is of especial interest for two further reasons. The first derives from its beginnings being based originally on its hereditary male membership. Forbears would have been ennobled at some time in the distant or recent past and the first born son would have automatically inherited the title and assumed his seat on the death of his father or upon reaching the age of majority at twenty-one. And secondly, the related aspect that the annual tug-of-war match between the Lords and Commons, until the culling of most of the hereditary aristocrats in 1999 by the Blair government, was invariably won by the former as it could always produce a team of eight men (by virtue of inheriting their titles at a young age) who were younger and fitter than their MP counterparts. After the House of Lords Act, however, the Lords would never win again.

Tony Blair failed to abolish all the hereditaries. The wily Lord Chancellor prevailed in proposing a minority of them should be retained to preserve some continuity by a form of election – an unprecedented element of democracy. This was taken up and championed by the former Speaker of the House of Commons – Lord (Bernard) Weatherill. He proposed an amendment to the Bill which received much support among peers, threatening to delay the necessary legislation forcing Blair to accept the so-called "Weatherill Amendment". This retained some ninety-two hereditary peers who on death are replaced via by-elections from the ranks of surviving aristocrats from outside the House.

Life peers were introduced in 1958 and, of course, their titles could not be passed on. The very nomenclature conveys a similarity between life peers and life prisoners but a main difference is that peers are entitled to six travel tickets a year for conjugal visits to Westminster, whereas prisoners get twelve annual travel grants for their spouses' visits. Life peers remained in the minority in the House until the culling.

An actuarial survey in the 1970s showed that whereas most husbands pre-deceased their wives, the opposite was the case among the aristocracy. The reasons for this are two-fold: first, a full diet eaten over succeeding generations; and secondly because of the care and attention they received as a result of sitting in the Lords: it was, and still is, the best day-care centre in the UK. And that is a main feature of the place. My colleague, Paul Tyler, later stole this description without attribution.

Another closely related feature is its archaeological character. It resembles in many ways a shipyard where ageing ships are harboured as their last destination, waiting to be broken up for scrap. The difference is that the lordly hulks are generally left stranded rather than salvaged. These two facets make the House of Lords the extraordinary anachronism it is and such a popular tourist attraction particularly for foreigners.

When I retired from the University of Ulster in 1999, I became available for more or less full-time attendance in the

House of Lords. As I have said, it is an extraordinary place. The late and engagingly amusing Lord (Michael) Onslow caught some of its flavour when he claimed new peers on their first day would enter the House's revolving door – the oldest one in London - and, on being welcomed by an attendant as "My Lord" would leave and re-enter just for the pleasure of being addressed by their new title once more.

Ostensibly it is the upper chamber of the UK Parliament, but it exhibits some of the features of a St James' Club. In one of the regular debates regarding its future, I spoke after lunch on the second day. I began by remarking that most peers would regularly be asked what it was like being in the Lords? I said, "I always reply, as occupational therapy goes it beats basket-weaving, but having heard the complacent and self-congratulatory speeches that have preceded me, basket-weaving is moving up my list of priorities". Partly aiming for a cheap laugh, I was also seeking to make the serious point that peers very much see themselves in the manner of tribal elders and as such collectively the repository of the wisdom of the nation. Such a view is encouraged by the House, it likes being venerated for the much vaunted collective expertise of its members. This is somewhat overdone as its expertise is rather more senile in character than embodying 'blue sky' state of the art thinking.

After 1999 it was assumed there would be further reform and, indeed, the Lib Dems tried to secure it during their time as junior partners in the Coalition government of 2010-15. This attempt was thwarted. Instead the Lords' membership continues to grow following the trend of expansion by successive prime ministers from Blair to Cameron. The result is that with a membership totalling around 775 peers and rising, it is second only in size to the National People's Congress of China amongst the world's legislative bodies. Overcrowding is such, that to guarantee a seat for the opening of the day with Questions, it is necessary to be sitting on the benches at least fifteen minutes before Prayers – "God works in mysterious ways", indeed! Scandals apart, it attracts, for the most part, little media attention. It exercises its main influence through its Select Committees (specialist subject) and legislative Standing Committees (reviewing and amending laws) largely away from the public gaze.

For most of my time in the Lords I have participated in the workings of many committees. My first Chief Whip, John Harris, put me on the sub-committee dealing with complementary and alternative medicine, chaired by the redoubtable Lord Walton of Detchant. It was filled with a galaxy of medical, veterinary and pharmacological elder statesmen. I felt I should establish my own provenance. I said "My Lords, I represent here the voice of the serious hypochondriac. Indeed, knowing I was coming onto the Committee I founded the International Federation of Serious Hypochondriacs and made myself Honorary Life President – but not for long, you understand!"

In March 2001 I was somewhat surprised to find myself chair of a full Select Committee on animals in scientific procedures which reported in July 2002. The topic was a 'red hot' political one; the use of laboratory animals for the testing of medicines and other goods had attracted much opposition and some of it of an extreme kind. A number of laboratories and distinguished scientists had been the focus of criminal attacks by extreme anti-vivisectionists. In particular, Huntingdon Life Sciences was under constant threat.

Until more recently it was fairly rare for a Lib Dem to chair a full Select Committee. Baroness Nancy Seear was asked to chair the Select Committee on Equal Pay many years before. Liberal Democrats only got chairs when the subject under review was so politically charged that neither Conservative nor Labour peers wanted to take it on. I was advised by Black Rod, who is in charge of Lords' security amongst other things, that I should seek the advice of the Metropolitan Police Special Branch about the personal safety of members of the Committee. Accordingly, at our first meeting a senior police officer came to address us. He said, "My Lords, we have intruded into the various animal rights terrorist bodies and I have to say, at the moment, your Committee has not appeared on their radar so, as far as the police is concerned, you are not a priority." I responded saying "Superintendent, I don't know whether to be relieved or insulted by your remarks!" He said the Metropolitan Police had advised the constabularies in which Committee members lived that an emergency 'phone call by us might well be prompted by attacks on our homes. I was contacted by the police in North Yorkshire who visited my wife and me. I observed that, "At least it is good to know that a 999 call would immediately register with your computers that this may well be an animal rights terrorist attack." To which the sergeant replied "What computer system?"

We had a considerable volume of evidence that was basically pro- or anti-vivisectionist. Nevertheless I felt that I had to read all the submissions that came into us. Thus there were only the two versions. The Committee visited "Dolly the sheep" at the Rosslyn Research Centre near Edinburgh. Michael Onslow talking to scientists there said "Explain to me how you would clone me?" Overhearing this I rushed across and said, "Please don't even think about it". Earl Onslow was a distinguished but somewhat irascible parliamentarian and a real character. He would regularly re-tell this story with much amusement.

We also visited the United States and went to Bethesda – the largest facility in the world for research into animals ranging from ants to elephants. We met with a distinguished group of scientists. The chairman asked, "Before we begin, is it true that all of you are related to the Queen?" I replied "there is only one true aristocrat as you Americans pronounce it, and that is Lord Onslow. The rest of us are time-share aristocrats!"

We then went to Johns Hopkins University which is the largest recipient of US Federal research grants in health. We moved north to New Jersey and into the Huntingdon Life Sciences (HLS) facility there. The situation was completely different from that of the company's headquarters in Cambridgeshire. Apart from security cameras, there was none of the barbed wire or other defences we had found at the Huntingdon HQ in Britain. The managing director of HLS was accompanying us and I asked him, why the contrast? He said it was because when the English activists came over attempting to recruit sympathisers in New Jersey, a court injunction was immediately sought and the protestors were banned for life from coming within a mile of the laboratory. Such a life ban would have been impossible to secure in the UK. New Jersey is particularly aware of its vulnerability because it has the largest concentration of pharmaceutical companies in the US and could not afford any kind of ricochet effect bouncing from Huntingdon to other laboratories.

We also visited Paris where most of the French pharmaceutical companies are situated in the Paris Basin. France had only two veterinary inspectors plus a half-time one to monitor the activities not just of the pharmaceuticals but also circuses and zoos. The US, too, had relatively few inspectors compared with the UK where supervision is extraordinarily strict by international standards.

Baroness (Mary) Warnock, the distinguished philosopher and educationist, was a member of the Committee. She had chaired and been a member of many official enquiries over the years. She subsequently wrote about her experience entitled *Nature and Mortality: Recollections of a Philosopher in Public Life* (2004) in which she said she had enjoyed our Committee as much as any and congratulated me on my chairmanship and had enjoyed my "sardonic personality" – praise indeed from such an experienced and authoritative source, even if she did get my full title wrong.

The Committee had the very good fortune in its Clerk. Thomas Elias became an official in the Lords with a brilliant academic track record, including a doctorate at King's College, Cambridge. He was a talented chorister and, as it turned out, one of the finest committee Clerks I have experienced. He invariably anticipated what was needed well in advance of my requesting it. I advised him that his talents were such that he should not remain in the Lords where promotion was on the basis of "Buggins' turn". He took my advice and read for the Bar. I wrote to him asking how he had got on in Bar Finals, "I expect you came top". He replied, "Yes I was top". He seemed to be able to turn his hand to anything with consummate dexterity - that's an Eton education for you!

Select Committees apart, my main task was to act as the Liberal Democrat Front Bench spokesperson for Northern Ireland from 2000 to 2011. Having only recently retired as Vice-Chancellor of Ulster University, I would have preferred to have had a break and taken on another portfolio. When I protested about my being type-cast in this way, my Chief Whip told me I was the only one who had seen the Giant's Causeway. While this was not strictly true, I could see the advantage of having a non-native from the region who was recently familiar with the developments in the peace process which had culminated in the Belfast Agreement, the referendum endorsing it and the creation of an elected Assembly at Stormont to which extensive powers had been devolved.

As it soon turned out, things went sour and Peter Mandelson, as Secretary of State for Northern Ireland, felt obliged to suspend Stormont and revert to direct rule from Westminster. When this decision was duly debated in the Lords I predicted it would not be a short suspension. The government intended it to be for up to a year in the first instance. A year later, with the need to continue the suspension, I reminded the House that I had warned it would be a very protracted affair. I said, "Sir Keith Joseph, when Secretary of State for Education, derided the social sciences because they could not predict the future and he changed the name of the Social Sciences Research Council to the Economic and Social Research Council. Social scientists might not have the predictive powers of the natural scientists, but some of them make very successful soothsayers in accurately foretelling the future." The Leader of the Lords (Gareth Williams QC), who had also assumed ministerial responsibility for Northern Ireland, replied, "You're right, but only on this one occasion." In the event, the suspension went on for a full five years before Stormont had its powers returned to it, though it was again suspended in 2017.

Direct rule from Westminster gave me a heavier burden than I had expected but involved working closely with Gareth Williams, which turned out to be a joy. He had a brilliant mind as befits a senior lawyer, but was even better as a politician. Previously he had been involved in the Thorpe trial. He was by far the best Leader of the Lords during my time and his untimely death in 2003 at a relatively early age (62) was a very great loss. We met frequently and cooperated very closely. I remember one time I went into his office saying I was putting down an amendment. He read it, lifted the 'phone to the Northern Ireland Office saying, "Lord Smith wishes to propose an amendment. I agree with it. Put it down in my name." He was an excellent orator, often "apologising" to the House for any failings to make himself understood as he was speaking in his second tongue. With him and his successors, I maintained an open and bipartisan approach.

This was necessary because the Ulster Unionist peers and their many Tory supporters would frequently be very obstructive. Debates on Northern Ireland quickly empty the Lords. I experienced many debates, dragging on well past midnight in which the Chamber consisted of the Labour minister and a whip, myself as the lone Liberal Democrat, and more than a dozen or so Tories and Ulster Unionists. Gerry Fitt would also be there to make his usual speech. A very amusing man, whom I liked, he was a member of the Social Democratic and Labour Party (SDLP). He had been the subject of an IRA assassination attempt at his home in Belfast but had drawn a pistol and drove the gunmen away. Although the SDLP was committed to Irish nationalism, doubtless because of the IRA attack, his one often repeated speech was essentially Unionist in all but name. He also spoke from the Labour benches which meant that Tories and Ulster Unionists could always cite what he said as offering support from across the floor for their arguments.

I recall another late evening debate when I remarked that we had heard much about the sensitivities of the Unionist and Protestant communities but absolutely nothing about the Catholic, Nationalist and Republican ones. You could have heard a pin drop and the glares I received from the Ulster Unionist Party (UUP), and Tory peers were murderous. The Irish Embassy counsellor was in the gallery and he told me he had to restrain himself from clapping. He had telegrammed my comments to the Irish Foreign Ministry overnight to show that there was at least one peer trying desperately to maintain some sort of even balance. It was very much an uphill struggle.

On another similar occasion I was pleased to be joined on the front bench by Shirley Williams, my then Party Leader. I was glad of her company and support. I spoke but afterwards she said I had criticised the Protestant paramilitaries but not the IRA. I remonstrated I had done no such thing, having condemned both equally. I had already passed on my speech to the Hansard writers. I complained bitterly about her to John

Roper, the Chief Whip, and showed him the Hansard Report of the debate which validated my version of events. He called over Shirley Williams who spoke some banalities but did not apologise to me. I threatened to resign as the spokesperson. Roper reported this to party leader Charles Kennedy who drunkenly implored me to stay on. I acceded. Roper agreed with me that Shirley's behaviour had been deplorable. As I have said, I admired her in the main, but on this occasion as over her choice of a "comprehensive" sixth form for her daughter, I did not.

Succeeding Secretaries of State hold regular cross-party meetings, under confidential "Chatham House" rules, with those peers interested in Northern Ireland. I recall one such occasion when Gerry Fitt said a rumour was going the rounds that Ian Paisley was to join the Lords. I remarked, "Well that will be the first time he'll have an authentic prefix to his name – the so-called Dr, so-called Reverend Paisley". The civil servants present had to stifle their laughter. I had always studiously called him "MR" Paisley since he had ordained himself into his own invented Presbyterian sect, while his doctorate came from the unaccredited "Bob Jones University." In person, Paisley could be an engaging man and quite humorous - that was one aspect of his personality. The other side of him could be outrageously bigoted, seditious, uttering murderous threats, even organising military-type mass demonstrations and proving to be opportunistic and unashamedly unprincipled. He maintained complete opposition to the Belfast Agreement, using it as a successful tactic to replace David Trimble's UUP as the main Unionist party in Stormont. He then quite cynically accepted the Agreement and assumed the position of First Minister. In the end, he was rumbled and was estranged from his inventions - the Democratic Unionist Party and the sect he had founded. Donald Trump, the president of the United States of America, is an extremely close facsimile of Paisley. Both are neo-fascist bully boys trading on an appallingly manufactured populism.

Together with the Northern Ireland portfolio was the concomitant duty of membership of the British-Irish Inter-Parliamentary Assembly which met twice a year, one time in the UK and the other somewhere in the Republic. Its creation had been the brainchild of Peter Temple-Morris, the moderate Tory MP for Leominster with the support of Labour's Kevin McNamara, who had been elected MP for North Hull at the famous by-election in 1966, which I remembered vividly from my time teaching at the University there. The sessions in Ireland were by far the best with plentiful hospitality, lasting two and a half days with tremendous sing-songs after dinner. The Irish Times gossip column once commended my rendition of *Some Enchanted Evening* from the musical *South Pacific*. In 2001, following Scottish and Welsh devolution these countries were also represented along with the Channel Islands and the Isle of Man.

Membership of the Assembly occasioned my coming across Dr Martin Mansergh, who had been a formidable 'fixer' for three Taoiseachs, and played a major role in the peace process which led to the Belfast Agreement. He came from a long line of Irish Protestants although brought up in Cambridge as the son of a distinguished history professor. I learnt that his secondary education had been as a boarder at the King's School,

Canterbury. A contemporary there was Charles Powell, one of Margaret Thatcher's chief fixers. His younger brother, Jonathan, later attended the school and became Blair's chief of staff who was also to be very involved in the Belfast Agreement. Did all three belong to the same House at King's School? If so, it ought now to be commonly known as "Rasputin's", for producing such a galaxy of behind-the-scenes courtiers. The three had pursued diplomatic careers prior to becoming fixers at the highest levels of government in their respective states.

During the Stormont suspension, the Assembly played an important role as a confidence-building device but with the return to "normality" it was much less influential, becoming little more than a talking-shop. It was modelled on the pattern of the Nordic Council but that remains an aspiration.

From 1999 to 2014 I was a member of one or more Lords committees. In addition to those already mentioned, these included European Law and Regulations, Communications, Works of Art, the Barnett Formula, Constitutional Affairs and, most enjoyable of all, Economic Affairs.

Parliamentarians are bombarded with letters and emails appealing for support for this or that project or cause. Most of them are extremely worthy but it is quite impossible to take on more than four or five at any one time. One has to limit oneself: parsimony and priority are the guiding principles to observe. Accordingly, I have maintained a continuing interest in corporate governance, constitutional problems, gender issues and particularly the equality of women, Northern Ireland and sickle cell disease.

During the course of the debate on Assisted Dying in

2014, both sides – those for or against euthanasia - sent peers a voluminous quantity of letters attempting to influence our votes. I remarked to colleagues, "So great has been the amount of correspondence, I was losing the will to live!"

I have a very ambivalent opinion towards the House of Lords. As a reformer, I went along with the view that membership should be elected. In 1999, I jointly authored with Lord (Raymond) Plant and Stuart Weir a pamphlet advocating an elected Senate for the UK. At the press launch, which was during the passage of the Bill designed to abolish the hereditary element, I said, "If Blair is having some difficulty in expunging the hereditary peers, it would be like nothing if he sought to get rid of life peers. There is not a mollusc in the oceans with stronger powers to cling on, to match the tenacity of a life peer similarly threatened with extinction." And so it has proved.

Virtually everyone agrees that, as presently constituted, the House of Lords is no longer defensible. The 2011 Bill to introduce further reforms, proposed by Deputy Prime Minister Nick Clegg during the Coalition government was ill-prepared, poorly presented and deservedly defeated, although I obediently voted for it. Various attempts have been made, among them by the Lords Speaker, Norman Fowler, to look again at how the Lords might be reformed to meet modern conditions. The chances of major reform remain slight. Brexit and its consequences will preoccupy parliamentary time and attention that will pre-empt the consideration of the future (if any) of the Upper House over the foreseeable future. It may be that the best chance will come during Parliament's expected move out of the Palace of Westminster for a prolonged period for much-needed physical renovation. One can only hope.

CHAPTER 11

THE WORLD OF POLITICS: PUBLIC AND DEMI-MONDE

Being part of that small minority active in politics makes me more deviant than those with criminal records, for a simple calculation shows that far more people have broken laws (from parking infringements to more serious offences) than there are political party members. The contrast must be even greater now than when I joined the Liberals in 1955, given the overall general decline in card-carrying members of all parties since then, despite occasional short-lived upsurges.

Political psychologists describe active political participation as 'displacement activity'. It is a way of avoiding coming to terms with some major problems facing the individual. In the case of male politicians, it is commonly suggested such displacement stems from relations with the opposite sex. In discussing the literature on this, I used to say to my students, "there may be something in this: Ted Heath could never get on with women and Lloyd George could never get off them".

Very frequently it revolves around mother/son relationships and Winston Churchill is cited as a prime example of this, though in US President Woodrow Wilson's case it was apparently a father fixation that was a major factor in his assuming a political career. In my own case, as I have recorded earlier, I think it is a combination of very politically interested parents and the intense dramas of a wartime childhood.

As previously observed I have had two overt manifestations of high-profile political activity – one at the beginning of adulthood and the other towards the end of my life. In the last half of the 1950s it began with the Liberal students, led swiftly on to joining the Liberal Party Executive, and culminated in standing as a candidate in the 1959 General Election. The second period dates from 1997 onwards when I became a Liberal Democrat life peer.

The Political Demi-Monde

In the intervening years I was very active though almost entirely behind the scenes. I participated in a few policy committees for the Party, most notably one chaired by Nancy Seear on the formulation of industrial relations policies and extending and modernising notions of co-ownership in industry. Also, briefly, I was adopted as the prospective candidate for West Ham South where, surprisingly given its social class make-up, the Liberals had a couple of local councillors. I resigned when I moved to Hull in 1962.

I was a fairly nominal, inactive member of the Hull North Liberal Party. My political activity was confined to teaching politics at the University and as previously noted broadcasting about politics, mainly on the BBC Radio Home Service (North Region).

The Joseph Rowntree Social Service Trust Ltd (JRSST)/ Joseph Rowntree Reform Trust Ltd (JRRT)

My return to a much more active role was when I became research adviser to the Joseph Rowntree Social Service Trust

Ltd (JRSST) in 1970. It was one of three foundations created in 1904 by Joseph Rowntree, the Quaker cocoa manufacturer, out of the vast fortune he had made late in life.

The directors felt they needed to beef up its organising capacity, particularly with regard to the research it sometimes commissioned. Philip Rowntree, the grandson of the founder Joseph, seemed particularly anxious to secure my involvement on a more permanent basis. I became a fully-fledged director five years later, chair of a newly created political committee in 1981 and overall chair in 1987 which I held for twelve years. I resigned from the board in 2006. Thus, I was clearly associated with the Trust for some 36 years and, as such, a major interest for much of my working life. I have never inherited so much as a penny piece, but Rowntree gave me access to a £25m fund.

The other two Trusts, the Rowntree Village Trust, now the Joseph Rowntree Foundation and the Joseph Rowntree Charitable Trust, were charities, but he had the prescience of mind to create a political fund as a limited company, the Joseph Rowntree Social Service Trust Ltd. At that time the term 'social service' did not have the precise connotations it has today and in 1990 it was decided to rename JRSST as the Joseph Rowntree Reform Trust Ltd (JRRT). Not being charitable, meant that in paying taxes it was free to make donations to help promote political causes. To this end, the JRRT had been the main and most constant funder of the Liberal Party ever since the collapse of Lloyd George's "cash for honours" slush fund. Joseph Rowntree enjoined the JRRT directors to "maintain a free press, ensure the purity of elections, to encourage and finance new radical political initiatives and support peace abroad." Most of his money was invested, along with the other two trusts, with his Rowntree Company, the chocolate and sweet manufacturer.

Shortly after I became research adviser there was a hostile takeover bid for Rowntree & Co from General Foods Ltd, the US giant. I remember visiting numerous stockbrokers as part of the effort by the three Rowntree Trusts to frustrate this from happening. They were successful in this since between them the Trusts held a majority shareholding. Unbeknown to them, however, Donald Barron the CEO of Rowntree & Co, was holding clandestine negotiations with the Mackintosh Company, who were also large chocolate and food manufacturers, on an agreed merger. He did this to protect Rowntree and Co but without consulting the Trusts and they were faced with a fait accompli with the consequent formation of Rowntree Mackintosh. It was my first encounter with the high jinks of high finance.

In 1975 I was invited to become a member of the board of directors of the JRSST Ltd. David Shutt, later to be ennobled as Lord Shutt of Greetland, active in the Liberal Party since his teenage years, was a West Yorkshire chartered accountant was also proposed. My main sponsor was Philip Rowntree, whose father had been the famous Seebohm Rowntree who had himself succeeded his father Joseph as managing director of Rowntree & Co. Philip was a pioneering sociologist of poverty, a chair of all three Rowntree Trusts who worked closely with Lloyd George in the production of the *Yellow Book*. Philip had known me from when I had joined the staff of the Acton Society of which he was also a trustee. I fully acknowledge him as one of my patrons to whom I owe a very great debt.

Shutt was proposed by Richard Wainwright, also a chartered accountant and very active in the Liberal Party who later became MP for Colne Valley. We were joined by Pratap Chitnis, later Lord Chitnis of Ryedale, who was then the secretary of the Trust having taken up that position promptly after his dismissal as director-general of the Liberal Party by Jeremy Thorpe, the then Leader. The prospect of Shutt and myself, both younger than him, joining the board, prompted him to insist that he also should become a director even though he was a salaried full-time employee. This is not a good working principle and the chair should have resisted Chitnis' demand.

At that time the other directors consisted of Bill Morrell as chair, Professor Roger Wilson, educationist and leading Quaker, Richard and Michael Rowntree, nephews of Seebohm, his son Philip, William Wallace, a former CEO of Rowntree & Co, Edward Goodman, an estate agent, Jo Grimond MP and Richard Wainwright. Four of them, of course, had known me from when I worked at the Acton Society Trust.

The JRSST Board was not known for its equality, in terms of gender or religion. Traditionally it consisted of about fifty percent Quakers and fifty percent others, indeed Chitnis was the first Roman Catholic member of the Board. It also consisted of zero percent women! J B Morrell (banker to Rowntree & Co) had succeeded Seebohm as chair and, like him, was a very pro-active chair. He, in turn, was succeeded by his son Bill, chairman of the Westminster Press Group, who was altogether more passive, somewhat politically squeamish, and as such allowed the Trust to fund a whole series of charitable undertakings including temperance reform. This was quite contrary to Joseph Rowntree's instructions. The Trust, however, had continued to fund the Liberal Party through some of its worst times. Wainwright, and to some extent, Grimond, continued to press for such funding.

Nevertheless, the majority of funded projects was still well outside the original remit. The JRSST had a small charitable fund, but the main Trust was often raided to supplement it. Richard Rowntree, for example, was a railway enthusiast and persuaded the Trust to give a good deal of money to finance the creation of the North York Moors Railway which is now a major tourist attraction. Delightful though the railway is, it nevertheless had nothing to do with politics as such and was a misappropriation of funds. He also persuaded his colleagues to fund *Music in Wales*, directed by his son-in-law, situated at Bangor University. Again this was a misappropriation of money and contrary to the founder's wishes. Similarly, Roger Wilson managed to get funds diverted to pay for a lectureship in development education in his department at Bristol University. Edward Goodman, for his part, was similarly indulged. Forced reluctantly to join his ailing father's estate agency, he was a philosopher manqué and contrived to syphon off money to finance a series of studies on the subject of toleration that, after a somewhat chequered start, ended up at the University of York. In such ways, money meant for demonstrably political purposes, was wrongly diverted to fund charitable activities.

Grimond, characteristically, was much more imaginative. One of his pet projects was to support community renewal in Greenock near Glasgow. He had met Baillie Gifford, a local Labour politician, who had persuaded him of the need for this. I vividly recall a meeting there. As a large municipal overspill housing estate, it had taken people from the slums of the Gorbals in Glasgow to a beautiful site overlooking the River Clyde. Typically, however, the governing Labour party of Scotland had simply built a modern version of the Gorbals ruining, in the process, some delightful countryside exactly as I had experienced in Lanarkshire in the early years of WWII. There were no shops except an off- licence with heavy bars on its windows. It was quite an appalling dumping ground, totally bereft of any essential amenities. The Trust duly supported this community renewal initiative.

Another director was Michael Rowntree who, like Roger Wilson and Richard Wainwright, had been a very active organiser of the Friends' Ambulance Unit in WWII and later a founder of Oxfam. At the time I met him, he was general manager of the Westminster Press's *Oxford Mail.* When I asked him how he got the job he replied, quite frankly: "nepotism". Unlike the majority of his fellow directors he did not seek to purloin any of the Trust's money for his own particular enthusiasms.

The three new directors meant that two of us – myself and Shutt - would be continuing to push for Liberal Party funding. Chitnis, smarting from his dismissal by Thorpe, managed to guide money to the party, but not to the central organisation and particularly not to Thorpe, but rather to groups within the party or to individual MPs who met with his approval.

In its giving, the Trust had been quite ecumenical. Although the vast bulk of its party political money went to support the Liberals and Liberal Democrats, it also supported "liberal" activities within the two main parties. For example, it had supported the Bow Group and the Tory Reform Group within Conservative ranks and similar moderate groups in the Labour Party. In his memoirs, *Across the Floor: A Life in Dissenting Politics* (2014), Peter Temple-Morris, erstwhile wet Tory MP and later Labour life peer, attests to the importance of JRRT money in helping to maintain moderate Conservatism.

Its practical support for devolution in Scotland and Wales was part of its wider interest in constitutional reform which was evidenced in its on-going support over many years for the Electoral Reform Society and its long-time director Dr Enid Lakeman.

Chocolate Soldiers

Likewise, in 1970, the JRSST created a scheme to provide for research support for frontbench spokespeople among the opposition parties in Parliament. Chitnis wanted to strengthen the role of the Parliamentary Opposition. Following the model of Congressional Assistants in the US, I suggested something along the same lines. Both the Labour and Liberal Parliamentary parties were the immediate beneficiaries of this largesse. Talented young people were appointed "Chocolate Soldiers" as they became known because of the Rowntree name. Among them were three future peers: Matthew Oakeshott who assisted Roy Jenkins; David Lipsey adviser to Tony Crosland; and Archy Kirkwood who served David Steel. While the parliamentary parties were free to make their own appointments Chitnis added a proviso that a member of the JRSST should also be in attendance at interviews. He invariably represented the Trust but, on one occasion, I substituted for him.

Jim Callaghan, then Shadow Home Secretary, was entitled to a special adviser under the scheme and wanted someone to help him with his brief that included Northern Ireland. He, together with Douglas Houghton MP then Chairman of the Parliamentary Labour Party, and I interviewed candidates. It came down to a choice between a young journalist on *The Economist*, an ex-President of the Oxford Union, and Roger Darlington who had been President of the Students' Union at the University of Manchester's Institute of Science and Technology (UMIST). Callaghan indicated that he was in favour of the Oxford alumnus for, as he put it, "Roy Jenkins has just appointed a postgraduate from Nuffield College" (Matthew Oakeshott). I had already elicited that the Oxford man had not renewed his Labour Party subscription whereas Darlington had always maintained his. I remarked that I favoured Darlington, arguing that "the man from *The Economist* was only President of the Union for one term as is the practice. He would dash off a speech for you and then likely tell his friends about it. Roger Darlington, on the other hand, had served for a year as President of the Students' Union and would be a devoted supporter working twenty- eight hours a day and eight days a week. He would be utterly loyal". Callaghan turned to Houghton, who had been dozing, and said "that's the finest advice I've ever had in politics." Reverting to me, he said "Why don't you become my special adviser?" I demurred, saying that I was not of his Party and in any case preferred being an academic.

At that time it was thought that Callaghan had no political future in the UK and would soon be departing its shores to head up an international organisation such as the International Monetary Fund (IMF). Of course, later, the wily politician survived to become Prime Minster.

I remember that day vividly because it coincided with the suspension of Stormont by Edward Heath. A Secretary of State for Northern Ireland was created (Willie Whitelaw) so that Callaghan lost his shadow responsibilities for Northern Ireland. Nevertheless, having been appointed, Darlington was transferred to Merlyn Rees MP when he became the Labour shadow NI spokesperson.

The Chocolate Soldier experiment was a prelude to the creation of the formal system of special advisers (SpAds) for Opposition front bench teams. In 1974 Edward Short, when Leader of the House in the second Government of Harold Wilson introduced the scheme formally into the practice of the Commons. What became known as "the Short Money", it has continued ever since and similar provision was made in the Lords in 1996, where it is known as "the Cranborne Money".

I now harbour some doubts as to the wisdom of the 'Chocolate Soldier' innovation. The continuous and seemingly relentless growth in the number of ministerial aides, particularly from the Blair government onwards, has had some deleterious consequences as I shall enumerate further below.

SpAds

The JRSST initiated another experiment that yielded similar results. When John Smith became Shadow Industry Secretary under Neil Kinnock, he approached the Trust for assistance with overseas travel. He wanted to maintain his independence and not be beholden either to lobbyist firms or host governments. The JRSST assisted him but stipulated that it had to be tourist class fares and a report submitted to the Trust after each trip.

After his first overseas visit the JRSST decided to make money available to Opposition spokespersons for overseas travel under the same conditions. Accordingly, a set sum was provided for the Labour Opposition, divided in half between Kinnock as Leader and John Smith who had been promoted to Shadow Foreign Affairs spokesperson. After a couple of years Smith's budget had been almost spent whereas Kinnock's had hardly been touched. I enquired of his Chief of Staff, Charles Clarke, why this was so. Clarke had laid down such strict criteria for disbursement that much remained in the kitty. I asked him to be less strict as it would be difficult to persuade my colleagues to renew the scheme if it had not been fully taken up.

Like the "Short" and "Cranborne Money", the Conservative Government under John Major adopted this scheme when Tony Newton was Leader of the Commons (1992-97). The Chocolate Soldiers – initially at least - and the overseas travel subsidy improved servicing senior parliamentarians in the course of their duties.

Poland Street

Away from the formal institutions of government there were two other noteworthy initiatives taken by the JRSST in the 1970s. Chitnis and I suggested that to harness the economies of scale a large building be acquired. Therefore, the Trust bought the lease of 9 Poland Street in London's Soho. The idea behind this was twofold. Financially it would mean a saving because many of the groups it funded also had to cover their rents, but giving them a free space in the new building would be a saving. Secondly, by having a number of groups of a liberal or left of centre persuasion would provide for a spirit of intellectual camaraderie and possible cross-fertilisation of ideas and methods – an early form of the 'co-working' spaces that are now so popular in cities the world over. Number 9 had previously been a garment manufacturers. Now it would house a variety of JRSST grantees. These included the then small Friends of the Earth, Gingerbread (one parent families), YouthAid (directed by Claire Short – later Secretary of State for International Development), the British Irish Association (directed by Nick Stadlen – later a High Court judge), APEX (white collar criminal rehabilitation), the 300 Group (promoting gender equality in Parliament), Comedia (radical publisher led by Charles Landry), Social Audit (promoting corporate responsibility and consumer affairs, founded by Charles Medawer) and the Acton Society Trust among others. It was dubbed by one journalist as the headquarters of the "counter civil service". Organisations, crammed in cheek by jowl, effectively and collectively created a sense of buzz and purpose.

The Thorpe Trial – What Other Accounts Have Not Revealed

The JRSST was indirectly involved in what became known as the "Thorpe Affair" that engulfed the Liberal Party in the 1970s which culminated in its then Leader being charged with conspiracy to murder Norman Scott, his former lover.

I first came across Jeremy Thorpe at the near-disastrous Liberal Party Assembly held in Torquay in 1958. Being on the

Party Executive I was entitled to sit on the platform along with its other members. Ronnie Fraser, a prominent parliamentary candidate, adopted something of a protective concern for younger Liberals. He came over to me sounding two warnings. He said, "Over there is Jeremy Thorpe from North Devon; watch him he's a predatory homosexual. And over there", pointing to an equally prominent parliamentary candidate, "Manuela Sykes, she's a man-eater." She was very attractive so I distanced myself from Thorpe and went closer towards her. Fraser proved to be correct in both his assessments.

After 1958 I became evermore aware of Thorpe's growing reputation as he won his seat in the 1959 General Election, became a well-known and popular Parliamentarian and ultimately succeeded Grimond as Leader in 1967. I had withdrawn from mainstream Liberal politics to concentrate on my academic career so I had no personal contact with him. But, along with most of the nation, I became increasingly riveted as the Thorpe Affair began to unfold from the mid-1970s. It culminated in Thorpe being charged with conspiracy to murder Norman Scott. It was a sensation.

Michael Bloch's much-acclaimed posthumous biography, published in the immediate aftermath of Thorpe's death, meticulously analyses the story, but it is lacking in one particular. Three of my fellow Rowntree directors closely involved themselves in securing the case against Thorpe in his up-coming trial. It seemed to be generally recognised that Peter Bessell, a former confidant of Thorpe's, would be a crucial witness but he was keeping low in the USA where he had been living for some years. While they had different motives for their combined operation Wainwright and Chitnis shared a deep loathing for Thorpe. The former had always taken against his flamboyance, affected mannerisms and his homosexuality, so had opposed him for the Leadership. While Chitnis bitterly resented Thorpe's peremptory dismissal of him as the Chief Executive of the Party. Richard Rowntree, scion of the family, would have shared some of Wainwright's views but, more importantly, possessed a very strong potential weapon in the matter. Whatever their specific reasons, their main aim was to contrive to get Bessell to give evidence at the trial.

Bessell, former MP for the Cornish seat of Bodmin, had been Thorpe's closest friend in the Commons, and to boot a womaniser, a dubious businessman and a hypocritical but popular Methodist lay preacher. On being declared bankrupt, he swiftly escaped to the USA to avoid his creditors of whom Richard Rowntree was one.

The three needed to make contact with Bessell and engage in what inevitably would turn out to be protracted discussions. International telecommunications then were a far cry from what has now developed. Accordingly, they took over the Trust's offices and hired the best means of trans-Atlantic telecommunications to facilitate the arduous and painstaking negotiations that would doubtless be necessary and would need to be recorded on tape. This was done without reference to Bill Morrell, the Trust's chair, let alone seeking formal permission from the full board. Chitnis, however, later confided to me what the three had been up to. The clincher that decided Bessell to give evidence was Richard Rowntree's undertaking to cancel the debts owed to him if he agreed to attest at the trial. He and Wainwright, who was also immensely wealthy, may well have paid off some or all of the debts he owed to others, as a condition of him returning to the British jurisdiction.

In the event Bessell was the Crown's prime witness. As John Preston shows, in his book of the trial *A Very English Scandal* (2016), Bessell was devastatingly interrogated by Thorpe's counsel, George Carman QC. He was also dealt with harshly by the presiding judge, Sir George Cantley in his summing up. It was not surprising that Bessell failed to convince the jury who considered him a very unreliable witness. Accordingly, after lengthy deliberation lasting over three days, Thorpe was acquitted of the charges against him. Although found "not guilty", the evidence was damming enough to irrevocably damage his career in politics. Earlier, he had been forced to resign as Leader and he lost his seat at the General Election of 1979. Thorpe became a very forlorn figure, particularly after he contracted Parkinson's disease. He was resentful that he was the only former Liberal Leader that had not received a peerage. He importuned every one of his successors to recommend him for one and repeatedly canvassed support from anyone he thought would influence a favourable response to his request. His relentless pursuit of ennoblement, which was bound to be as fruitless as it was humiliating, revealed just how far flamboyance had transmogrified into an all-consuming fantasy. A modern morality play if ever there was one.

As I have described elsewhere at different points in these memoirs, it was one of the main remits of the JRSST/JRRT Ltd to be involved in the politics of the UK. Usually this was completely overt and subject to full publicity but occasionally covert for a brief period if that was what beneficiaries wished because annual accounts had to be transparent. The use to which my three colleagues put the Trust's office in the run-up to the Thorpe trial was of an altogether different nature and they should not have sequestered them for their own purposes. At the very least, they should have sought the chair's permission which should then have been conveyed to the full board. Who paid for the installation of the telephonic equipment was never vouchsafed to me. At a guess, I would reckon it was obscured in the generality of the British Telecom charges; I was remiss in not enquiring. The Bessell tape recordings, to the best of my knowledge, remain in the safe of the JRRT.

British Broadcasting Reform

The 1970s also witnessed much interest in the future of broadcasting. In 1976 the Independent Television Act was due for renewal as was the BBC Charter. There was much speculation about the creation of a fourth television channel. Two groups applied to JRSST for funding. One was the '76 Group led by such luminaries as Anthony Smith, Philip Whitehead, David Elstein and other producers. To the left of them was the Free Communications Group (FCG). The latter was led by Gus Macdonald (later a Labour Peer and a Blair Minister) who was the editor of the pioneering Granada television programme *World in Action*, Nicholas Garnham from the BBC, Stuart Hood the distinguished BBC broadcaster and former spy, the academic James Curran and Neal Ascherson, *The Observer* columnist. Both groups attracted much support in their endeavours to preserve the best of public service broadcasting.

They had to tackle a good deal of corporate and commercial lobbying on the part of television companies and commercial broadcasters. Hughie Green, the famous quizmaster, was very active on behalf of the commercial lobby.

I was concerned that the two progressive groups might adopt stances that were too distinctive from each other, thus enabling the government to dismiss them, by using the traditional divide and rule tactic, to show that the progressives were at odds. I proposed, therefore, that the two be brought together under the umbrella of the Standing Conference on Broadcasting (SCOB). This would facilitate the production of a common agenda while allowing the two groups and others also to make different points if they so wished.

The high-powered Committee on the Future of Broadcasting was appointed under Lord Annan in 1974 which reported in 1977. The Report owed much to the views of Richard Hoggart. This was to have a great influence on the future nature of broadcasting. Among other things it recommended the creation of Channel 4, a second independent television conduit. It set up the Broadcasting Complaints Commission, it proposed the privatisation of local radio and sought to ensure as far as possible the political independence of all broadcasting media. All four measures were set up in 1980. There can be no doubt that SCOB greatly influenced the outcome of the Annan Committee and indeed Whitehead, by then an MP, had served on the Committee itself. Another of SCOB's legacies was the publication of *The British Broadcasting Journal* that aims to promote high standards and which continues to flourish.

As I remarked earlier, the '70s and '80s were a period that

unleashed great passion for constitutional reform. For most of the twentieth century this had not loomed large on the political agenda particularly in England. The revival of interest, when it came, was initiated in Scotland and Wales and remained an enduring problem for the governance of Northern Ireland. Rudyard Kipling in his poem *The Puzzler* (1909) captured the contrasting English predisposition rather well when he ends by saying:

> "And while the Celt is talking from Valencia to Kirkwall, The English – ah, the English! – don't say anything at all".

International Politics

The Trust confined itself mainly to the United Kingdom but with some exceptions, especially Africa. First, it supported the Methodist Bishop Muzorewa who led the opposition to Ian Smith, the Prime Minister of Rhodesia, who had decreed Unilateral Declaration of Independence (UDI) from Britain. The Rhodesian secret service was much more efficient than the Bureau for State Security (BOSS), its counterpart in South Africa. This made it very difficult to get money into the country to help the bishop. Chitnis used his life-long connections with the Jesuits to get funds transported to Muzorewa via them. St Ignatius Loyola, himself, would have proudly blessed this subterfuge and the finesse with which it was executed.

Following the successful outcome of negotiations conducted by Sir Christopher Soames, that brought to an end Ian Smith's UDI in Rhodesia, it was agreed there would be a democratic general election in 1980. Chitnis had been in Salisbury and had made contact with his fellow Roman Catholic, Robert Mugabe, who as leader of the Zimbabwe African National Union-Patriotic Front (ZANU-PF) was one of the main candidates. He offered to be his main election agent. Chitnis' previous experience of organising Liberal election campaigns, essentially, so to speak, 'of cold starts on a February morning' (most notably organising Eric Lubbock's famous victory at the 1962 Orpington by-election) made him fully equipped this time for 'a cold start' in the tropics. To his credit, Mugabe said that his main opponent, Joshua Nkomo, the leader of the Zimbabwe African People's Union (ZAPU), the smaller liberation party, was also in need of an assistant and Chitnis arranged for a fellow Liberal agent to assist Nkomo.

Mugabe won the election and assumed full power as Prime Minister while offering Nkomo the nominal Presidency. Mugabe began almost immediately to act dictatorially and to lay the foundation for his lengthy period of total autocratic power. Years later in 1983, Nkomo fled for his life to London where he was installed in Claridges Hotel by Tiny Rowland, the head of the Lonrho business empire which had extensive interests in Zimbabwe. Mugabe threatened to nationalise all of Lonrho's Zimbabwean assets unless Rowland ceased to support Nkomo. The JRSST moved in to pay the rent for a very modest bedsitter in the Edgware Road where Nkomo was housed. Later, there was some reconciliation and Nkomo returned to Zimbabwe.

In the late 1990s, the Trust returned to an interest in Zimbabwe when it financially supported Morgan Tsvangirai's Movement for Democratic Control that sought unsuccessfully to oppose Mugabe.

Chitnis, together with James Cornford, was provided with funds from the JRRT and the Nuffield Foundation to establish training courses between 1990 and 1994 for potential African National Congress (ANC) ministers as and when the Apartheid regime collapsed in South Africa as it did eventually in 1992.

The Trust also supported independence movements in Portuguese dominated Africa. It avoided Angola, on the grounds that it could not decide which of the various independence factions there merited support. However, it did support the Mozambique Liberation Front (FRELIMO). It also helped the equivalent movements in Guinea Bissau in West Africa and when the Portuguese abandoned Mozambique almost overnight, the Trust had to provide FRELIMO with a tele-printer to enable it to communicate with the outside world. Richard Wainwright trekked through the jungle of Cape Verde Island, to meet with the independence leaders and came back clutching a heavily carved wooden statue which was a token of thanks to the JRSST. It is proudly displayed in the Joseph Rowntree Reform Trust offices in York.

In Europe, the Trust funded activities behind the Iron Curtain. In Hungary and Czechoslovakia, this took the form of literature, mainly bibles, smuggled into those counties by dissident religious groups. More importantly, it paid for a printing machine for *Solidarity*, the successful anti-Communist movement, led by Lech Walesa that had originated in the dockyards of Gdansk.

While most of the political party budget went to the Liberals, the Trust also financed Mec Vannin (the sons of Manx), a short-lived party which sought to challenge the hegemony of the tax-dodging ruling elite in the Isle of Man and, later, Plaid Cymru in Wales alongside the Ulster Unionist Party (UUP), the Progressive Unionist Party (PUP), the Alliance Party of Northern Ireland (APNI), the Ulster Democratic Party (UDP), as well as the Social Democratic and Labour Party (SDLP) in Northern Ireland.

When Michael Rowntree succeeded Bill Morrell as chair in 1981 he clearly intimated that he was less interested in party politics than most of his colleagues. That was true and, if anything, he was a Labour supporter. The Trust decided to appoint a political sub-committee of which I became chair. In that capacity I took the lead in negotiating Liberal Party funding with David Steel who, by that time, had taken over from Thorpe as Liberal Leader.

Grassroots Politics

Post the General Election of 1983, the results were poor and far worse than expected. When the JRSST analysed the outcome, I persuaded my colleagues to devote almost all of our Liberal funding to the Association of Liberal Councillors (ALC). We were already providing its accommodation in Hebden Bridge and, if the Party's fortunes were to have any hope of reviving, it was essential to build up and strengthen its local councillor base. I thought this was a more realistic prospect than continuing to fund the centre. We required the ALC to design a business plan, targeting the most promising local government areas and offering them financial incentives as a reward for success. A new medium-term plan strategy was implemented and the gamble paid off, despite protestations from the central leadership.

In September 2012, *The Sunday Times* quoted from a recent *Liberator* magazine article I had written criticising Nick Clegg's leadership of lacking strategy and resembling that of "a cork bobbing on the waves." Lorely Burt, then a Birmingham MP, questioned this and inquired who I was. In a quite unsolicited e-mail, Bill le Breton – who had been very active in the ALC – wrote of my article on the Social Liberal Forum's website:

> "This is a very powerful piece from one of the Party's best thinkers. But Professor Smith has also always been an activist. Few will realise just how influential he was in the Party's performance in the 1997 election.
>
> So when he speaks the leadership should listen. But they won't because very few of them will know how influential he has been in getting them into the position they now occupy....
>
> Professor Smith was also responsible for making sure the Alliance's advances in the 1985 counties election were with help and advice on the ground..."

In a similar vein, Dick Newby, when Chief Whip in the Lords, told Ms Burt she owed the fact she had been elected to Westminster to my earlier build-up of her local municipal support. In its way, the diversion of funds away from the main party to the ALC proved something of a triumph.

British party politics was becoming even more fluid. One

manifestation of this was the creation of a Liberal-Labour pact in order to sustain the Callaghan government in power. Another was the formation of the Alliance between the Liberals and the newly- formed Social Democratic Party (SDP) created by the "Gang of Four" breakaway from Labour under the leadership of Roy Jenkins. The SDP had had a small start-up grant from the JRSST but the bulk of its early money came from David Sainsbury. Chitnis and I negotiated with Sainsbury and David Owen over the financing of Alliance publicity and propaganda for the general election of 1983.

The political sub-committee was abolished after I succeeded Michael Rowntree as the sixth chair of the Trust in 1987. I was to remain its chair for the next twelve years. I sought to emulate both Seebohm Rowntree and J B Morrell by being very pro-active in leading the Trust and not simply acting as chair of its quarterly Board meetings. My following six successors in the chair chose to be much less high profile.

Constitutional Reform

As luck would have it, my motivation to be a pro-active chair coincided with just the right moment. Unlike most of the twentieth century in the UK, the late 1980s were years of considerable political tumult and in particular there was a strong revival of interest in constitutional reform.

First, there was the Constitutional Convention for Scotland which the Trust financed. This was the catalytic precursor that led to the referendum and consequential establishment of a devolved Scottish Parliament. Similarly, the Trust financed the "Yes" campaign for devolution in Wales which, in contrast, was only very narrowly won, but which led to the creation of the Welsh Assembly.

Peter Hain MP, my former tutee and at that time a junior minister in the Welsh Office responsible for the Referendum, wrote to me after the result, that the JRSST's role had been crucial and that he had reported this to Prime Minister Tony Blair.

The year 1988 was the tercentenary of the 1688 Glorious Revolution, which was being celebrated in a very stuffy way. As recorded previously I was on the board of *The New Statesman*, having taken part in the merger with *New Society*. Stuart Weir, the Statesman's editor, came to me with an exciting idea. He wanted to publish a democratic charter, entitled Charter 88, in the magazine and to recruit a wide spectrum of 888 eminent people – artists, politicians, musicians, writers, and academics – to sign it. He saw his charter in part as a good promotion scheme for the Statesman, but his chief executive refused to fund it and he asked for a £5,000 loan to make it possible. His idea and the proposals in the draft charter for improving democracy and protecting civil liberties coincided exactly with my own thinking. I instantly agreed to secure the loan from the Trust. The launch of the Charter was a great success; some 349 well-known people signed the charter and it became a major talking point in the media. Weir wrote in his account of the formation of Charter 88, that it was fortunate that the Trust's "directors included Trevor Smith who as chairman.....was pressing ahead with a democratic agenda. Trevor is the unsung hero of Charter 88 (and many other democratic initiatives)."

The formation of Charter 88 was to prove a major stimulus

in the new movement for constitutional and political reform. Indeed, it was later acknowledged, though doubtless somewhat reluctantly, by the Daily Telegraph to be the most successful pressure group of the 1990s decade. Originated by Stuart Weir, editor of *The New Statesman* and directed by Anthony Barnett, a columnist for that magazine, it mobilised the forces of progress, which were growing increasingly restless during the torpor of the John Major years.

At the time it was founded there were two other competitors for Trust money. One was Samizdat, a magazine edited briefly by Ben Pimlott, and another pressure group Tactical Voting. I suggested we gave all three of them a grant for a year at the end of which we would decide which one was most worthy of major funding. Charter 88 won hands down.

Under the brilliant leadership of Weir and Barnett, Charter 88 harnessed hitherto dormant radical opinion. It attracted the support and interest of John Smith MP, by then Leader of the Labour Party. He was very concerned with constitutional reform. Fortunately, his untimely death did not halt the progress he had started. Tony Blair, his successor, was not in the least interested in constitutional reform and he derided the establishment of a Scottish Parliament as akin to being little more than a parish council. Nevertheless, the momentum built up by Smith was such that Blair had to continue with this legacy which led, of course, to the establishment of devolved legislative institutions in both Edinburgh and Cardiff.

While the Freedom of Information Campaign research was mainly financed by the Joseph Rowntree Charitable Trust, it relied upon the JRSST/JRRT, for the bulk of its campaigning funds. That, too, was an issue that Blair had inherited from Smith and thus assured its implementation in partial form in the Freedom of Information Act 2000 – something he later regretted.

Broadening the Board

When I became chair of JRSST, (later JRRT), I determined to broaden it in two ways. Elinor Goodman, the political television broadcaster and daughter of Edward Goodman, succeeded him as a director and became the first woman on the board. Later, Mandy Cormack, whom I proposed, and Tina Day, Diana Scott and Pam Giddy joined the Board as did a second Roman Catholic, Professor Peadar Cremin, a distinguished Irish educationist and peace activist from Limerick.

As well as beginning to redress the gender imbalance I also wanted to broaden the political outlook amongst the Board to include politically active people who were not necessarily card-carrying Liberals. My friend and colleague at QMC, Professor David Currie, had been a member of the Communist Party but had been converted to the modernising Labour Party. His mentor and patron was Maurice Peston who himself had been an adviser to two Labour ministers – Reg Prentice and Roy Hattersley. He suggested that Currie should advise the then Shadow Cabinet. I was anxious to harness his considerable talents on behalf of the Trust. I knew it would be near- impossible for me to get him appointed to the Board straight away but I did contrive to have him join its investment committee on the grounds that his economic advice would be invaluable. After an apprenticeship of some two years I then managed to install him as a Director which, I claim, was his first company directorship – albeit unpaid. He went on to become Chair of Charter 88, Deputy Dean of London Business School, Dean of the Cass School of Business, a Labour Peer, Chair of Ofcom (Office of Communications) and later first chair of the Competition & Markets Authority formed in 2013. On being appointed to Ofcom he had become a crossbench peer, having also earlier resigned from the JRRT.

State of the Nation

In order to strengthen the promotion of constitutional debate within England, the JRRT, at my behest, set up a series of *State of the Nation* opinion polls.

In 1991, I began the series by consulting various democratic organisations to suggest topics for the questionnaire and engaging Sir Robert Worcester at Market & Opinion Research International Ltd (MORI) to design it. I invited Weir and Patrick Dunleavy, the polymath at the LSE, to a meeting with Worcester to approve the final draft. A row broke out. Weir and Dunleavy argued robustly that the MORI draft of what were rather minimalist questions, aiming for neutrality, would leave most respondents adrift. They put forward more explanatory questions to which Worcester objected vigorously and bitterly. I came down on the side of Weir and Dunleavy and the distinctive series of State of the Nation polls across a wide democratic agenda was born and carried on for 13 years, at first briefly with MORI, then with ICM Unlimited.

There were at least two significant outcomes. First, the polls showed a majority of respondents took on board and favoured the idea of proportional representations; secondly, they tested attitudes towards economic and social rights and found that people rated free health-care and a right to housing as highly as they did traditional civil and political rights (as later the Northern Ireland Human Rights Commission confirmed, finding consensus-level approval across both communities for four basic social-economic rights).

Although, as noted, Kipling had observed constitutional matters did not usually have huge salience amongst the English, when prompted, they showed considerable support for reform, and in particular for reform of the House of Lords. These surveys by themselves did not have a great deal of influence but they exerted a strong 'trickle-down' effect on the debate and certainly helped to encourage John Smith in his endeavours.

It is difficult to capture the intensity of radical politics in the last two decades of the twentieth century which, unusually, made deep inroads in the more conventional modes of UK politics. Much of this was due to the serendipitous confluence of a number of crucial factors. First, of course, was the propitious climate of public opinion which was desperate for some kind of transformation. Secondly, was a coterie of quite remarkably talented people who came and worked together at this time. I have already alluded to the intellectual entrepreneurialism of Weir and Barnett who still had more innovative initiatives to launch. They were ably assisted by a small number of outstandingly gifted academics who were dedicated to the cause of reform: Professor Dunleavy; his highly expert computer-literate colleague Dr Helen Margetts, who joined the State of the Nation team. She was later to hold chairs at both UCL and Oxford and the accomplished Leeds political theorist, Professor David Beetham, who developed new methodologies for assessing the scale and quality of democracy in nation states for a further inter-Rowntree trust initiative – Democratic Audit.

Thirdly, and equally crucial, I was able to persuade my JRRT colleagues to will the financial means to develop the necessary campaigning to advance the reforms and the ideas behind them. The Joseph Rowntree Charitable Trust (JRCT), for its part, made generous grants towards funding the equally vital research effort needed to underpin the whole exercise. Someday, a bright young researcher will write up a comprehensive history of this fertile, almost unique, reformist movement.

Open Democracy

However, the new reformism still had some way to run. Barnett, in 2001, having moved on from Charter 88, initiated *Open Democracy* an online inter-active forum for the propagation and discussion of reformist ideas and policy. Both the JRCT and the JRRT provided the necessary start-up backing. It was a brilliant idea, embracing as it did, the advent of what has become known now as "the social media". The explosive increase in mass communications has had a transforming effect of considerable magnitude on the conduct of politics, as well as on other aspects of contemporary life. Barnett struggled successfully to obtain funds from other sources to keep going and he was thus able to increase the menu with the introduction of *Our Kingdom* that concentrated on the problems of the UK and its devolved elements. Barnett continues to be one of the most enterprising commentators on contemporary UK politics.

Democratic Audit

Before that, the inter-Trust initiative had been in the making. I had been co-opted onto the JRCT'S Democracy sub-committee, chaired by the redoubtable Grigor McClelland. He had served with Michael Rowntree in the Friends' Ambulance Corps during WWII, had inherited Laws, the large departmental store in Newcastle and had become the first Dean of the Manchester Business School. Like me, he too was despondent after the 1987 general election, the sclerotic condition of the UK's machinery of government it revealed and the consequential very labile public mood it engendered. I suggested the UK polity needed a regular review akin to that undertaken by the National Institute of Economic and Social Research (NIESR) regarding the UK economy. I proposed it be called The Democratic Audit of the United Kingdom. The concept and title was approved and tenders were sent out.

The two best responses came in from Weir on behalf of Charter 88 and another from Beetham at the politics department at Leeds University. We suggested that they combine which they did to great effect. From the late 1980s they produced a number of single studies on various aspects of the constitution and also published more comprehensive commentaries most notably. *The Three Pillars of Liberty* (1996) Francesca Klug, Keir Starmer and Stuart Weir and *Political Power and Democratic Control in Britain* (1999) Stuart Weir and David Beetham. Later, Beetham's very important and detailed analysis of the extent to which corporate power influenced the public agenda *Unelected Oligarchy* (2011) was published by Democratic Audit.

Democratic Audit was hosted first at Professor Kevin Boyle's Human Rights Centre at Essex University, then moved to Liverpool University with Dr Stuart Wilks-Heeg as its director, and is now at LSE under Professor Dunleavy. The Hansard Society adopted the concept of political audit and has been publishing its own surveys over the past decade so the earlier momentum continues to be maintained.

Both intellectually and politically, for my part, it was exciting to work with such a talented group of colleagues and to help in their complementary endeavours, as part composer, part conductor, part orchestrator and part impresario.

By that time, I had long since ceased to be chair and I resigned from the JRRT in 2006. Since then the Board has reverted to being composed almost exclusively of card-carrying Liberal Democrats – a backward step in my view particularly given the nature of the post-Blair state of UK politics, which continues to cry out for a Joseph Rowntree sense of vision that encompasses the growing fragmentation of politics including the populism thrown up in part by the digital communications age.

PART 2: FURTHER REFLECTIONS

CHAPTER 12

TEN LIBERAL LEADERS – 1955-2018

I joined the Liberal Society at LSE in October 1955 which automatically afforded membership of the Liberal Party. This was some months before Clement Davies resigned as Leader. I have always stressed this timing because I did not want to appear to have been enticed by his successor Major Joseph (Jo) Grimond, the MP for Orkney & Zetland. Grimond's undoubted charisma attracted many of my later contemporaries, but I wanted to assert my independence from such populist appeals and rely on my political principles.

1/ Clement Davies (1945-55)

A long-time MP he had veered between being a radical and a supporter of the pre-war Conservative/National Liberal administration under Stanley Baldwin. During WWII he had advocated a Liberal withdrawal from the Churchill Coalition. He became Leader when Sir Archibald Sinclair unexpectedly lost his seat.

I invited him to be guest of honour at the annual dinner of the LSE Liberal Society when I was its chair. He spoke well and was very affable and showed no signs of his long-term alcoholism.

2/ Jo Grimond 1955-67

He was the Leader I came to know best because we spent many years together with the JRSST. He was a director (1967-85) and I was associated with it first as its research adviser from 1970 and then as a director (1975-96), so there was a considerable overlap.

He enjoyed an exceptionally charmed life with everything falling in his lap. He was handsome, charismatic and a good speaker. Equally, he was vain, lazy and something of a snob. Born into a very wealthy Dundee firm of jute manufacturers, he lacked for nothing. Educated at Eton and Balliol, he was a self-admitted lackadaisical house captain but must have exerted himself at Oxford where he graduated with a First in PPE. He qualified as a barrister but never practiced and worked shortly as a research assistant before being called-up and commissioned in the army. He had a carefree war, being stationed in Northern Ireland for the duration involved with troop training. In 1945 he was offered the candidacy without any other contenders and narrowly lost Orkney & Zetland. Again, without any others being considered, he was appointed secretary of the National Trust for Scotland and spent most of the time looking for a superior tied-house that would go with the job. He won the seat in 1950 and it was expected Frank Byers would succeed

Davies as Leader in due course. Byers lost his Dorset seat in the 1951 election, Grimond succeeded him as chief whip and later took over from Davies as Leader.

His vanity was to be seen in his refusal to wear spectacles despite poor eyesight or hearing aids despite equally poor hearing. His laziness was reflected in his often vacuous speeches. His good delivery helped obscure the fact that the content was often randomly constructed with little logic.

He had the merit of appreciating that Lloyd George's Yellow Book policies needed up-dating and attracted a number of top-rate academics to help devise new ones. He also called for a "realignment of the Left" following the Tories' third General Election success in 1959. This clarion call was later to be remembered when the SDP/Liberal Alliance was formed and he wallowed in the glory of being so prescient. In the intervening years, however, he had become very right-wing, privately expressing appreciation for some of Thatcher's policies.

His snobbery may seem surprising to some for he showed he could mix easily with princes or peasants alike. This disguised a disdain for the middle classes – which, of course formed the bulk of his political support – precisely because he regarded them as, by definition, mediocre. He had this very much in common with Roy Jenkins whom, despite numerous virtues, I found exuded a similar brand of snobbery.

Grimond was invariably very good company. Although intellectually lazy, I witnessed a flash of his innate intelligence when we attended an Acton Society seminar addressed by Michael Ignatieff, the acclaimed philosopher and later disastrously failed Canadian Liberal party leader. I was most impressed by Grimond's contribution to the discussion.

His other attribute was his capacity for alcohol drinking. His consumption was prodigious. I often shared a session with him, usually in company with Pratap Chitnis and the journalist Robert Oakeshott. I never once saw Grimond the worse for wear; it must have been his tall height – the booze could have only reached his knees while our brains had become befuddled.

3/ Jeremy Thorpe (1967-1976)

I hardly knew him as a personal acquaintance. As I have recalled I saw him first at the disastrous 1958 Liberal Party annual conference in Torquay when Ronnie Fraser warned me of his sexual proclivities. A brilliant public orator, there was little else to commend him, though I did approve the policies he advanced for dealing with Ian Smith, the Rhodesian prime minister who had declared Unilateral Declaration of Independence from the UK. Thorpe urged the use of RAF airpower against the rebellious regime. This earned him the opprobrium of the right-wing press, who called him "Bomber Thorpe". Again, as I have re-called, I learnt more about him from the activities of Richard Wainwright, Pratap Chitnis and Michael Rowntree before and during Thorpe's trial for attempted murder.

4/ David Steel (1976-1988)

On the night Thorpe resigned I sought out Steel and Chitnis who had been dining together. I remember we went into Thorpe's office and Steel tried out the desk for size. The two of them had already decided that Steel would run for the leadership with Chitnis organising his campaign. I tried to persuade him to wait for the next time round but to no avail and subsequently he beat John Pardoe for the post.

"The Boy David", as he had been called when he entered the Commons in 1965 as the baby of the House, became more outgoing after he ceased to be Leader. As Leader, he played his cards fairly close to his chest, though Chitnis remained a very close confidant. I always found him affable.

He agreed to the Lib-Lab Pact which lasted for some eighteen months (1977-78), by which support would be given to the Callaghan government. To a degree this appeared to echo Grimond's post-1959 call. However, when I asked Grimond, he said he had wanted to work with the far left of the Labour Party – Sydney Silverman and the Bevanite rump and not the Croslandite revisionists; he thought the former more libertarian and the latter too statist. It is generally now regarded that Steel should have struck a much harder bargain with Callaghan.

Steel enjoyed something of a political Indian Summer when he became the first Presiding Office of the devolved Scottish Parliament.

5/ Paddy Ashdown (1988-99)

The JRSST had provided the necessary finance to sustain him as a candidate for Yeovil for which he became MP in 1983. Like Grimond he has adopted a number of seemingly opposed policies over the years especially concerning defence; he strongly supports strengthening the Royal Marines, into which he was commissioned on leaving school, while flirting with the Campaign for Nuclear Disarmament (CND) when he first was elected. Again, like Grimond, he sought to prepare for a Lib-Lab pact with Tony Blair before the 1997 General Election which was scuppered by Labour securing an overwhelming majority. His inherent promiscuity later led him to encourage Nick Clegg to join in Coalition with David Cameron's Tories to form a Coalition government which was to have disastrous electoral consequences for the Liberal Democrats.

Ashdown's qualities included an ability to rapidly acquire knowledge; for instance he learnt Mandarin while stationed in Hong Kong and later Serbo-Croat when in the Balkans. However, he suffered from something akin to Attention Deficit Hyperactivity Disorder (ADHD). Accordingly, he was better at tactics but very bad at strategy. I observed, if you were the sergeant of a platoon which he commanded and surrounded in no-man's land, you would have to say to the squaddies: "if we're to stand any chance of escape, we'll have first to shoot our lieutenant!"

It is generally agreed that he served a very good four-year term as the EU's High Representative in Bosnia Herzegovina (2002-06) which contrasted with a very varied time as party Leader.

6/ Charles Kennedy (1999-2006)

By general consent Charles Kennedy was one of the most successful of the Leaders. He had abandoned post-graduate studies in the US to successfully fight the remote Highland seat of Ross, Cromarty & Skye for the SDP.

Although lacking in experience, his innate intelligence and political *nous* were of a very superior order indeed. This was especially to be seen in his critical decision to oppose the war in Iraq. Subsequent events, proved how right he had been. His performance gained much popular support and 62 Lib Dem MPs were elected at the 2005 General Election.

However, like Davies, he became severely alcoholic, but much more so than Davies. This made him unable to fulfil his political and parliamentary duties with increasing frequency and his MPs forced him to resign. It was a crying shame that his time as Leader was prematurely terminated in this way.

7/ Menzies (Ming) Campbell QC (2006-07)

Ming Campbell won the contest to succeed Kennedy as Leader. An Olympic athlete he had enjoyed a very successful career at the Bar. This equipped him to be a formidable debater both in the Commons and in the media. He chose foreign affairs and defence as his special policy areas and was always accorded a very respectful audience.

Handsome, charming and always immaculately attired – we once shared the same bespoke tailor - and he exuded a strong personal presence. By any reckoning his many positive attributes should have enabled him to have a good run as Leader. It was not to be. His health deteriorated and he couldn't muster the necessary energy. The truth was that he should have sought the Leadership after Ashdown, but felt he could not beat Kennedy. He paid the price and lasted for less than two years.

8/ Nick Clegg (2007-15)

Nicholas Clegg served as an EU *fonctionnaire* working for Leon Brittan when he was a UK Commissioner in Brussels. A talented multi-linguist and very committed European, Brittan was very attracted to both his EU commitment and, it has to be said, his boyish good looks. The latter caused Clegg much discomfort.

Brittan wanted to help advance his political aspirations while being aware Clegg would eschew the Tories for not being wholeheartedly European. Accordingly, he approached Ashdown, strongly recommending Clegg as a potential Liberal candidate. Ashdown got Chris Rennard, then chief agent, to contrive Clegg's adoption to fight a winnable Midlands constituency for the European Parliament. Clegg served one term as an MEP when, fortuitously, Richard Allen decided to stand down as the Lib Dem MP for Sheffield Hallam and not contest the 2005 General Election. Clegg took over as the candidate and he duly held on to the seat.

When Kennedy resigned, Clegg stayed loyal to Campbell and would not contest the Leadership. But when Campbell gave up, he fought the succession. It turned out to be very fortuitous. Despite the euphoria of 'Cleggomania' which the 2010 General Election campaign generated, it could not be sustained and the Lib Dems lost some MPs. However, the resulting hung Parliament led to the formation of a Coalition with Clegg becoming Deputy Prime Minister (DPM) under David Cameron. Clegg's parliamentary career had advanced very rapidly indeed but it also sowed the seeds of his undoing.

First, the Lib Dems had allowed the Cabinet Secretary to contrive a Coalition Agreement with the Tories which, like Steel's Lib/Lab Pact, gave too little power to them – they should have pondered all the implications for much longer and struck a harder bargain. Secondly, as a consequence, Clegg & Co had no major policies that they could achieve and claim as their own for their Tory partners did not support electoral reform when a Bill was introduced.

Underlying these two factors was how Clegg deported himself during the Coalition years. I described him in the *Liberator* magazine in 2012 as "a cork bobbing on the waves". This was taken up on the front page of *The Sunday Times*. The fact was that Clegg spent too much of his time enjoying the spoils of office as DPM, as shown spending weekends with his family at Chevening, and ignoring the over-riding consideration of being party Leader. The result was that at the 2015 general Election the Lib Dems were reduced to a rump of eight MPs, back to where the Liberals had been for so long after 1945. Clegg's reversal of a hardline stance to a "yes sir, David sir" was particularly damaging to students' opinion of the Lib Dems.

As I have said, his parliamentary rise had been too rapid. His apprenticeship had been too short to equip him for the Leadership and Cabinet office and he had absorbed too little of his party's ethos or previous policy history. His departure from high office was as spectacular as had been his swift rise to it.

9/ Tim Farron (2015-17)

Farron's leadership was as brief as Campbell's. I described him as "the Lib Dems answer to Cliff Richard" with his much-proclaimed Evangelicalism. He adopted some good radical policy stances but did not stick to them. His leadership style, if such it can be called, was to run the Party as he did his constituency without appreciating the vast differences in scale.

He was forced to quit as Leader by a group of senior party dignitaries immediately after the 2017 General Election.

10/ Sir Vince Cable (2017 -)

In many ways, Cable shares much in common with Campbell. He had a varied experience of work in both the public and private sectors and before becoming an MP, he had been Shell's senior economist. On his own specialist topic, in his case economics and industry, Cable displayed a mastery as had Campbell on foreign affairs. Before all other MPs he had predicted the 2008 world economic crisis. He could also be a compelling orator, once ridiculing Prime Minister Gordon Brown as "Mr Bean".

His experience as a businessman was much less than he liked to project. Essentially, he was more of an adviser than an executive and in this not dissimilar to the job of a barrister. So, like Campbell, he had not been a manager of people prior to becoming Secretary of State for Business in the 2005-10 Coalition. In that post, he had responsibility for the big rise in university fees - a policy reversal which caused long-lasting damage to the Lib Dem's credibility.

Like Clegg he allowed himself to relish the spoils of Cabinet office rather than be decisive, resign and challenge Clegg to a leadership election. He contemplated it, as he did other options, but decided against. In the event he left it too late: Clegg had irrevocably damaged the Party which the later Farron interlude only exacerbated. Cable will find the task of reversing the Lib Dems' electoral fortunes difficult, if not impossible, during his tenure as Leader.

CHAPTER 13

POLITICS AFTER DEMOCRACY - AND THE RISE OF THE TENTACULAR STATE

With the exception of India and Botswana, democracy has not firmly taken root outside the Western world. Now it is in the retreat even in what was its heartland. This has been a recent development in the USA, the Nordic States and the Low Countries but, by contrast, the process has been a long, on-going one in Britain.

Brexit was proclaimed to lead to the return of unalloyed national sovereignty to the United Kingdom. Implicit in that claim was it would simultaneously usher in greater democratic interaction between the governors and the governed. Two reservations need to be made. First, is to question how far national sovereignty is achievable anywhere in a multi-national, globalised world. And, secondly, greater democracy is by no means a guaranteed corollary. Most governments are to a greater or lesser extent sovereign, very few are democracies.

The history of British government since the end of WWII, devolution apart, reveals a continuing series of retreats away from democracy and parliamentary oversight of the executive. This will continue if recent rumours that most of the erstwhile functions exercised by the EU Commission will, on repatriation, be farmed out to a host of newly-created QUANGOs (Quasi-Autonomous Non-Governmental Organisations). Yet, arguably, the rise of Quangocracy itself contributed in no small measure to the malaise and ultimate alienation of the public which sparked off the populist wave that resulted in the vote in favour of Brexit.

Occasionally, leading politicians have been aware of the deleterious effects of the enormous growth of, and resort to, QUANGOs and other arm's length measures. On entering office David Cameron undertook to reduce their number but in practice there was to be no reduction whatsoever in the growing recourse to such agencies.

QUANGOs are not new. The Brethren of Trinity House were sub-contracted to run Britain's lighthouses as long ago as 1514. It meant that Ministers of the Crown could avoid day-to-day responsibility. The big game-changer came with the Attlee government's nationalisation program post-1945. It adopted the 'Morrisonian' concept of the public corporation to manage the operations of the industries that had been taken into public ownership. Although successor Conservative administrations de-nationalised a few, they kept on with the device of the public corporation to manage the remaining state enterprises. Ted Heath, during his 'Selsdon Man' phase when Leader of the Opposition, threatened wholesale privatisation of industry, but it was left to Margaret Thatcher to actually introduce this. It was finished off by her successor John Major, who sold off British Rail in a very botched way.

A good example of the process is to track the history of the General Post Office (GPO). Postal services were set up as a

State monopoly in 1660 under the direct ministerial control of the Post-Master General (PMG). The GPO later acquired electronic communications in 1869 with the coming of the telegraph and in 1912 it absorbed telephones. The PMG model endured until 1969. Tony Benn was the last PMG under Harold Wilson who created the Post Office Corporation along the lines of the public corporation. Thereafter, Ministers would never again bear direct responsibility for an enterprise. British Telecom and the Post Office went the way of all flesh and were subsequently privatised.

The wholesale privatisations of the Thatcher and Major eras were heralded as a return to the free market but they were no such thing. They were examples of what Karl Marx termed "monopoly capitalism". The workings of the free market, then, could not provide any form of regulation. This was tacitly acknowledged by government who appointed a growing army of regulators to ostensibly safeguard the public interest. By and large they have proved very feeble, not least because they have been recruited from the very industries they are meant to oversee and to which, at the end of their stint, they often return. The "revolving door" principle of poacher-turned-gamekeeper thrives in the operations of such agencies. At very great expense to the public exchequer, these so-called regulators offer very poor accountability to the public which only adds to the general sense of cynicism which feeds the populist reaction.

The combination of the effects of the public corporation and the successor rise of the regulatory industry are but the more overt examples of the very widespread movement away from direct ministerial involvement with the machinery of modern government. Professor Preston King, has vividly termed this phenomenon as "the tentacular state" to encompass the growing devices by which central power seeks seemingly inexorably to extend itself. Most of these are much less in the public eye than the public corporations and regulators, but they can all be seen as diverse elements in what now comprises the practice of contemporary government.

Butskellism

The Conservatives returning to power in 1951, maintained almost all of the nationalised undertakings along with the Welfare State that also had been greatly expanded under Labour. This continuation by the new government of its predecessor's innovations gave rise to a sense of inter-party consensus for which *The Economist* coined the phrase "Butskellism", being an amalgam of the surnames of Rab Butler, Tory Chancellor of the Exchequer and his predecessor Hugh Gaitskell. It served as the prevailing policy paradigm for most of the 1950s.

Towards the end of that decade, Britain was undergoing transformation. The Suez crisis of 1956 was a precipitator and signalled the end of Imperialistic adventurism that had characterised the foreign policy of the UK over previous centuries. The UK was in no sense the 'Great Power' it once was although nostalgic residues unfortunately persisted. This military humiliation coincided with rumbling economic troubles at home. The economy while still advancing had slowed and was not performing as well as its European neighbours – in particular France.

Harold Macmillan was fully apprised of the situation

but played it down for the 1959 General Election where he blatantly and successfully appealed to the electorate's hedonism with his "You've Never had it so Good - Don't let Labour Ruin It!" message. But he knew full well the relative weakness of the underlying economy.

Planning and the First Modern QUANGO

Macmillan was attracted to President de Gaulle's approach of 'indicative', as opposed to Soviet-style 'directed', Five Year Plans that were drawn up in close collaboration with the main representatives of both industrialists and the trade unions. These French plans were widely regarded as promoting growth and prosperity. Macmillan's not very original contribution to the debate on planning in the 1930s was part of the British reaction to the USSR along the lines already suggested by Sir Arthur Salter. It was important precisely because of his position as one of the leading Conservative younger MPs. It meant he would be particularly receptive to the ideas behind the later French experiment.

Accordingly, he set about emulating them with his creation in 1962 of the National Economic Development Council, the NEDC or 'NEDDY' as it colloquially came to be known. It was the first big modern QUANGO, consisting of a tri-partite forum bringing the unions, employers and government round the same table together with a few independent experts. It would be presided over by the Chancellor of the Exchequer, though the Prime Minister himself would be present on important occasions. It was generously staffed by the National Economic Development Office (NEDO) and would later spawn a number of National Economic Development Committees ('Little Neddies'), also tri-partite in composition, to supervise and plan the modernisation of major industries.

The NEDDY caught and reflected the mood of the time and easily survived the defeat of the Conservatives at the 1964 General Election. Harold Wilson, the incoming Labour Prime Minister, was even more enamoured with planning than Macmillan, evidenced by his creation of the Department of Economic Affairs (DEA). The hope was that the DEA, with a wider planning remit, would counter-balance the Treasury and its narrower fiscal concerns which Wilson thought had too dominant an influence on the formulation of policy in Whitehall. So, in its turn, the consensus of Butskellism yielded to 'the planning of the two Harolds', as the new prevailing paradigm.

This new consensus differed from the old in what was to become an increasingly significant and influential way. A war-time Treasury civil servant, and later President of the Board of Trade, Wilson put great store by the use of experts. As he said in his election campaign, he wanted a Labour government to "harness the forces of the white heat of the technological revolution" that he saw as taking place.

The Fulton Report

It was taken as axiomatic that planning would necessitate the employment of expert skills, but Wilson also thought new skills might be brought in more generally throughout the senior echelons of Whitehall. To this end he appointed his old Balliol College economics tutor, John Fulton to preside over a Committee on the Civil Service. Its brief was to examine the role and performance of the top Administrative Class and make recommendations as to how it might be improved, including its recruitment procedures which, many suspected, drew too exclusively from the narrow 'Old School Tie' sources of Oxbridge and its feeder Clarendon public schools.

Fulton duly reported in 1968, recommending a wider pool of recruitment, providing Whitehall officials with mid-career placements in the private sector, and encouraging the recruitment of mid-career personnel from the private sector directly into the Civil Service. Prior to Fulton the senior Civil Service almost invariably drew new entrants straight from graduation and employed them until retirement. Fulton criticised this for consolidating "the cult of the amateur". Innocuous enough, or so it may have seemed, the Fulton proposals were to have a much wider and enduring impact. The Report also formalised, promoted and encouraged the acceleration in practice of the main underlying operational principle behind the tri-partism of NEDDY, namely the co-optation in policy making of skills and experience from without the traditional apparatus of the state. Tri-partism brought in new skills but also had the added advantage for ministers of the comfort and protection of being able to lay off total responsibility for any poor decisions by spreading the blame, while claiming full credit for good outcomes.

In effect, tri-partism and Fulton were the midwives that facilitated the birth of the notion that "private sector = good/ public sector = bad". It was a notion that was to burgeon without constraint and be used to justify the many ensuing manifestations of the tentacular state – which culminated in the catastrophic collapse of Carillion in 2018.

QUANGOs and Task Forces

The QUANGO revolution has been one of the foremost illustrations of that State, of which NEDDY was a prime example. Wilson had followed it up with a framework of Economic Planning Councils and Boards in the ten Regions of the UK that were to replicate on a territorial basis what NEDDY was attempting on a sectoral one. Edward Heath's particular contribution was to create in 1971 a Central Policy Review Staff (CPRS), attached to No 10, to assist the Cabinet in its collective deliberations. It consisted largely of experts recruited from outside Whitehall directed by Lord Rothschild; the CPRS was intended to reinforce the implementation of centralised decisions that, of course, included planning. Wilson re-elected in 1974 and his successor James Callaghan retained the CPRS, staffing it with their own appointees.

NEDDY was retained by six Prime Ministers, including Thatcher, but was finally dismantled by the seventh, John Major, though some of the ideas behind it were not killed off – they remained dormant until revived by Blair. Assuming office in 1997, he promoted a series of 'Task Forces' to advise on a variety of policy matters. These were essentially informal ad hoc groups of outsiders, mainly businessmen, appointed by ministers. So many task forces were spawned that the government could not keep track of them. Anthony Barker, from Essex University, uncovered 295 actual and 318 estimated task forces in a report for Democratic Audit. The minister, Lord Falconer, tried to deny these figures and, as recorded in the Lords Hansard 23.2.2000, insisted there were only 48.

The agencies that were invented, the public corporations, NEDDY, the REPCs and task forces constituted the more visible aspects of what was happening, but the totality of the Quangocracy has grown exponentially in recent decades. They cover a host of different roles: there are Executive ones like the Prison Commission and the Environment Agency; Advisory ones such as the Low Pay Commission; and Adjudicatory ones as with the Valuation Tribunals. There are also Monitoring bodies overseeing Immigration Centres and the like.

Their recent growth has been phenomenal and precise numbers are correspondingly difficult to determine. In 2005 some 529 were counted, rising to 827 two years later, but falling to 766 in 2009. In those last two years, however, while the total fell by around ten per cent through mergers and takeovers, more staff were engaged and at a greater cost. Some 111,000 officials cost £46.5 billion. Both the Coalition government and its Conservative successor promised to drastically reduce their number but with no evident success.

Thatcherism - Revolution or Mutation?

The intention of the 'Thatcher Revolution' was aimed at reducing the scale of the State, particularly with the wholesale privatisation of the nationalised industries. Thatcher incorporated to a large extent the intentions behind the policies of Heath's 'Selsdon Man' which he abandoned as soon as he came to office. Despite the rhetoric, however, privatisation did not by any stretch of the imagination rekindle the free market:

it merely installed a system of "monopoly capitalism" – not dissimilar to the oligarchies created by Vladimir Putin in Russia - to use the term of Karl Marx's accurate prediction. The one exception was telecommunications where globalisation makes for a greater measure of the interplay of the forces of the free market, but the other enterprises retained their monopolistic character when owned by shareholders instead of the state. Ironically, many of these shareholders were themselves foreign state-owned industries.

Since privatisation did not mean that the interplay of free market forces would self-regulate these firms, a new form of accountability had to be devised to replace that of the state. This emerged in the form of the 'Regulatory Agency'. A plethora of such bodies were invented including OfWat (Water Services Regulation Agency) and OfGem (Office of Gas and Eletricity Markets), although they were also used to oversee a diverse range of other areas of activity, such as the Independent Police Complaints Commission, the Quality Care Commission (NHS and care homes), OfSted (education and orphanages), the Competition & Markets Authority and others. Indeed, the regulators became a major industry in themselves, adding yet another dimension to Quangocracy. Like the public corporations, regulatory agencies enabled ministers to distance themselves from direct responsibility for the performance of these various sectors. The agencies, however, do not constitute a uniform system and they exhibit wide divergences in powers, terms of reference, composition and to whom they are answerable. They create as big a problem of accountability as those they are meant to hold accountable, thus adding to the constitutional chaos that is so prevalent in contemporary Britain. During the Coalition Government (2010-15) almost all of them came under criticism for falling short in their performance, sometimes very severely, which regularly and inevitably continues. The Quality Care Commission is a particular case in point. Its functions were first out-sourced to some major charities, but then privatised to Remploy, a former employer of the disabled which itself had been privatised, whose main shareholder is "...the US outsourcing giant Maximus." (cf The Independent 29.1.16). One wonders if a super monitoring agency should not be created in order to regulate all of the regulatory agencies, it could be called the Efficiency Office or EffOff for short. (cf Lords Hansard 04.03.2015)

The Thatcher government had two main results. First, it created the concept of TINA (There Is No Alternative) to ward off criticisms of its policies. Thatcher loathed all talk of "consensus", which she saw as compromising one's own principles. As we have seen, the sort of ersatz technocratic consensus that began with Butskellism played its part in downplaying ideological discourse, but nowhere near as forcefully as TINA which by its very name implies aims to abolish outright any form of criticism, let alone discourse. Adopted by successive governments, it has become one of the axiomatic cornerstones of the tentacular state and anti-politics as is evidenced by Theresa May's more recent emphasis on "strong and stable government".

Secondly, Thatcherism merely transferred the managerialist cadres away from the planning apparatus and into the privatised entities and their regulators. In a very real sense, continuity was maintained and enhanced with the regime which had preceded it.

One of the major problems associated with regulatory agencies is that identified as the 'Revolving Door', whereby senior staff are recruited from the very ranks of those who are to be regulated. This makes it all too easy for 'agency capture' by the regulated. Professor Anat Admati has warned that "Regulatory, political and even an 'intellectual' capture is a concern". (Quoted by Brooke Masters, "Enter the Revolving Regulators", *Financial Times* 24.4.2012).

The Volkswagen (VW) scandal that exploded in September 2015 is a recent illustration both of agency capture and corresponding failures on the part of the relevant regulatory agencies. United States law enforcers uncovered that VW cars had been doctored to disguise the high levels of toxic emissions being released. Volkswagen admitted to such transgressions and allegations of government complicity, across Europe, were suspected in hushing up the truth. The US authorities later prosecuted VW and the reverberations continue and will do for some time to come.

The VW crisis is of a kind anticipated by President Dwight D. Eisenhower in his remarkably prescient 1961 valedictory address to the American people. He spoke of "the coming military-industrial crisis" that would usurp public policy-making. Eisenhower warned "against the acquisition of unwarranted influence... (and) the potential for the disastrous rise of misplaced power exists and will persist". Later, Dick Cheney, when George W Bush's Vice-President, personified the military-industrial complex and the immense power it wields.

Since Eisenhower, of course, that complex has stretched far

beyond the confines of military matters and defence procurement and now undue corporate influence intrudes over a very wide range of policy areas, as the VW scandal vividly illustrates. The Trump presidency appears to be extending commercial corporate power over the public agenda even further – the White House is in danger of becoming just another department in the Trump empire.

In Britain these developments were greatly accelerated under Blair's New Labour government. Terms such as "UK PLC" (Public Limited Company) and "Cool Britannia" were deployed as rhetoric to suggest innovation. Gordon Brown once described the relationship between himself as Chancellor of the Exchequer and Blair as Prime Minister as analogous to that of CEO and Chairman of the Board. In keeping with the business emphasis the incoming government adopted the practice of producing Annual Reports, aping those that publicly quoted companies on the Stock Exchange who were legally obliged to publish such documents. The innovation lasted for three years before it was silently abandoned. Apparently, no questions were asked, let alone lessons learnt from this brief attempt to emulate business practice. Rather the reverse, as the relentless quest continued apace.

Private Finance Initiative/Public/Private Partnerships

To pay for the construction of the express train from Paddington to Heathrow, the Major government had come up with the novel idea of what it called a Private Finance Initiative (PFI) which would be less of a drain on state funds. It was ingenious, providing private funds for a relatively small-scale project that generated a cash flow which would re-pay the initial private loans. It was a self-contained project. The concept was seized upon by New Labour and greatly expanded in practice. Re-named Public/Private Partnerships (PPPs) they would be deployed to finance a vast number of infrastructural projects that included hospitals, schools, fire, police and ambulance stations, computer programmes and others. There were over 800 such schemes, of which the NHS accounted for 125 and the latter yielded £831 million in profits to the firms running them in six years. This is because the profit margins run at around 40% added to which are the estimated £21.2 million which the NHS spent since March 2016 on servicing them (*The Times* 30.8.17).

The PPPs were devised in secret (because of the need for commercial confidentially, or so it was claimed) by consortiums of architects, lawyers, accountants, engineers, financiers and banks who would bid for the government contracts that typically would last for thirty years. These PPPs were intended to be 'off balance sheet', thus not adding to the government's borrowing figures. The problems generated by this wholesale recourse to PPPs became readily apparent. First, was the tight secrecy surrounding the compilation of such bids which meant, for example, local authorities could not know anything about schools being PPP-built in their areas. Secondly, the civil service felt itself ill-prepared to procure the contracts and employed consultants and accountants to act on its behalf to negotiate with the successful bidders. Thirdly, as reported above, the successful contracts proved to be exorbitantly costly and tightly drawn, making any future changes (inevitable over a thirty year period) prohibitively expensive.

Fourthly, unlike the Heathrow Express, these projects did not generate their own cashflow so that the costly re-payment of the initial loans would fall on the Exchequer. Fifthly, if PPPs were abandoned by the contractors – as has happened in some cases, the contracts would have to be picked up by the government and returned to being a charge on the public purse.

The PPPs were ill-conceived in many respects, not least in that so little regard was paid to protecting the true public interest. Civil service doubts as to its own procurement ability were all too correct: it couldn't even insist that its outside advisers should put the main priority on safeguarding the public interest. The money to be made from PPPs, is to be seen in the fact that a secondary market in PPPs quickly emerged whereby the contracts have been sold on – often many times – making the monitoring of contract compliance that much more difficult. But the PFI/PPP saga was born in large part by the desire to keep the provision of public projects as far away as possible from the responsibility of ministers and to seem to show they were not a charge on public funds. In reality, of course, they have proved very expensive and a drain on the Exchequer and now have to be included on its balance sheet; the sleight of hand, which they represented, could not be sustained.

In this, they were all-of-a-piece with the vast use of outsourcing erstwhile state activities. Nothing is sacred. Even the Victorian advocates of "The Night-Watchman State", argued that government should restrict itself to and preserve its monopoly of the conduct of defence and foreign affairs, internal security (justice, prisons and police) and broad but limited direction of the economy. Nowadays, a third of prisons and detention centres, most of the probation service, and internal security have been outsourced. The armed forces have been cut back and corresponding greater reliance placed on mercenaries and security firms to assume bigger tasks in theatres of war. In Afghanistan, at the height of the Allied intervention there were more such employees than all the western coalition's regular forces put together.

The tentacular state thrives on constant innovation, indeed, it is an intrinsic and necessary element for its survival. It has an underlying motive to mobilise ideas and practices from the outside commercial world and import them into what were once the traditional corridors of power. A kind interpretation would be these innovations were attempts to develop a better lateral thinking capacity.

"Tsars"and Non-Executive Directors (NEDs)

One such attempt was the creation of a cadre of what became known as 'Policy Tsars', to advise on improving specific areas of policy. The idea behind this came from US experience and they were to advise ministers in promoting change and reducing red-tape. In 1998 Chief Constable Keith Hellawell was the first of this new species, being asked to deal with the issue of illegal drugs; he later received much controversial publicity as board chair of Sports Direct.

Other areas covered by tsars have included medicine, social mobility, the weather, high streets, veterans, the promotion of enterprise and financial technology. According to a study undertaken by King's College, London (KCL), between 1997 and 2015 over 300 tsars have been appointed. The study found much variation among them as in the Regulatory Agencies as noted above. Some were paid, others not. There was little conformity in job specifications and they were recruited from a wide spread of backgrounds with the majority coming from business and others from academia and the public services. The KCL study commented that tsars are "not subject to any existing codes of practice (and that) current arrangements are vulnerable to ministerial idiosyncrasy, opaque procedures and lack of accountability" all in keeping with the precepts of tentacular government. Tsars have endured much longer than task forces and they were appointed at a faster annual rate by the Coalition than they were under the Blair or Brown administrations. Their effectiveness, however, is almost impossible to determine, given their very nature. It would seem the main purpose is to demonstrate ministers are dealing with pressing issues thrown up by the moment but in fact are being kicked into the long grass unless and until they rise up again. Symbols of urgency serving also as fig-leaves disguising procrastination would be as good a description of any of the tsars.

Another attempt was to be seen in the appointment of Non-Executive Directors (NEDs) to the so-called 'Boards' of Whitehall departments that were enthusiastically embraced by the Coalition. Unusually, their role was codified and enhanced very publicly in the 2005 up-dated Ministerial Code. Five years later the Conservative government of David Cameron added to the Code that NEDs "should be largely drawn from the commercial private sector". By 2014, some sixty-nine had been appointed, led by the former British Petroleum (BP) boss, Lord Browne of Maddingley, himself being appointed to the

Cabinet Office. NEDs, it was said, were to be the eyes and ears of the Prime Minister (and his Deputy) "to ensure the effective running of government by participating in enhanced departmental board meetings". In the Ministerial Code it was also claimed NEDs would facilitate relations between ministers and their senior civil servants, advise on the performance of Permanent Secretaries, the composition of business plans, risk management, relations with QUANGOs and outsourced contractors and whether policies should be returned in-house if their political content merited it. Lord Browne was succeeded as lead NED by Sir Ian Cheshire, former CEO of Kingfisher, in April 2015.

The Financial Times reported that "civil servants at times struggled to incorporate the external figures into Whitehall", which is not surprising given their 'double agent' remit in the Ministerial Code. In 2012, Lord Browne told MPs he would give the system of departmental boards a performance mark of "two out of ten" (*The Times* 9.4.2015). Unless this rating can be greatly improved, it is likely that NEDs will suffer the same fate as task forces and be allowed to fade slowly away without fanfare.

Extended Ministerial Offices (EMOs), Major Projects Authority (MPA) and Behavioural Insight Team (BIT)

However, this was to be some time off, given Cameron's predilections that fired his determination. He sought to strengthen the rationale behind NEDs with the creation of Extended Ministerial Offices (EMOs), whereby outsiders from industry and commerce would be appointed on five year civil servant contracts. None were appointed during the period of Coalition rule, but the idea resurfaced again in 2015 with five Cabinet ministers forming their own EMOs. Ministers would be allowed to recruit up to ten officials from either outside or favoured officials from inside Whitehall ("Is he one of us?" as Margaret Thatcher would ask). They were soon dubbed "Downing Street narks" according to *The Times* (21.7.2015). Theresa May at first seemed bent on counteracting this trend towards ministerial autonomy but after her devastating defeat at the polls in May 2017 she was so weakened she had little or no control over her Cabinet colleagues.

Apart from these more generalised reforms, particular attention was focused on improving the procurement ability within Whitehall. This followed a long history of failures, especially in commissioning large-scale computer programmes and armaments purchases. Accordingly, the Major Projects Authority (MPA) was established in 2011 "to import skills more common in the private sector, such as managing risk, learning from competitors and improving supply chains." (*The Economist* 9.8.2014).

Complementing the MPA's efforts would be the Commissioning Academy, set up in 2013, which would recruit 1,500 commissioners located throughout both central and local government. A further addition came a year later with the formation of the Crown Procurement Service (CPS) in 2014. The MPA monitored some 191 procurement projects in 2013, 199 in the following year and188 in 2015, plotting their performance on a red, amber, green traffic light spectrum.

The Coalition created the Behavioural Insight Team (BIT)

in 2010 within the Cabinet Office. The "nudge unit", to give it its colloquial name, is designed to persuade organisations and people to adopt policies which the government wants without recourse to formal instructions; yet another device to keep ministers from exercising direct responsibility. The BIT was part-privatised in 2013 and sells its services both to the British government and foreign powers.

Given the often extensive lead times associated with all these programmes, it will be some time before a full assessment of the activities of the MPA, the Commissioning Academy, the CPS and the BIT can be made, but all four initiatives are illustrations of the modus operandi that underpins the tentacular state.

Whitehall Chief Executive Officer (CEO)

A further and very striking example came with the, perhaps inevitable, creation of a major new post – that of a Chief Executive – to preside over all the departments of Whitehall. Reporting to the Head of the Civil Service and effectively his deputy, the appointee would seek to induce change away from the direct provision of services to commissioning them from private contractors, Blair's "UK PLC" in all but name.

The Financial Times reported difficulty in attracting suitable candidates from the private business world to fill the post but John Manzoni, who had been Lord Browne's deputy at BP and later head of the MPA, was appointed. Apparently and surprisingly or not, depending on one's viewpoint, Lord Browne was a member of the selection panel (cf *The Guardian* 11.10. 2014).

In 2015, with the advent of the new Cameron government,

Manzoni instructed all government departments to draw up corporate plans in the manner of the private sector lest there be any misunderstanding. His memorandum is the most starkly explicit statement articulating the aim of dismantling much of what had been seen essentially as public administration and substituting for it private business management and methods. It thus brought to a temporary fruition phase of the pattern of thought that had developed apace since at least the Fulton Report and even before..

The apparatus and personnel of the tentacular state that I have described requires, somehow or other, to be kept going or, in its own terms, "managed". In the distant past, governments were presumed to have been "led". It is somewhat ironic that most academic commentators regard "management" as being subordinate to "leadership". Things seem to have changed. What accounts for this? It would appear that either the exercise of leadership is all but impossible in modern political conditions, or it has been overwhelmed by management as rampant technocracy prefers to call itself. This has led to the cultivation of a new breed of professionals to serve or keep going the managerialist technocracy of the tentacular state.

Special Advisors (SpAds), "Government of all the Talents (GOATs)

Special advisers (SpAds) to ministers go back a long way. Churchill employed Professor Lindemann (later Lord Cherwell) as his scientific specialist and Brendan Bracken as his media adviser during WWII. His prime ministerial successors continued the practice but from Blair onwards there was an unprecedented increase in their numbers. Blair attached them to ministers in order to liaise with civil servants to ensure party policy was being followed. Indeed, at No 10 he gave his own Chief of Staff, Jonathan Powell, and his Head of Communications, Alastair Campbell, - both essentially superior SpAds – formal official status which gave them authority to instruct regular civil servants. This was quite unprecedented at the time and has not been directly repeated, although the appointment of a Chief Executive in the case of Manzoni shows how the practice endures and develops further.

According to the Constitution Unit, some 626 SpAds were appointed between 1979 and 2013. In 2010, there were sixty-three in post after the General Election which, despite promises to reduce the number, had grown to ninety-eight after the next Election (cf Ben Young & Robert Hazell. *Special Advisers* 2014). The annual cost of hiring SpAds rose from £8.4m in 2013-14 to £9.2m in the following financial year. In Gordon Brown's last year as PM (2009-10) there were 71; at the start of 2015 the number had grown to over the hundred mark. Their median age is thirty-four and they usually earn considerably more than they did in their previous employment and subsequently receiving hefty annual pay increases (cf *The Guardian* 18.12.15).

Apart from assisting ministers in a various ways, SpAds are also something of a protective shield for their masters in that they are easily expendable and can be blamed for any unfortunate events that occur, as has actually happened in some cases. They also constitute a new pool of recruitment for future MPs and ministers. David Cameron, George Osborne, the Miliband brothers and Nick Clegg, for example, all entered the Commons and ultimately ministerial office via this conduit. Their careers feed the criticism, increasingly being made, that the contemporary political class lacks any experience outside of politics. This is seen to be to the detriment of the wider body politic and is becoming all too extensive. In the past of course, William Pitt the Younger and William Gladstone are examples of little wider experience, but these were the exceptions to what now appears to becoming the rule. Just before the 2005 General Election I was tempted to put down a Parliamentary Question (PQ) asking "If the Government would hold a referendum as to whether Masters Cameron, Osborne, Clegg and the Miliband brothers should be allowed to wear long trousers?" – the PQ would have been disallowed, but you can see what I meant.

There may well have been a connection between the consequences of the mushroom growth in the numbers of SpAds and equally steep rise in the recruitment of GOATs – so named after the 1806 Grenville administration which was depicted as the "Government of all the Talents". Gordon Brown borrowed this term to describe a plethora of ministerial appointments under New Labour.

It is not that uncommon to bring in ministers from outside Parliament. In WWII, for example, Churchill imported three such into the Cabinet: Max Beaverbrook, the newspaper tycoon, Fred Woolton, who ran Selfridges, the well-known Oxford Street department store; and Ernest Bevin, the General Secretary of the mighty Transport Workers' Trade Union. All three proved great successes. War conditions may make success easier; in peacetime such outside recruits reveal a much more patchy record as ministers.

In their much greater reliance on GOATs, both Blair and Brown followed Thatcher's example. Many more were appointed but with mixed results. Some stayed a very short time; some were acceptably competent but there were many poor or indifferent performers. The most successful was Paul Myners. Coming from modest Cornish beginnings he trained as a schoolteacher but soon abandoned that career for work in the City. His progress was meteoric as a financier and he gathered a portfolio of directorships in major corporations. His unusual career path may have given him his high degree of political adroitness that stood him out from the generality of GOATs.

The Coalition government and its Tory successor made extensive recourse to GOATs and it has to be asked why the practice proved so popular with Prime Ministers. There are a number of possible reasons which may combine to foster the practice.

First and foremost, of course, is the incessant belief in the over-riding supremacy of business managers and their methods over public administrators and their ways of doing things: hence the mantra 'private good/public bad' which, as in the examples cited, continues to gain ground. Secondly, the increasingly restrictive backgrounds from which MPs are now drawn, including SpAds, means that there is a smaller range of skills amongst them, which is perhaps why PMs look farther afield in choosing ministers. This is compounded by the growing preference of constituency parties to select parliamentary candidates from their own localities. These factors in turn conspire to put off more people from seeking elected office.

Thirdly, power has ebbed away from Westminster as a result of globalisation (including the EU) and the power of corporate influence in determining the public agenda. These factors all play a part in the growing use of GOATs which, itself, feeds the notion that government should be run much more on the lines of business. This is almost a self-fulfilling prophecy, being seen as inevitable – yet another manifestation of Thatcher's TINA. This is mostly implied and taken for granted almost like a religion. Rarely is the notion openly argued which is a great intellectual failing on the part of those who covertly accept it. It is all part of the Burkean hangover which is used to disguise the fact that the UK's governing arrangements now no longer evolve gradually but are part of a whirligig which twists and turns with increasing rapidity.

A New Nomenclatura and 'Revolving Doors'

The tentacular state, in effect, has also spawned its own type of *nomenklatura*, so to speak, to sustain and keep it going. As was the case in Soviet Russia, it is now almost impossible to discern the backgrounds from which this new breed of fixers come. Are they lobbyists and spin doctors, management consultants, erstwhile civil servants, businessmen/women, academics, or what? Sometimes, indeed, they combine many past roles. Sir Howard Davies is the doyen of this new breed. His career includes serving as a civil servant in both the Foreign & Commonwealth Office and Her Majesty's Treasury, as a management consultant with McKinsey & Co, as a lobbyist as Director-General of the CBI, Controller of the Audit Commission, Bank of England deputy Governor, and academically as Director of the LSE and a professor in Paris. He advised on additional airport capacity for Heathrow or Gatwick and his latest role is chairman of a leading bank. He is the quintessential personification of the nomenklatura.

The main requirement of the generality of members of the fixers that comprise the nomenklatura is not so much that they know about anything in particular but that they know their way around – that is vital.

A major problem thrown up is that of the so-called 'revolving door' as fixers move from one job to another, a major feature of the corporate direction of government. David Beetham in *Unelected Oligarchy: Corporate & Financial Dominance in Britain's Democracy* (2011) and Stephen Wilks in *The Revolving Door and the Corporate Colonisation of UK Politics* (2015) have analysed this in detail. It is especially acute in appointing people to the regulatory agencies: these are frequently appointed from the ranks of those they are to regulate. It is all too easy for 'agency capture' to occur in such cases. Similar to the VW crisis outlined previously, this is another illustration of President Eisenhower's prediction. His prediction was in turn validated by C Wright Mills' notion of the power elite in *The Power Elite* (1956) which gave scholarly backing to Eisenhower. To be sure, the passage of time has amply endorsed both of their arguments.

Politics and Business – Discrete and Distinctive Entities

As has been continually repeated in this chapter, the problem with the managerialism of the tentacular state is that it takes as axiomatic the transferability of skills as between the public and private sectors. Digby Jones, a former CBI Director-

General who served briefly as a junior Trade Minister under Blair, concluded that GOATs, like him, were unable to fulfil their potential as ministers as Whitehall did not make for an amenable working environment precisely because it did not approximate closely enough to the private sector. In other words, and this is very revealing, politics and business constitute very different worlds and the methods of the latter should have supremacy.

Of the more successful GOATs, Lord Drayson, is one of the very few people to realise that the two worlds are, indeed, quite different. A millionaire businessman and entrepreneur, he served as a minister under Gordon Brown. Reflecting on the two worlds, he was quoted as saying,

> "It is much harder to be a government minister than a chief executive. In business, you build the team, you have the numbers that show how you're doing. You have a sense of control and clarity. My experience of politics was completely different. You have to persuade and build consensus. It's a very different to running businesses." (cf *The Times* 7.10.15).

This observation is very well made and is a very rare appreciation of the inherent distinctions between the two worlds of business and politics, especially coming as it does from one who has direct experience of both. To conflate business and politics is, to use a philosopher's term, to make a category mistake. Another factor is the sheer difference in size and scale of government activity for the most part compared with that of business. For example, UK government computer contracts are amongst the largest in the world, which probably accounts for their many failures. Only a few multi-national corporations get anywhere close to these dimensions and the complexities they give rise to.

It is interesting to conclude that political skills seem more readily transferable to the private sector than vice versa to judge from the large numbers of retired senior civil servants and ex-Ministers snapped up by businesses (cf *Daily Mirror* 11.1.2015). Both are meant to get permission from the Advisory Committee on Business Appointments (Acoba) which has received over 800 such applications to determine possible conflicts of interest. But it has no powers of enforcement. It can only express its concerns when it identifies possible conflicts (cf *The Sunday Times* 10.1.2016), adding to the failure of formal power. In practice, it chooses to turn a blind eye; George Osborne, the former Chancellor of the Exchequer, did not bother to inform Acoba when he assumed the editorship of London's *Evening Standard*.

The Rise of Populism

In almost every respect, tentacular government in all its ramifications is the operation of what I termed "anti-politics" in a book of that title published nearly fifty years ago. Anti-politics severely curtails and circumscribes debate on public affairs; increasingly distances ministers from their responsibilities and from the general public; and helps constitute a tortuous maze-like extension in the executive branch of UK government. When saloon bar Johnnies reflect on politics, they frequently conclude, "We don't know the half of it", but this is a gross under-estimate. The truth is that contemporary politics is almost impenetrable. This means that Ministers, parliamentarians, the civil service, the media - let alone those in the saloon bar - are severely handicapped in comprehending the totality of what is going on: public accountability is at a colossal discount which is very detrimental for democracy and parliamentary government. Those who are meant to rule - Ministers - and the plethora of associated outliers are thus largely insulated from those who are ruled. The European Union, or its institutional network, by contrast, is relatively transparent.

The Nobel prize-winning economist, Oliver E Williamson, fully understood this. He argued that with the imposition of each new additional tier of authority there are associated communication costs and control loss, both of which should be appraised beforehand as to whether they are worthwhile. It is surprising coming from so authoritative a source that Williamson's strictures are ignored, for there is very little evidence that changes are systematically examined for the costs and benefits they incur. To take two examples: the failed attempts at out-sourcing and privatisation of Hinchingbrooke Hospital and uniting Care in Cambridge and Peterborough vividly reveal the enormous dis-benefits involved.

Were more appraisals to be undertaken, the myriad of agencies and the rise of the nomenklatura that characterise tentacular government, would provoke adverse public reactions. Without such audits they remain largely indiscernible and below the surface. Recent developments, however, suggest there is something of a sea change occurring. As remarked at the beginning of this chapter, there is a growing sense of unease and dissatisfaction among the electorate with how politics has been carried on over the past half century and more. Outbursts of populism appeared in the 2015 General Election with the surge in support for the Scottish National Party (SNP) and the UK Independence Party (UKIP). The opinion polls got the results spectacularly wrong. People were thrashing out against what has become the established way of conducting the affairs of the nation.

The UK's politics is in a parlous condition. Of course, party leaders have been aware of this for some time and they have endeavoured to re-engage with the electorate by, among other ways, the use of rhetorical symbols. For example, rather unconvincingly, Thatcher recited St Francis of Assisi's prayer outside No 10 as she assumed office. Major talked of a peaceful nation at ease with itself with old ladies cycling to church, the sound of leather balls on willow cricket bats and the taste of warm beer. He also called for a "Back to Basics" return to traditional moral values. Slightly more practically, he also arranged for a telephone hot-line to receive complaints about the excessive deployment of traffic cones on motorways. Blair tried to evoke an atmospheric sense with "Cool Britannia", emphasising the modernity of New Labour. Cameron, in contrast to Thatcher, sought to re-unite government and community with talk of fostering the "Big Society". He later invoked Disraeli's nineteenth century notion of "One Nation" soon after Ed Miliband sought to purloin it for the Labour Party. Theresa May, for her part, advocated "a fair society". None of these appeals has successfully caught the imagination of the voters. They are seen for what they are – empty rhetoric. As such they are wholly counter-productive and only serve to foster greater public alienation, cynicism and dis-engagement.

There is a crying need for a formal examination of the UK's woes. Top of the list, there is a case for attempting to provide a defined framework for accommodating the devolved character of the UK. The creation of regional legislatures in Belfast, Cardiff and Edinburgh were all responses to crises rather than the results of a pre-meditated constitutional approach at the centre to modernising the conduct of public affairs: though devolution did chime in with greater out-sourcing away from Whitehall. But a worked-out system for devolution is still unfinished business.

Then there is the advent and continuing very rapid development of social media. These, in their various forms, are already making their influence felt at all levels of politics from grass-roots canvassing and petition rising to instantaneous mass, usually short-lived, moments with news potential, news circulation, that includes whistle-blowing and the release of State secrets. It has introduced a new form of direct democracy which will be very difficult to combine with representative parliamentary democracy as Tony Benn and Jeremy Bray had once hoped.

The impact of the blogosphere can also to be seen in successive governments having recourse to referenda as a device for dealing with major political questions – a real plebiscitary exercise in direct democracy. Other straws in the wind along these lines are the placing of increasing emphasis on so-called "Red Lines" which cannot be crossed and highlighting manifesto commitments. Labour, ostensibly at least, has always been committed to internal validation of its policies through constituency, trade union and Conference votes but now all political parties point to such pledges either being upheld or ignored.

Another plebiscitary symptom is evident in moves towards the hypothecation of taxes, like the Commons vote in 2015 to make legal provision for 0.7 % of annual GDP to be reserved for overseas development aid. The less formal undertakings to 'ring fence' specific government expenditures for defined periods is another illustration of trying to assure the electorate that ministers are true to their word and can be trusted.

Nor can the ethics and professional integrity of those who staff the nomenklatura be regarded as one of the principal safeguards to ensure propriety and good conduct in the exercise of power simply because, in the light of continuing scandals, public trust in banking, insurance, retailing, accountancy and cognate vocations is at an all-time low; polls show that hairdressers rank higher in esteem.

Thus there are very large issues to be addressed were a Constitutional Convention or some such formal review be set up to make proposals for a more effective re-ordering of the nation's affairs. The overall reaction in the immediate aftermath of the 2015 General Election, as enumerated earlier, made it seem likely that so un-British an attempt might be made. It is now less likely for a number of reasons.

It is not in the nature of UK ruling parties, of whatever stripe, to warm to such an idea – they would rather have us believe they were fully capable of handling the problems piecemeal as and when they arise. If that is the case, the big question remains whether tentacular government in all it trappings, coupled with the rise of social media with all its intrusions for good and ill, makes representative parliamentary government anachronistic and beyond recovery? Parliament and even the Cabinet seem on the way to being consigned to the "dignified" part of the constitution, to employ Bagehot's terminology.

Are the notions of *collegium* and *hierarchy* now becoming increasingly redundant? If so, how is public accountability over those who exercise power to be enforced? After all, accountability is the hallmark of democracy or is that principle no longer possible to operate? Have we now to recognise that the sheer pace of the activity of contemporary government, and the concomitant velocity of change that is inherent in that, means a re-arrangement of the division between *collegium* and *hierarchy* is near-impossible? Would it not be better to accept that the exercise of the 'governing of men and women' should be subsumed into the 'managing of things' undertaken by elites cocooned in their bubbles? That follows inevitably from the irrepressible impulses behind the tentacular state. In the next phase of our history, UK government will likely share more in common with the governing systems of Xi Jinping's China, Putin's Russia and Trump's USA than its erstwhile pursuit of parliamentary democracy.

May, Maybe, May Not – Almost Certainly Won't

When asked what he most feared about causing unpredictability in politics, Harold MacMillan, then prime minister, is alleged to have replied, "Events, dear boy, events".

Whether wrongly attributed or not, the catchphrase is a useful alembic through which to view the tumultuous character of the political drama that has ensued in the aftermath of the 2015 General Election.

It began, of course, with David Cameron's disastrous decision to call for a Referendum on whether or not the UK should remain in the European Union. To much surprise, the country decided to quit the EU by a margin of fifty-two to forty-eight per cent.

Cameron immediately resigned as Prime Minister, Tory Leader and as an MP. After very unseemly fratricidal in-fighting among the main Brexiteer contenders to succeed him, all withdrew to give the Home Secretary, Theresa May a free run.

She quickly proved to be even more cack-handed than her predecessor. Having declared repeatedly she would carry on with her small majority, she suddenly called a snap election. She claimed to offer "strong and stable" leadership that no-one else could: essentially, she was attempting to promote an even stronger version of TINA.

In the event she lost thirteen MPs and had to preside over a minority administration and had to do a costly (both financial and even worse political) deal with the ten-strong Northern Irish Democratic Unionist Party (DUP) in the Commons to provide her with a majority on a "confidence and supply" basis.

Before the 2017 General Election *The Economist* had asked "Theresa May or Maybe?" The answer has swiftly turned out to be "May Won't". "Events", indeed, have returned with a vengeance to dictate the politics of the UK with potentially fearful consequences. China, Russia and the USA here we come.

CHAPTER 14

THE MEDIA AND ITS CONFLUENCES

For everyone the prevailing culture, particularly in their earlier formative years, helps shape their lives in a very lasting manner. That was especially true for me during my childhood and as a teenager. Cultural determinants were particularly diverse and dynamic in the 1940s and 1950s and almost as much as they are today.

BBC radio, or "The Wireless" as it was then referred to, had become firmly established as the major medium largely as a consequence of the war. Because of its immediacy, both in the transmission of the latest news and its deliverance in the home, the BBC Home Service became the main source of regular information. It largely displaced the monopoly exercised previously by newspapers. The press could still claim scoops from time to time and engage in specific campaigns but the BBC assumed the predominant role. This spilled over to the Light Programme and Third Programme with their provision of differing kinds of entertainment. The former offered popular variety programmes including light music while the latter was confined to classical music, drama and serious talks.

Books & Comics

As with earlier generations, reading, both voluntary and school-driven, was a major pre-occupation. My literary odyssey, like others, began with the recitation of nursery rhymes, progressing to the very popular stories of *The Famous Five* by Enid Blyton. These were succeeded by Richmal Crompton's *Just William* books and those, in turn, by Frank Roberts' Billy Bunter's antics at boarding school where the 'Owl of the Remove' was the bane of Mr Quelch, his form-master. I recognised elements of Quelch in many of my schoolmasters.

My reading habits burgeoned with two discoveries. The first was the introduction to almost the entire corpus of Captain W E Johns' Biggles stories – the greatest fictional flying ace. Very well written, they easily caught the imagination of a boy, about to enter adolescence, who had experienced the Battle of Britain and followed news of subsequent air battles. I gathered a very large collection of Biggles books.

It occurs to me, looking back, that all of the books I have mentioned displayed a very middle-class penumbra. The schools attended by the various characters were, implicitly or explicitly, in the private sector and, as such, chimed in well with what I experienced in the several schools I attended.

My second source of avid reading, came from my rapidly acquired addiction to four weekly comics: *The Adventure*, *The Wizard*, *The Rover* and *The Hotspur*. I didn't care for *The Dandy*, *The Beano*, *Film Fun* or *Radio Fun* which were the other weeklies on offer. My favourite four were all very well-written and composed. They offered something by way of an antidote to the books, for the chosen themes often reflected a different social class emphasis. For example, one depicted Hogan, the player/manager of a struggling lower division soccer team, and another an apprentice plumber Alf Tupper, a natural runner, who was so poor, he often had to run to far-flung venues to compete. Disability was also treated with 'Limp Along Leslie' who adapted his handicap into an unstoppable goal-scoring technique, thereby becoming a famous soccer star.

Later, I bought *The Eagle* when it appeared. I was particularly taken by the exploits of Captain Dan Dare of the International Police Force fighting off the Mekon who led the invaders from outer space. It was a good preparation for the Liberal Party which, when I joined, had the creation of a UN Police Force as one of its main policy planks. I used to dip into the monthly *Boy's Own Paper* but it was too disparate in its coverage and appeared altogether too shallow for my tastes.

I have always been grateful for the compulsory school element of my reading. Although sometimes reluctant, I'm particularly pleased how much poetry was forced upon me, not just to read but to learn off by heart. When I bought *The Faber Popular Reciter*, edited by Kingsley Amis, which appeared in 1978, I was delighted to find almost all of his selected poems were very familiar and many of which I could still recite bits of, having been made to rote-learn them decades before. Again, though, as with the fiction I read, much of the poetry reflected an idealised 'merry England'. Nevertheless, compulsory poetry made me aware of the delights it affords and prepared me for the works of Dylan Thomas, Philip Larkin and, later, Seamus Heaney. When I conferred an honorary doctorate on Heaney, I asked him to sign my various volumes of his poetry. Pat, his wife, urged me not to: "He's signed so many, virgin copies would be much more valuable!"

The famous crime writer, the late Ruth Rendell, and a fellow member of the Lords, warned of a decline in book reading amongst present-day youngsters caused by alternative access to computers and the like. I share her fear. It is also certainly true that being required to learn poetry off by heart has long been abolished from the school syllabus. Both have deleterious consequences for developing children's imaginations which is an issue to which I shall return later.

Of equal contemporary relevance is the exposure to pornography, now a commonplace, which was almost non-existent in my adolescence days. There were "Adult Only" cinemas, I remember one in Tottenham Court Road, but under-21s were disallowed admittance. I saw a *Folies Bergere* show once with my cousin Alan in Brighton in my early teens, where the scantily clothed cast had to stand still throughout the performance. The only recourse in my time was to two magazines: *Health & Efficiency*, ostensibly a weekly journal for practising naturists and *The National Geographic* magazine with its photographs of bare-bosomed African women. Brendan Behan, in his novel *Borstal Boy*, remarks that the latter was in great demand at 'lights out' during his time of youthful incarceration. These two magazines comprised the meagre stimulus for sexual fantasies for my youthful generation.

The Radio

On the wireless *Children's Hour*, as the title implies, catered for younger listeners on weekday afternoons from five o'clock. Hosted by 'Uncle Mac', who always concluded with "Goodnight children, everywhere", it often included a *Larry the Lamb* episode with Mr Mayor, Mr Growser sir, Dennis the Dachshund, the Inventor and Larry himself played by Ernest

Jay. He lived near us in Boston Manor and was father to the more famous Anthony Jay, creator of the highly-rated television series *Yes, Minister. Norman and Henry Bones – the Boy Detectives* was another, somewhat inferior, serial on *Children's Hour* but one which prompted a lifelong addiction in me to whodunits. It was the heyday of 'steam radio' as it is now called.

The early attempts on television to cater for younger viewers were poor. *Muffin the Mule,* a puppet manipulated by Annette Mills, was popular, and my father and his partner sold many copies of the puppet, but its appeal was not the result of a quality programme but lay rather in the sheer novelty of television. Production quality later improved with the likes of *Andy Pandy, Thomas the Tank Engine, Paddington Bear, The Wombles of Wimbledon, Postman Pat, Animal Magic* and *Blue Peter* which my children enjoyed.

Among adult and family radio programmes, I vaguely remember Tommy Handley and *ITMA*, but was very familiar with Franklin Engleman compering *Down Your Way*, Cliff Michelmore and his wife Jean Metcalfe's *Two-Way Family Favourites* transmitted on Sunday mornings, *In Town Tonight* broadcast early Saturday evenings reviewing the goings-on in London and other such regulars.

In sport, I particularly enjoyed listening to boxing contests: Bruce Woodcock, Freddie Mills and Randolph Turpin were the British hopefuls at the time. I vividly recall the boxing commentaries of the Canadian Stewart MacPherson with inter-round summaries provided in the dulcet, received English of W Barrington Dalby. The accents of the two commentators contrasted markedly in much the same way as the later television election broadcasts hosted by Robert Mackenzie and David Butler. Looking back, MacPherson and Dalby were something of a trailer and I always wondered if a BBC producer had transferred from sports radio to political television where he employed the same successful Anglo-Canadian formula? The Test match cricket commentaries of John Arlott held the same fascination for me.

Music and song were also much listened to. I vividly remember the first song I learnt. "*Little Sir Echo... won't you come over and play?*" came out in 1939 and was popularised by Bing Crosby. Its lyrics captured the loneliness of the baby bust age cohort and should be seen as its anthem.

The 1940s were essentially the decade of crooning. Deanna Durbin, Vera Lynn, The Ink Spots, Bing Crosby, Fats Waller and a young Frank Sinatra were favourite singers as well as the bands of Duke Ellington, and Louis Armstrong. Petula Clark, a child prodigy and six years my senior, captured my heart and I have followed her very long and always successful career ever since.

One tune stuck vividly in my mind – "*The kids all called him Johnny Zero....*" This Song Spinners title came out in 1943 and referred to a US Air Force gunner. At high school his academic results were so poor his fellow students gave him the nick-name "Johnny Zero". In flights over the Pacific in the war he shot down a record number of Japanese fighters which were called "Zeros". Hence the tune ended with "Johnny Zero is a Hero today".

I remember bands of 'the two Vs' – Victor Sylvester and his strict tempo orchestra and Vic Oliver, violinist, comedian and briefly Churchill's one-time son-in- law, together with Joe Loss, Ted Heath's Big Band Sound, Harry Hall and his Orchestra, Mantovani and his Strings, Geraldo and Edmundo Ros who imported Latin American rhythms into the UK. On Sunday evenings from an Eastbourne seaside hotel came The *Palm Court Orchestra* playing to large audiences, while the pianist Alberto Semprini, played his weekly half-hour serenades of "new ones, old ones, remembered ones, forgotten ones" to similar acclaim. Because of his popularity, Donald Peers, a Welsh tenor, merits recalling. Not a great voice but one that appealed to middle-aged women, he made a successful comeback towards the end of his singing career. His signature tune, *By a babbling brook*, close a shady nook... that heralded his programmes stuck in my mind as such tunes so often annoyingly do – hence the description 'ear worms'.

The late 1940s and '50s spawned a run of particularly awful songs. Especially excruciating were Gilly, Gilly Ossenfeffer Katzenellen Bogen by the Sea, (I'd Like to Get You on a) *Slow Boat to China*, The Maharajah of Mogador, Mairzy Doats and Dozy Doats and Liddle Lamzy Divey. *While I'm Walking Behind You on your Wedding Day* and *On the Street Where you Live* would now be regarded as a stalker's anthem. Leading singers such as Bing Crosby, Eddie Fisher, Max Bygraves and even Ella Fitzgerald and Frank Sinatra recorded some of these songs. They were the pits.

At the beginning of the 1950s a new US generation of crooners emerged replacing boogie-woogie and be-bop rhythms that had dominated the popular music of the previous decade. The innovation of Hit Parades produced weekly rankings of the most popular songs measured by retail sales. Al Martino, Johnnie Ray, Frankie Lane, Andy Williams and Rosemary Clooney emerged to acclaim together with a re-invented Frank Sinatra.

This coincided with the introduction, on a mass and cheap scale, of 78 rpm vinyl records. This helped to create and shape the emerging phenomenon of the teenage market. Previously, of course, youngsters left school and went straight to work. A raised school-leaving age and increasing affluence, created a new transition from childhood to adulthood that in turn spawned its own commercial market for which, obligingly, the Hit Parade and its discs catered.

The new wave of crooners, in turn, gave way to rock music that burst in with Bill Haley and the Comets, a fashion for which Elvis Presley was to be the main and posthumously enduring performer. Cliff Richard, of *We're All Going on a Summer Holiday* fame kept alive the tradition of crooning with a persistence that lasted well into the next century.

Traditional jazz enjoyed its most successful run in Britain in the 1950s. Sid Phillips, Cy Laurie, Chris Barber, Ken Colyer, Humphrey Lyttleton and others performed in Soho and nationwide and were particular favourites at student hops in the universities.

The lighter side of radio and the nascent television consisted of comedy shows hosted by the likes of Charlie Chester, Ted Ray, Kenneth Horne, Tommy Trinder and others - later to be followed by Frankie Howerd, Benny Hill, Ken Dodd and Morecambe & Wise, Kenneth Williams, Bob Monkhouse - all of whom became household names.

Panel games were also very popular, most notably, *What's My Line?* The idea was a US import, the British version of which opened in 1951 and continued for the next decade. Ordinary people would mime an activity that reflected their job in front of the panel which had to guess what that was. Someone more famous was also included to mime an aspect of their work, but with the panel blindfolded. The regular panellists became even better well-known stars. They included the irascible Gilbert Harding – who earned the sobriquet "the rudest man in Britain", though he considered himself to be merely a "tele-phoney", a conjuror David Niven, Barbara Kelly, actress wife of Bernard Braden – a popular compere/comedian in his own right - and Lady Isobel Barnett. Eamon Andrews, the start of a tradition of Irish interviewers and disc jockeys on British media, usually chaired the programme.

Workers' Playtime was introduced soon after the outbreak of hostilities with Germany, and broadcast every weekday around lunchtime, from different factory canteen locations, to offer good cheer with the aim of boosting morale and the war effort. It consisted of a mixture of songs and comedy and among its regular performers were "Gert and Daisy", real names Ethel and Dorothy Waters and sisters of the actor Jack Warner. The programme continued well into the Attlee government to help stimulate the very weak post-war economy. Wilfred Pickles' *Have a Go* quiz, was another enduring weekly fixture throughout the 1940s and '50s. Successful participants were rewarded after the cry, "Give them the money, Barney", Barney Collahan being the producer of the programme.

Desert Island Discs, was created by Roy Plumley in 1944. He conducted interviews with prominent personalities tracing their life stories and asking them to select their eight favourite pieces of music, together with a luxury and a book "apart from the Bible and Shakespeare" which would come washed up alongside them on the island. For his book, the famous society solicitor, Arnold Goodman, chose *Who's Who* so, as he said, that he could call to mind his many elite clients. The best choice came from a Russian male ballet dancer who selected for his "eighth and final record" the programme's signature tune. A startled Plumley asked the reason and the dancer replied, "If you can stand *The Sleepy Lagoon* all these years, it must have something going for it!" Its appeal was established from the outset: who has not pondered their own choice of eight records and regularly revised them? It became something of an accolade - akin to a major public honour - to be invited to appear on Desert Island Discs. The comedian Arthur Askey was brought back an unprecedented three times. It retains very high audience ratings to this day.

Police programmes found wide public support to which, as I said, I was inducted by the Bones brothers. These ranged on the radio from *Dick Barton, Special Agent* accompanied by his assistants Jock and Snowy. Barton, clearly the product of a public school, Jock, a Scot, and Snowy, a Cockney, were together a representation of UK society. *Paul Temple*, by contrast, was definitely a toff, living in Mayfair with his cut-glass speaking wife, Steve, and a butler Charlie. Temple was a freelance private investigator in the manner of Sherlock Holmes who was always sharper than those in the higher echelons of Scotland Yard. *Dixon of Dock Green* was decidedly salt-of-the-earth working class. The programme saw the promotion of Dixon, played by Jack Warner, from constable to sergeant and the programme itself from radio to television. Later *Z Cars*, *Inspector Morse*, *Midsomer Murders* and others continued the tradition.

Medical programmes, like the police, were to become an established feature in the repertoire of broadcasting. On the radio, *Mrs Dale's Diary*, involving her GP husband Jim, was later succeeded on television by *Emergency Ward Ten* and *Dr Finlay's Casebook*. The subject of hospitals remains a constant standby as a theme for television producers. Cookery programmes are also a regular feature. Philip Harben was the first to host these but, much to my annoyance, Fanny Cradock is always referred to as being the first one.

On the less frivolous side, partly because of WWII and the ensuing Cold War, there was serious reporting of news and current affairs. Richard Dimbleby, the founder of what was to become a broadcasting dynasty, was undoubtedly the doyen of commentators (especially memorable was his account of entering Bergen-Belsen concentration camp while the sonorous tones of Alvar Lidell presented the dire news endemic to those dark days).

During the war and after, *The Brains Trust* appeared on the Home Service, with the Birkbeck College philosopher, Dr Cyril Joad, wrongly promoted to 'Professor' in the public mind. Along with other eminent people, he pontificated weekly on the events of the moment. However, he was instantly removed after being found guilty of fiddling his rail tickets. The programme was replaced by *Any Questions?* That has become an established feature of the radio scene at this time and, as with *Desert Island Discs*, apparently, for all time.

Television

Two programmes that appeared on the nascent BBC single black and white television channel were *In the News* and *Current Affairs*. Both were essentially radio programmes transmitted onto the screen in the living room. In the News lasted thirty minutes during which two topical political questions were debated. Bob Boothby, a Tory MP, and William J Brown, an ex-Independent MP, representing the Right, faced Michael Foot, a future Labour Leader and Alan J P Taylor, an Oxford historian and later a famous "teledon", representing the Left. Frank Byers, a Liberal politician, presided. Although it was all very contrived with the four contestants playing up to their public political personae, I was riveted and rarely missed this Sunday post-lunch programme.

The other, *Current Affairs*, appearing on a weekly evening, was hosted by Christopher Mayhew. He had been a Labour MP, holding a junior post at the Foreign Office in the Attlee government and later at Defence in the first Wilson administration. In a very didactic manner he would discourse on contemporary matters of foreign policy which I found enthralling. Much later he joined the Social Democratic Party (SDP) and became a Lib Dem life peer but by then he had, to my mind, adopted some rather strange, idiosyncratic views that made me reconsider him. But the earlier Mayhew's commentaries I found most instructive to a politically interested young adolescent.

Two other programmes stick in my memory as both were broadcast before 8 a.m. on the Home Service, just as I was breakfasting before leaving for school. One, *Lift up your Hearts*, was a five-minute Christian homily and survives to this day in a more ecumenical form as *Thought for the Day*. The other was *The Radio Doctor* which gave out seasonal medical tips. It was presented in avuncular tones by Dr Charles Hill. At that time he was General Secretary of the British Medical Association and wouldn't have seen a live patient for years past let alone knowing anything about antibiotics. I remember him extolling the virtues of "rubbing a little Vaseline on the chest now that winter's here". He later became a Conservative MP, Cabinet Minister and successively chairman of both the BBC and of ITV.

Films

Films also constituted a major cultural influence. The cinema, "going to the flicks", was another mainstay of our existence. War films, Westerns and Musicals formed the staple diet, with supporting 'B movies', so that you invariably got two feature films, a cartoon (often Disney) and a Pathé, Gaumont or Paramount newsreel containing the previous week's news.

Some films were unashamedly straight patriotic propaganda such as Will Hay's 1942 *The Goose Steps Out* and, more subtly, Laurence Olivier's *Henry V* in 1945. But the war unleashed a mass of films extolling the valour British armed forces displayed under fire. They continued years after 1945 and have been well catalogued but three or four stand out for me: *A Matter of Life or Death*, *The Way to the Stars*, *The Cruel Sea* and *The Sea Shall Not Have Them*. The last, starring Dirk Bogarde and John Mills, I recall if only because Noel Coward, passing the Dominion cinema in Tottenham Court Road where the film was showing, is recorded as saying "The sea shall not have them - why not? Everyone else has!"

Danny Kaye, starring in *Up in Arms*, was a very humorous American antidote to these sombre depictions of war. Three post-war films made lasting impressions as they reflected different aspects of conflict. The first was *The Third Man*, written by Graham Greene and starring Orson Welles, with its haunting "Harry Lime Theme". It was the first pictorial treatment of what was to become "The Cold War" between the USSR and the West and set in Vienna mid-way between the two power blocs. This was followed by *The Planter's Wife* in which Jack Hawkins took on the Chinese Communists who led the major insurgency in Malaya. Equally terrifying was *Simba, Sign of Mau Mau* that covered the Mau Mau uprising in Kenya.

Cinema-going was almost universal in the war years and in the aftermath and for children, there was the additional provision of "Saturday morning Pictures". Most local Odeon, ABC and Gaumont cinemas, the main circuits, put these on. They re-hashed old films like Hopalong Cassidy, Robin Hood, Abbott & Costello, Laurel & Hardy, Lassie and similar fare, together with cartoons. Saturday mornings were not replete without going on these excursions.

However, it differed totally from watching television for long periods on a daily basis. In the 1950s films were superseded as the main source of mass entertainment. For their part, films came in discrete packages and were easy to assimilate and ponder over – to digest, in other words. Today's instant news, twenty-four hours' transmissions, with incessant offerings on social media is altogether much more indigestible. It is also less 'social' because they are for the most part, heard, seen and absorbed mainly in isolation. In my formative years, the media was more 'social'. People would discuss radio and television programmes and the films they had seen.

In the mid-1970s the Acton Society was actively researching into the expected burgeoning of television on a multi-channel basis. As part of this, my research assistant Julia – later my wife – and I interviewed leading experts. One was Milton Shulman, the well-known media critic of the London *Evening Standard.* Commenting on the coming explosion of multi-channel tv, he said the entertainment of an earlier generation of cinema goers meant that they could digest the film on their way home, often acting out memorable scenes. Hours of watching television offered no such opportunity. At least in the immediate post-war years the single BBC channel, aping the theatre, had fifteen minutes interludes between programmes with windmills circling, swans swimming and potters moulding in silence. Shulman made the further observation that viewers could remember TV series but not individual episodes. I can attest to this as the only distinct memories I have of individual programmes are *Cathy Come Home* and *Abigail's Party* because of the social poignancy they engendered.

Social Media & The Blogosphere

The mono-cultural and almost monochrome childhood of radio and films that characterised my childhood and early teens meant that entertainment was a series of more or less discrete episodes each delineated by distinct boundaries and regularly up-dated. Each had the potential, at least, of its own memory, however fleeting or enduring it turned out. Early in the last century, the Welsh poet, William Henry Davies asked: "What is this life if full of care we have no time to stand and stare?" If it was a valid question a century or more ago, it is even more so now. Today's children, overwhelmed by the incessant importunities of the ubiquitous social media are denied such opportunities for relaxation and reflection. Ask yourself when last you spoke, heard or read the words "pondered", "cogitated" or "ruminated"? And now there is recourse to a single emphasis – the word "really" – while the comparatives, "very", "more" and "most" have been all but abolished from our vocabulary.

The changes induced by the advent of the blogosphere have been and continue to be both profound and seemingly unending. That is commonly agreed but there consensus ends. On the one hand, the school of optimists thinks the potentialities of social media will see a liberation of the human spirit and imagination much greater than that afforded by Johannes Gutenberg and William Caxton who ushered in the era of printing and mass circulation publication. The school of pessimists, on the other hand, are deeply worried by the extent of changes in the very essence of life that social media is likely to wreak.

Two members of the Lords, both Cross Benchers, share this concern. The neuro-scientist, Professor Susan Greenfield, has warned of what she calls the *Mind Change* (her 2014 book title) by which future generations will think and feel: she questions "the impact of modern screen technologies on the human brain." Brought up on an unrelentingly constant diet of e-mails, text messaging, Twitter, Facebook and the like, may give rise to a screen-watching isolated set of near-hermits. Such individuals, will find difficulty coping with the social world because they exist largely in the cocoon of a virtual world. For many adults changes in the patterns of work, hot-desking, working at home, digital communication, continuous surveillance etc. are already with us and indicative of manifold developments in the shape of things to come which will be even more disorienting for future generations.

The other Parliamentarian, the noted film-maker, Beeban Kidron, in her *In Real Life* reveals the impact of pornography in the lives of young teenagers derived from the internet. As she has remarked: "There is a new world order and our children are carrying it in their pockets".

Julia Hobsbawm in *Fully Connected* (2017) shares the concerns expressed by Greenfield and Kidron. She speaks of "an age of overload" occasioned by the new media technology which produces "a glut" of information. This, paradoxically, leads many people to feel misinformed, disconnected and quite overwhelmed. This new situation, which makes the digestion of information very difficult – if not near-impossible – can lead to very real mental health problems and it also contributes to the growing political populism with its demands for simple answers.

Greenfield, Kidron and Hobsbawm are from liberal, progressive backgrounds and far from the mind-set that inspired Mary Whitehouse, Malcolm Muggeridge, Cliff Richard and Lord Longford in their 'Clean up' media campaigning during the last three decades of the twentieth century. Did Whitehouse and company in their way anticipate the concerns expressed by the three more recent commentators? Had Whitehouse and company not wrapped their crusade up in the strident tones of Moral Re-Armament and evangelical Christianity, they might have received a better public hearing?

Had he witnessed modern developments, would Karl Marx have reframed his observation, to the effect that the social media have replaced religion as "the opium of the people"?

The question almost poses itself: is the blogosphere a mine of information or a barrage of lethal hand grenades? The academic in me invites you to discuss it while there's still time: it's an issue that will continually need addressing.

Almost time for me to turn out the lights...

APHORISMS & ADAGES

Life is not a bowl of cherries – it's a series of trade-offs.

Of course I'm a conspiracy theorist: "cock-ups", after all, are only failed conspiracies.

When saloon-bar Johnnies say of politics, "we don't know the half of it", they are guilty of serious under-estimation.

When Prime Minister, John Major stated he wanted to put the UK "at the heart of Europe". Unfortunately, the Tories could never tell their Aarhus from their Elba!

The Twentieth century was shaped largely by the thoughts of Marx, Freud and Darwin. Two Jews and one Gentile – just the right proportion.

Plato classified people in three categories – those of gold, silver and bronze. I'm more parsimonious: they come as either plumbers or poets and, as Byron said, it's the poets who set future agendas.

"White collar, blue collar, dog collar: speculations on the emerging ecclesiastical/industrial complex" (Title of a spoof article published 1985 *Universities Quarterly)*.

As occupational therapy, attending the House of Lords beats basket-making.

The difference between a Life Peer and a Prisoner for Life is that Peers are entitled to six travel tickets a years for conjugal visits to Westminster, whereas prisoners get twelve annual travel grants.

The growth of regulatory agencies like OfWat, Ofsted, OfGem, OfCom and the like, means that they too now need regulating. A super monitoring agency is called for. It could be called the Efficiency Office or EffOff for short.

The happy medium is best found among Spiritualists.

NAME INDEX

N

O

SUBJECT INDEX

Education

Entertainment & Periodicals

Geography: London

Geography: Non-London

Politics & Organizations

Publications

Dominance in Britain's Democracy. Democratic Audit, 2011, 290
Behan, Brendan *Borstal Boy*, London: Hutchinson, 1958, 302
Berle, Adolf A., Gardiner Means, *The Modern Corporation and Private Property.* London: Macmillan, 1932, 128
Birch, Anthony Harold, *Small Town Politics: A Study of Political Life in Glossop.* Oxford: Oxford University Press, 1959, 140
Birch, Anthony Harold, *Representative and Responsible Government.* Sydney: Allen & Unwin Australia Pty, Ltd., 1964, 154
Bowen, John, *Storyboard.* London: Faber and Faber, 1960, 131
Crosland, Anthony, *The Future of Socialism.* London: Jonathan Cape, 1964, 128
Dunn, Seamus, Helen Dawson's *An Alphabetical Listing of Word, Name and Place in Northern Ireland and the Living Language of Conflict.* Lampeter: Edwin Mellen Press, 2000, 200
Fishman, William, *East End Jewish Radicals* 1875-1914. London: Duckworth, 1975, 160
George, David Lloyd, *"Yellow Book,"* 1928, 120, 227
Goldthorpe, John, David Lockwood, *The Affluent Worker.* Cambridge: Cambridge University Press, 1976, 123
Greenfield, Susan, *Mind Change: How Digital Technologies are Leaving Their Mark on Our Brains.* London: Random House, 2014, 314
Greenleaf, William H., *The British Political Tradition Vol 1: The Rise of Collectivism.* Abingdon-on-Thames: Routledge, 1983, 142, 153, 154
Greenleaf, William H., *The British Political Tradition Vol 2: The Ideological Heritage.* London: Methuen Publishing, 1983, 142
Greenleaf, William H., *The British Political Tradition Vol 3: A*

Much Governed Nation. Abingdon-on-Thames, Routtledge, 1987, 142

Greenleaf, Willaim H., *The British Political Tradition Vol 4: The World Outside.* London: Methuen, forthcoming, 142

Hobsbawm, Julia, *Fully Connected: Surviving and Thriving in an Age of Overload.* London: Bloomsbury Publishing, 2017, 315

Hoggart, Richard, *Uses of Literacy: Aspects of Working Class Life.* Piscataway NJ: Transaction Publishers, 1957, 144

Jacques, Eliot, Wilfrid Brown, *The Changing Culture of a Factory.* Cambridge: Tavistock Press, 1951, 150

Kennedy, Benjamin, G.H. Halam, Julie Kennedy, Marion Kennedy, Thomas Page. Kennedy's Revised Latin Primer, 55

Kipling, Rudyard, "The Puzzler", in *Actions and Reactions.* London: Macmillan & Co, 1909, 241

Klug, Francesca, Keir Starmer, Stuart Weir, *The Three Pillars of Liberty: The Political Rights and Freedoms in the United Kingdom.* Democratic Audit of the United Kingdom. London: Routledge, 1996, 253

Koestler, Arthur, *Darkness at Noon.* London: Macmillan, 1940, 106

Mills, C. Wright, *The Power Elite.* Oxford: Oxford University Press, 1956, 290

New Orbits Group, *High Time for Radicals.* London: New Orbits Group, 1960, 122

Packard, Vance, *The Hidden Persuaders.* London: Random House, 1957, 130

Preston, John, *A Very English Scandal: Sex, Lies and a Murder Plot at the Heart of the Establishment.* New York: Viking Press, 2014, 238

Rée, Harry, *The Essential Grammar School.* London: George G. Harrap & Co Ltd, 1956, 146

Rose, Richard, *Governing Without Consensus: An Irish Perspective.* London: Faber & Faber, 1971, 199

Salway, Peter G, *Roman Britain.* Oxford History of England Series. Oxford: Oxford Clarendon Press, 1982, 63

Shanks, Michael, *The Stagnant Society: A Warning.* London: Pelican Books, 1964, 123

Smith, Trevor, *Anti-Politics: Consensus, Reform & Protest in Britain.* London: Charles Knight & Co, 1972, 154, 292

Smith, Trevor, *British Politics in the Post-Keynesian Era.* London: The Acton Society Trust, 1986, 156

Smith, Trevor, "The New Orbits Group, 1958-c. 1962", *The Journal of Liberal History*, Summer 2017, 126

Smith, Trevor, *The Politics of the Corporate Economy.* Hoboken NJ: Blackwell Publishers, 1979, 154

Smith, Trevor, *Town and County Hall: Problems of Recruitment and Training.* London: The Acton Society Trust, 1966, 158

Smith, Trevor, Michael Argyle, Training Managers. London: The Acton Society Trust, 1962, 139

Smith, Trevor, Anthony M. Rees, *Town Councillors: A Study in Barking.* London: The Acton Society Trust, 1964, 140

Temple-Morris, Peter, *Across the Floor: A Life in Dissenting Politics.* London: I.B. Tauris, 2014, 231

Tressell, Robert, *The Ragged Trousered Philanthropists.* New York: New York University Press, 1955, 78

Vilnay, Zez, *Israel Guide.* London: Ahiever Publishing Ltd, 1979, 89

Vinen, Richard, *National Service; A Generation in Uniform* 1945-1963. London: Penguin Group , 2014, 14
Vinen, Richard, *National Service: Conscription in Britain 1945-63.* London: Allen Lane, 2014, 116, 117
Warnock, Mary, *Nature and Mortality: Recollections of a Philosopher in Public Life.* London: Continuum Publishing, 2004, 216
Weir, Stuart, David Beetham, *Political Power & Democratic Control in Britain: The Executive, Parliament and the Rule of Law in Britain.* London: Routledge, 1999, 253
Whyte, William, *The Organisation Man.* New York: Doubleday, 1956, 128
Wilks, Stephen, *The Revolving Door and the Corporate Colonisation of UK Politics.* London: High Pay Centre, 2015, 290
Young, Ben & Robert Hazell. *Special Advisers: Who They Are, What They Do and Why They Matter.* London: Bloomsbury Publishing, 2014, 286